Governor James Rolph and
the Great Depression in California

Governor James Rolph and the Great Depression in California

James Worthen

McFarland & Company, Inc., Publishers
Jefferson, North Carolina, and London

LIBRARY OF CONGRESS CATALOGUING-IN-PUBLICATION DATA

Worthen, James.
   Governor James Rolph and the Great Depression in California / James Worthen.
      p.   cm.
   Includes bibliographical references and index.

   ISBN-13: 978-0-7864-2574-1
   ISBN-10: 0-7864-2574-1 (softcover : 50# alkaline paper) ∞

   1. Rolph, James, 1869–1934. 2. Governors—California—Biography. 3. California—History—20th century. 4. Mayors—California—San Francisco—Biography. 5. San Francisco (Calif.)—History—20th century. 6. Depressions—1929—California.
   I. Title
   F866.W93   2006
   979.4'053092—dc22   2006016742
   [B]

British Library cataloguing data are available

©2006 James Worthen. All rights reserved

No part of this book may be reproduced or transmitted in any form or by any means, electronic or mechanical, including photocopying or recording, or by any information storage and retrieval system, without permission in writing from the publisher.

Cover photograph ©2004 Brand X Pictures

Manufactured in the United States of America

McFarland & Company, Inc., Publishers
   Box 611, Jefferson, North Carolina 28640
      www.mcfarlandpub.com

In memory of Raymond J. Sontag,
who brought history to life

Table of Contents

Preface	1
Introduction: "The 'Humanest' Human Being I Ever Knew"	9

PART ONE: The Citizen Politician
1. "Mission Jim"	17
2. From the Earthquake to the Mayor's Office	22
3. Moving Through Cheers	30
4. Friends and Family	38

PART TWO: A Civic "Hereditary" Monarchy
5. Second-Term Challenges	47
6. Wealth and Generosity	53
7. Strange Interlude — The First Run for Governor	56
8. Reversal of Fortune	59
9. Third Term — Growing Conservatism and Passivity	61
10. Hetch Hetchy and Municipal Ownership	67
11. Overdoing the Good Life	73
12. A Strong Finish	78

PART THREE: Moving On to Sacramento
13. The 1930 Campaign for Governor	89
14. Great Expectations	98

15. The Appointment Wars	106
16. Rolph and the Legislature	109
17. The Permanent Campaign	115

PART FOUR: The Long, Downhill Slide

18. The Depression Worsens	121
19. Capital Punishment and the Mooney Case	125
20. 1932 — A "Most Troublesome Year"	135
21. A Government Divided	142
22. The Firestorm Over Taxes and Spending	146
23. 1933 — In the Eye of the Storm	152
24. California's Tax Revolution	159
25. Embattled, Fatigued and Broke	170
26. The Farm Labor Crisis	174
27. Preparing for the 1934 Campaign	179
28: The San Jose Kidnapping	182
29. The Central Valley Water Plan	187
30. 1934 — Recovery and Ruin	192
31. A Final Accounting	198
Chapter Notes	209
Bibliography	219
Index	225

Preface

In late 1929, James Rolph, Jr., was nearing the end of an unprecedented fifth consecutive term as mayor of San Francisco. He was a flamboyant, charismatic man, whose warmth and genuineness had made him an icon in the Bay Area and one of the most admired politicians anywhere in the country. He had raised his beloved city from the ashes of the Great Earthquake of 1906 and restored it to its rightful place as the "gayest, lightest hearted, and most pleasure loving city of the western continent."[1] President Herbert Hoover called Rolph a "public institution."[2]

Still ambitious, and with nothing left to prove in San Francisco, Rolph made a fateful decision. He would give up what Will Rogers termed his civic hereditary monarchy[3] and enter the race for governor of California. He had every reason to believe he would win. After all, he had run in the gubernatorial primaries of 1918 and received more votes than any other candidate, though he had been disqualified on a technicality. Now, he had an added advantage — a 20-year record of civic accomplishment. This time, he would reach the summit and write the final chapter in a dazzling political career.

Four years later, Rolph was a broken man, a victim of his own success. He had won election as governor in 1930, but he had miscalculated the magnitude of the challenge in store for him. California was descending into the Great Depression, a situation he could only hope to make less difficult, but not to reverse. Little went well during his term of office. His relationships with the state Senate and Assembly deteriorated, and his chief lieutenants fell into warring cliques. As matters worsened, his health went downhill and he succumbed to a series of ailments, including a stroke, in June 1934.

The conventional wisdom among historians is that Rolph lacked the necessary experience and breadth of understanding to be governor of California during a time of crisis. He has been dismissed as an "amicable

Republican knucklehead"[4] and mocked as having "all the virtues except brains and moral courage."[5] Merritt S. Barnes summarized the prevailing consensus: Rolph was "ill-equipped intellectually, politically and temperamentally to cope with the overwhelmingly complex problems presented by the state's impending financial collapse."[6]

Yet no U.S. governor was able to save his state from the ravages of high unemployment and declining revenues. Many states threw in the towel early and went hat in hand to the federal government for assistance. Rolph showed that he was not a prisoner of the prevailing mainstream Republican economic ideology. In the face of protests from economy-minded legislators, he spent down the state's $30 million budget surplus in order to help the needy and stimulate the economy—hardly the action of a "Republican knucklehead."

In fact, Rolph resisted political classification. He was a contradiction—a nominal Republican and one-time pillar of the business establishment who treated the private sector with unmistakable deference, but also a bleeding-heart humanitarian, a strong backer of organized labor and, like the Progressives of his era as well as the New Dealers to come, a believer in the power of government to get things done. He backed Republican—and fellow Californian—Herbert Hoover in his bid for reelection as president in 1932, but when Hoover lost, he enthusiastically supported President Franklin Roosevelt, a Democrat. As troubles mounted in California, Rolph's pragmatic approach to governing seemed to bode well for his ultimate success.

So we must ask again: Was Rolph truly an ill-equipped, incompetent governor? Or did other factors—such as politics, poor health, and bad luck—conspire to turn a solid effort into disaster?

The Rolph story bridges two distinct periods in twentieth-century California history—the exuberant post–World War I boom, and the years of economic free-fall that began as he moved into the statehouse. Rolph's sunny optimism and relaxed approach to governing were a perfect match for the mood of the 1920s, but the dismal Depression years put a greater premium on mettle and policy acumen. The bad times would test not so much his intelligence or his courage as his flexibility and seriousness of purpose.

With the steadily worsening economy as a backdrop, the Rolph administration held office during a tumultuous period in California history. Many questions had to be addressed:

- How should the state help the unemployed? How could people be put back to work?
- How could the state's tax system be changed so that it was both fair to everyone and responsive to the budgetary needs of rapid growth?

- How should political power be redistributed to recognize the burgeoning population of southern California?
- What could be done for and about the thousands of immigrants to the state — both Mexican farm workers and down-and-outers from America's heartland?
- How could unrest among unionized urban workers in the state's major cities be dealt with?
- How should the state deal with society's latest scourge — a wave of kidnappings that spread fear and anger throughout the country?
- Had Prohibition been a failure? Should the 18th Amendment be repealed?
- Should the state use its scarce resources to pursue the ambitious Central Valley Water Project, which would divert water from the north to the arid south?
- To what extent should the governor's right to appoint loyalists to high state office be restricted?
- How should Republicans deal with the great popularity of President Franklin Roosevelt?

This book, however, is less about the state's many problems during the early 1930s than about the job of governor as Jim Rolph experienced it and shaped it. He was far more prepared for the office than some of his successors, yet his difficulties showed that a sense of direction is more helpful to success than a strong record in politics. Adaptability and administrative skill are also key. Governors must decide among the many possible ways of allocating their time. They face limits on their ability to influence events. They must interact with other centers of political power. They must spend large amounts of time on unexpected developments that may interfere with their agenda. Their work styles, personal habits, and self-discipline — or lack of it — help to determine the kinds of choices they make.

Rolph's reign in San Francisco had been a highly personal one. He believed that the mayor should be accessible to all who wanted to see him, regardless of their importance. Interacting with ordinary people was for him the whole point of public office. How else, he reasoned, would he know what they wanted him to do?

Once he became governor, Rolph continued his courtship of the electorate, only now the electorate stretched 500 miles in either direction from Sacramento. Despite mounting policy challenges, he traveled the state at a frenetic pace, attending county fair openings, judging beauty contests, laying cornerstones, speaking to Rotary clubs, all the while leaving exhausted reporters and staffers in his wake. The state media and legislative leadership criticized him relentlessly for this activity, which they considered pointless.

Rolph's lengthy record in San Francisco provided an accurate guide to his later behavior as governor. It may have taken some digging, but the voter in the 1930 election could have learned of Rolph's hunger for the public spotlight, his tendency to overdelegate, his distaste for conflict, his penchant for big-picture thinking, and his preference for loyalty over competence in subordinates. Or perhaps the voter knew all these things and was more taken by Rolph's charm, optimism, and humility. The electorate cannot know in advance which of a candidate's qualities will be most in demand by circumstances.

Like all of California's chief executives, Rolph would have the important responsibility of preparing a budget and getting it enacted by the legislature. The best-known governors had a strong impact on state finances:

- The Progressives, led by Hiram Johnson (1911–1917), applied the principles of scientific management to state government by developing California's first system of financial oversight.
- Three-term governor Earl Warren (1942–1953), a liberal Republican, was able to reduce taxes because of a huge budget surplus created by the post–World War II boom.
- Edmund G. "Pat" Brown (1959–1967), a liberal Democrat, raised taxes in order to develop the state's transportation and education infrastructure.
- Conservative Ronald Reagan (1967–1975) sought massive tax reductions and draconian spending cuts in an effort to reverse the momentum of the Brown years.

Of all the issues Rolph faced, the budget was the most urgent. After years of expansion, revenue shortfalls beginning in 1930 left the state government facing chronic deficits. Unrelenting pressure was brought to bear on the governor, first to cut spending on state services and then to raise taxes, at a time when the state could least afford either. It would be a far cry from running prosperous San Francisco during the flush 1920s.

One of the more remarkable aspects of Rolph's tenure was the ferocity of political combat in the capital — a city that the *Sacramento Union* called a "boiling cauldron" during those years. By the time the new administration was only a few weeks old, Lt. Gov. Frank Merriam had already declared his candidacy for governor in the next election. Many influential state senators made no effort to disguise their contempt for the governor, and he in return declared that he had "no use for the Senate." The mutual hostility between the legislative and executive branches rendered a productive working relationship almost nonexistent, especially after a Senate investigation of the administration began in January 1933. It was an especially stressful environment for a governor who put a high value on harmony.

In order to understand Rolph's response to what became an unenviable and perhaps impossible administrative challenge, we will first explore his political evolution in the city he loved. Prior to the age of 40, he had no thought of running for public office. He was a successful businessman who gained public recognition for his selfless relief activities in the aftermath of the devastating San Francisco earthquake of 1906. A group of leading citizens pushed him into running for mayor in 1911, because in a city polarized between labor and capital, he had close ties to both.

By the time he had served five terms in office, he had lost much of the momentum he started with, but he had compiled a solid record as a builder and, more important to his future, had established a formidable political machine. This strong organization and a campaign strategy that highlighted his sunny presence and winning personality helped him defeat a sitting governor in the 1930 Republican gubernatorial primary and then brought him victory in the general election against weak Democratic opposition.

This book pays special attention to the campaign of 1930, because it marked the dawn of the media candidacy in America. That year, an unusually charismatic politician arrived on the state scene just as new technology began to allow political messages to be widely disseminated. Rolph ran a virtually issueless campaign, but he made unprecedented use of the airplane and automobile and managed to visit every county in California. For those who missed seeing him in person, the radio and motion picture newsreel brought his cheerful countenance into their homes, and fascinated reporters described the Rolph magic for newspaper readers. Rolph did not win the election because he was well qualified. He won because he employed modern communications to make an emotional connection with the voters.

Any appraisal of Rolph's ill-fated governorship also must take into account the sad condition of his personal finances and his advanced age upon taking office. Once a wealthy shipbuilder who gave away his money freely to anyone in need, he suffered crippling business reverses in the 1920s that left him deeply in debt and dependent on others for the funding of his political campaigns. The loss of his fortune undoubtedly caused him psychological distress as well as real concerns about providing for his family and his old age.

When he arrived in Sacramento, old age was not that far off. He was 62 when he became governor — probably the equivalent of 70 or 75 today — and though his energy seemed inexhaustible, his health already showed signs of decline. Illness sidelined him frequently during his term and eventually caused him to abort his plans for a reelection campaign.

No other detailed history of the Rolph administration in Sacramento exists. The source material for this account consists of newspapers from the period, recollections of contemporaries, records of the state Senate and Assembly, and more recent books and journal articles on specific issues that drew national attention. The most dramatic of these issues were the appeal of convicted anarchist Tom Mooney for a pardon in 1931 and the aftermath of the lynching of two kidnappers in San Jose in 1933. Rolph's response to these two challenges dramatically displayed two important aspects of his personality—his raw emotionalism and his cold political calculation.

I have used the *Sacramento Union* as the newspaper of record for Rolph's entire term as governor. Its coverage of state politics seemed fair, balanced and comprehensive. Its summaries and analyses captured the mood of the times and put political developments into context. I supplemented this record with many other California dailies.

Rolph's San Francisco years are far more richly documented than his years in the capital. The mayor was constantly in the local headlines, and he often received attention in national journals. His personal papers, held at the California Historical Society in San Francisco, contain voluminous (if mostly trivial) correspondence from all five terms of office.

Among the many other sources of information on Rolph's political and personal evolution, four may be singled out. The most detailed analysis of his actions and policies while mayor is *The Political Career of James Rolph, Jr.: A Preliminary Study*, by Herman G. Goldbeck.[7] Tidbits on Rolph's private life are supplied in Jerry Flamm's entertaining *Hometown San Francisco: Sunny Jim, Phat Willie, and Dave*.[8] Days before his inauguration as governor, Rolph sat down with journalist Elenore Meherin and provided many colorful details of his early life and career. A series of articles based on these interviews was published by the *San Francisco Chronicle* in December 1930 and January 1931. Loren B. Chan is the author of the most positive assessment of the Rolph administration—an article in the *Southern California Quarterly* in 1981.[9]

This book would have been easier to write 30 years ago, when it was still possible to get first-hand recollections from family members and contemporaries of Rolph. I have, however, received invaluable help from Nancy Rolph Welch, the governor's granddaughter, who has become the custodian of the family's memorabilia, photos and clippings from the period. I hope she and the many other members of the Rolph clan find this interpretation objective and reasonable.

I want to thank the reference staffs at the San Francisco Public Library, the California State Library, the Bancroft Library at the University of California, Berkeley, and the Sacramento Archives and Museum Collection Center for their professional and timely assistance. I would also like to thank my fiancée, Claudia Harmon, for her patience and encouragement, and David Overton for his thorough perusal of the manuscript and excellent suggestions for improvement.

Introduction: "The 'Humanest' Human Being I Ever Knew"

In the hours following Jim Rolph's death in June 1934, a woman named Rosie Lavender rose from her tiny apple stand on a Los Angeles street corner and made her way to the main road going north. There she began to hitchhike, and 30 hours later, close to collapse from fatigue, she arrived in San Francisco, where the former mayor and governor was being laid to rest. People heard a "piteous cry, a muffled struggle" as she attempted to breach the circle of presiding notables. "I've come so far — please — just to look on his kind face once more — oh, please." Rolph, it seemed, had ended her precarious effort at making a living several years before by financing her modest apple-selling enterprise and paying for her first stock. "You see," she said as they let her through, "he was my friend."[1]

That same month, leading San Franciscans established a fund in Rolph's memory and began soliciting donations from the public. Most people could barely afford life's necessities in 1934, but the contributions listed in the *Chronicle* included many tiny sums sent by anonymous working people from all over the city. Typical of these was one in the amount of 25 cents from an "Auntie Lillian," who wrote simply: "Sunny Jim help me."[2]

The year before Rolph died had been one of unimagined humiliation for such a popular man — a man who had won three-quarters of all votes cast for governor in 1930. The State Grange had led a movement to recall him. The legislature had launched an investigation of his administration and, when that faltered, simply refused to deal with him. As the state's economic crisis deepened, the new sales tax he signed into law was derided as "a penny for Jimmy." His public approval of a lynching in San Jose caused a firestorm of criticism from all over the nation.

Yet when he died, Californians put aside their frustration and unleashed a torrent of tears and tributes. "Only romantic, golden California could have produced such a glittering political figure," said the *Sacramento Union*. "He lived for the people of California and loved them, and couldn't understand why they didn't have at all times the same affection."[3] Rolph was "a fighter and a master political strategist," wrote the *San Francisco Chronicle*. "He had color, glamour, simplicity, diplomatic genius, and a dogged persistence as component parts of an extraordinary personality that was impossible to analyze."[4] His best friend and advisor, Matt Sullivan, called him "the 'humanest' human being I ever knew."[5]

Rolph was arguably the most unusual and original American politician of his era. Voters, first in San Francisco and then all over the state, responded not to his ideas or intellect, but to the sheer force of his personality and the generosity of his spirit. He was a man who could hobnob with civic leaders by day and then drink with dockworkers by night; who gave people a lift to work as he drove along his route to the city hall; who gave his own money away to anyone down on his luck; and who remembered the name of nearly everyone he had ever met. Above all, people felt he was just like them—flawed and sometimes wrong but doing his best.

Rolph's distinctiveness began with his physical appearance and manner. As governor, he was a "beaming, balding man, a little corpulent with advancing age but nonetheless handsome, with blue laughing eyes, a fringe of white hair, and a finely trimmed white mustache, accenting a round, florid face."[6] Everyone agreed that he made a memorable appearance. "He was an interesting person to look at," said a local journalist.[7] "Dapper, ebullient and utterly charming," a historian recalled.[8] "He was not a large man," remarked San Francisco's best-known madam, "but he had a voice that turned the most casual statement into a graceful speech."[9] In a tribute to his soothing public persona, the *Los Angeles Times* judged that "heaven intended him to be the permanent chairman of all the Christmas costume balls to be given by all the Rotary clubs."[10]

Rolph's manner of dress also reflected a sense of style and individuality. He was never seen in public without handmade, immaculately polished leather boots, of which he was reputed to own 40 pairs, and a fresh gardenia or carnation in his lapel. He wore a morning coat and striped trousers "at the slightest provocation"[11] and a high silk hat or a cattleman's huge Stetson. Tailors supplied him with four-in-hand ties in a special shade of blue and custom-made soft white shirts with detached collars.[12] Overall, he cut quite a figure. He was "a real-life version of Hollywood's screen caricature of a big-city mayor"—a "photo editor's dream."[13]

Rolph's presence alone added life and color to any occasion. A man who watched him enter the Belmont Hotel in New York said that the atmosphere simply changed when he walked in.[14] "He was a charmer, and he genuinely liked people, and people could feel it," said author Jerry Flamm. "When he came into a room, he would light it up. That is a cliché, but it was true."[15] A few detractors suggested that Rolph's style was at least in part political calculation, but it was almost certainly the result of a naturally buoyant and extroverted nature. "You can't resist that magnetism," wrote journalist Elenore Meherin, "any more than you can chill the sun."[16]

Central to Rolph's appeal was his success in being simultaneously aristocratic and democratic. The same man who as mayor of San Francisco presided over the Pan Pacific International Exposition in 1915, charming visiting world leaders with his sophistication and urbanity, was once late to a lunch in Alturas because he stopped his car en route and talked to a schoolteacher and her brood in a pouring rain for 20 minutes.[17] The same man who "radiated an imperial aplomb, a regal splendor" in becoming the "monarch" of American mayors[18] regularly received the poor and unfortunate, "men and women without the slightest political influence," in an attempt to relieve their distress.[19] Once, when he was shown the guest list for a party to be held in his honor, he saw only celebrities, so he added two policemen, a professional wrestler, an actor, and "other miscellaneous ragtags."[20] As *Sunset* magazine wrote in a 1928 profile, "He wears a high hat, but doesn't have a high-hat manner."[21]

Everyone who knew Rolph agreed that he functioned from the heart rather than the head. This was not so much a slight to his intelligence as a tribute to his humanity. "He dispensed love lavishly, generously and indiscriminately," one journalist wrote.[22] Rolph's surviving desk calendars are marked with birthdays and anniversaries of friends rather than meetings or engagements. "He was touched by the suffering of all, and he wanted to help them all," political reporter Earl Behrens eulogized.[23] He was barely able to pass a homeless man on the streets of San Francisco without jumping out of his car and offering assistance. Members of his staff joked that they had to keep him away from the poorer sections of the city because "he was a soft touch.... He would give away his pants."[24]

Even after his shipbuilding business collapsed and he had gone hopelessly in debt, Rolph continued to give what he had to anyone in need. As governor, not wanting to worry about money, he asked an aide to hand him an envelope full of currency whenever he needed cash. Rolph wondered one day why the $1 bills were always on the outside and the larger denominations in the middle. "Hang it all, Governor," the aide replied, "I've got to do that because every time some down-and-outer comes to you with a hard-luck tale, you reach into the envelope and hand him the first bill you put your fingers on."[25]

Like Franklin Roosevelt, whom he much admired, Rolph always wore a smile and exuded bonhomie. During his mayoral campaigns, he often framed the issue with his opponent as one of "optimism versus gloom." He was elected governor in part because, in a state known for its contentious political climate, he refrained from criticizing the other candidates and had "no sourness in his platitudes." California, said *The Nation*, "wanted Jimmy Rolph for a sunbeam." His public behavior communicated a sense that "the world is full of gay and decent fellows, regardless of minor differences of customs and opinion."[26] He strove to get along with everyone.

Part and parcel of his optimism was an excellent sense of humor, which could not be extinguished even by the slings and arrows directed his way in Sacramento. He insisted throughout his life that he was a descendant of Pocahontas and her English husband, John Rolfe. To add to the believability of this running gag, he sent two secretaries on a mission to find a wooden Indian for his office. They both failed, but a friend located a life-size replica of Chief Powhatan, father of Pocahontas. This statue was purchased and installed next to the mayor's desk.[27] Even during his final illness, Rolph was able to keep fun in his life: instead of using a bell or some other conventional means of summoning his nurse, he fired a pistol loaded with blanks.

All of these qualities, plus his penchant for showmanship, made Rolph an unbeatable candidate for public office. He thrived on events that other politicians considered sheer drudgery. He attended county fair openings and cornerstone layings. He milked cows, kissed babies, and rode white stallions in parades. Whenever possible, he was attired in a costume appropriate to the occasion. Included in his wardrobe were a train engineer's uniform, a canary-yellow festival outfit, and the formal attire of a Spanish don.

The political results spoke for themselves. Rolph ran five times for mayor and once for governor, never coming close to defeat. Looking back at his career from today's more cynical age, when elected officials seem to act and speak primarily in calculation of political advantage, it is hard to grasp the genuineness of the affection people had for him. He was "one of the few who could provoke a spontaneous public ovation without sending runners ahead to make sure it was spontaneous."[28] Even his opponents conceded that they could not dislike Jim Rolph — or win a popularity contest against him. It was "his human understanding, his kindliness, his sincerity, and the memory of countless little acts and courtesies ... that brought him the votes."[29] He was, in short, a "political dreamboat."[30]

When Rolph was first persuaded to run for mayor in 1910, he was a

41-year-old businessman, unskilled in the political arts. Though he lacked polish and eloquence, what impressed his audiences was his utter sincerity. "I appear before you as just plain Jim Rolph of the Mission, your neighbor," he would humbly begin.[31] Because he was not a politician, he did not come across as one. "So marked is this intense human quality," one journalist reported, "that even in his first public appearances it caught the populace."[32]

After five mayoral campaigns, he had become a mesmerizing public performer. An acquaintance of Charles Lindbergh recalled a San Francisco appearance of the famous aviator in the late 1920s at which Rolph presided:

> When the meal was over and cigar smoke began to cloud the room, Mayor Rolph introduced the nation's hero. James Rolph was a handsome, silver-haired man, and he had just the right kind of deep, sentimental Irish voice for a moment like this. After a standing ovation, Lindbergh began to speak. His voice was high-pitched, almost squeaky, and after the mayor's graceful words, he seemed ill at ease.[33]

Most politicians of the era lacked Rolph's ability to connect across class, religious and ethnic lines. Though he was a Protestant, he was an intimate of Catholic prelates and an honorary member of a local synagogue. He could walk into any church in town and feel completely at home and familiar with whatever rituals were being conducted. "He could attend a Catholic mass and tell you when to sit and when to stand better than you knew yourself," said one of his political rivals.[34] As the Lindbergh anecdote shows, he frequently impressed Irish audiences as one of their own, though he was not. And his successful identification with labor unions and advocacy of the closed shop, even while running several businesses of his own, was a big factor in his political success. "I will be mayor of the whole city, and not the mayor for any particular section," he promised in 1911.[35]

All these qualities would seem to make Rolph the perfect governor during a time of troubles. To learn why they did not—and why San Francisco's "hereditary mayor" could not transplant his success to Sacramento—requires a brief examination of his political and personal evolution.

PART ONE
The Citizen Politician

1

"Mission Jim"

Jim Rolph's buoyant personality and natural charm were the product of a happy childhood and a close-knit family. He inherited his urbanity and love of the city from his father and mother, who were born in London and Edinburgh and later met on a ship while en route to the United States. They married shortly after arriving in San Francisco in 1868. A year later, James Rolph, Jr., the first of seven children, was born. The family settled in the then-unfashionable Mission district, first residing on Minna, just south of Market Street, and later moving to a home on Guerrero. James Rolph, Sr., took up work as a bank teller and remained one for the rest of his life.

By all accounts, Rolph's childhood was idyllic. He once told an interviewer that the children knew they counted very much to their parents, and that he grew up with a feeling of "happy importance."[1] The family often read to each other at night, took many traveling vacations together, and willingly shared household chores. Rolph idolized his parents, especially his father, and when he married in 1900 he chose their anniversary as his wedding date. "They made sacrifices for us and we knew it," he later recalled. He took dancing lessons and learned the flute "because mother wished it."[2]

Early on, Rolph showed an extroverted nature, a knack for making friends, and an ability to lead. He had a zest for life and limitless energy. "We wanted fun," he told a journalist in 1930, "and were willing to meet the dawn to get it."[3] He wandered all over the city with his friends, excelled at bird trapping, fishing, and swimming, and was involved in school sports. He developed an early love of the sea, stimulated by Rolph Sr.'s part-time responsibilities as San Francisco agent for his brother in London, who had a shipping firm. Living in a maritime city allowed the young man to spend many afternoons watching ships from all over the world unloading cargo at the wharf.

The unique urban environment in which young Jim Rolph grew up shaped the development of his values and political outlook. San Francisco

The Rolph family in 1875. James Rolph, Jr., right with his mother behind him. Sitting are brothers Ronald, left, and George. In rear are Rolph's father, left, sister Mildred, and brother William. Rolph idolized his parents — he scheduled his wedding on their anniversary. When his mother died, he put his career on hold for nine years in order to help care for the other children (courtesy of the Bancroft Library, University of California, Berkeley).

was at the summit of its prestige as the political, economic and cultural capital of the west. It was world-renowned for its urbanity, sophistication and cosmopolitan appeal. But it was also a working-class city whose isolation from the rest of the country had given its industrial labor force enormous bargaining power with employers. Businesses had long observed the closed shop, agreeing to hire only union workers.

In the 1860s and 1870s, the favorable environment for labor began to change. The combination of a national depression and the completion of the transcontinental railroad brought unemployed workers from elsewhere in the country to compete with locals for jobs. Just as threatening was the arrival of large numbers of Chinese, who were willing to work for pennies. Living in a working-class neighborhood, the Rolph family may have sympathized with the labor discontent that frequently roiled the city.

But San Francisco was also a prosperous place with a strong business community, and Rolph had ambition and an entrepreneurial bent. By age

The family residence on San Jose Avenue in San Francisco. A childhood spent in the blue-collar Mission district helped make Rolph's later mayoral candidacy acceptable to labor (Nancy Rolph Welch Collection).

15, using a stake provided by his father, he was breeding squabs at home and selling the hatched chicks to the city's epicures. He also raised prize cocker spaniels. During the summers, he held down more conventional employment as a cashier at a department store. One of the neighbor boys, Matt Sullivan, though he was Rolph's senior by 12 years, was attracted to young Jim because he seemed always to be at the center of the action. Sullivan was to become Rolph's closest friend, advisor and confidant.

Again deferring to his mother's wishes, Rolph attended a local parochial school — the Trinity Academy. Mrs. Rolph was a devout churchgoer, and her pastor was also head of the academy. Here, the boy "reveled in both education and social activity"[4] and ended up as class president in his senior year. The day after graduation, Rolph went to work as a clerk for DeWitt, Kittle & Co., a shipping firm. He proposed to his high school sweetheart — a girl named Annie Reid — and they resolved to marry when the time was right.

Rolph later recalled an incident that helped shape him as an orator and politician. In readying himself for a school debate, he had memorized a large body of material, but once in front of the large crowd looking on, he froze with stage fright after reciting one sentence. From that moment, he overprepared for any public appearance, saying to himself, "There must be no slip." Though he later learned to extemporize skillfully, on important occasions he wrote down every point on note cards as a precaution. He was never able to overcome last-minute jitters before speeches. His nervousness often brought a hot flush to his face that, according to his future personal secretary, his opponents incorrectly ascribed to excessive drinking.[5]

The first big test of Rolph's character came with the death of his mother when he was 20. He had many plans, including marriage and medical school, but his father was now the sole parent of seven children, including two babies. Rolph quickly decided that his place was at home. His father sent for his 50-year-old unmarried sister, Mary, who lived in Toronto. She left Canada the day after receiving his letter, arrived in San Francisco a few weeks later, moved in, and devoted herself from that day forward to raising the Rolph children. Jim Rolph put his future on hold and remained a clerk — unwilling to marry or pursue a serious career — until his youngest brother was almost grown. By then, he would be almost 30.

Even during these years of increased familial responsibility, Rolph was not obliged to sacrifice material comforts. In the mid–1890s, he was earning $125 a month — a sum that allowed him to hire an occasional cab to take him and Annie to the theater or opera house. On New Year's, he rented a rig and made calls on his many friends, leaving a decorated card with a "pretty sentiment" at the home of each.[6]

Rolph's long friendship with a young man named George Hind led to a business opportunity that would launch them both into San Francisco's moneyed elite. In 1898, they each put up $2,500 — a significant sum in those days — and Hind's father, a wealthy sugar plantation owner in Hawaii, contributed sufficient additional capital for the boys to establish the Hind, Rolph Shipping Company.[7] Its primary responsibility was to act as agent for the Hind ships and plantation.

The firm was immediately successful and soon was shipping goods up and down the coast as well as abroad — first using the bottoms of the elder Hind's ships and then buying their own. After only three years as a shipping executive, Rolph was named head of the San Francisco Shipowners' Association. In 1900, he was sure enough of his financial future to stage an elaborate wedding and take a seven-week honeymoon in Hawaii.

Rolph's people skills and business acumen marked him as a man to watch. In 1901, Rolph saw a chance to bring a much-needed bank to the Mission district. At his urging, the Bank of California opened a branch in the Mission — the first branch bank to be established in the city's residential area. Then it made Rolph its president. The energetic young man had

Young Rolph, left, and George Hind, with a stake provided by Hind's father, founded a shipping company in 1898. The firm was immediately successful. By the middle of the next decade, Rolph had already earned his first $1 million and bought a 160-acre ranch (Nancy Rolph Welch Collection).

become a leading voice in local business circles by mid-decade as president of the Merchant's Exchange and the Mission Promotion Association and a leading figure in the Chamber of Commerce. Soon his net worth was almost $1 million.[8]

At this point in his career, Rolph seemed prepared to rest on his laurels. Certainly he did not entertain any notions about entering politics. His only ambitions were to have a family and live the good life — "to raise my own cows and chickens, to have my own stables, and pick fruit from my own trees," he reflected many years later. He had already purchased his first ranch — a 160-acre spread in Los Altos. He had the money to take his family on annual jaunts to Europe. Rolph was supremely happy with his life: "I wanted my place in the sun. And, by heaven, I had it."[9]

2

From the Earthquake to the Mayor's Office

Turn-of-the-century San Francisco had a well-deserved reputation as a wide-open and free-wheeling city. It was also a place of sharp economic contrasts. Enormously wealthy businessmen lived in mansions on exclusive Nob Hill surrounded by a sea of working-class neighborhoods. The average San Franciscan lived an enviable, though hardly luxurious, life. Thousands of saloons and a variety of free-lunch counters provided workers with midday refreshment. There, a nickel not only bought a mug of beer but also a filling, if plain, meal. After dark, neighborhoods like the Barbary Coast, notorious for "low gambling houses thronged with riot-loving rowdies in all stages of intoxication" and "fetid brothels which dispensed delight and disease in about equal portions," attracted a varied and enthusiastic clientele.[1]

Aggressive expansion of labor unions aided the fortunes of the city's working class during the 1890s. Many union organizers were anarchists or socialists who employed fiery, class-conscious rhetoric to galvanize their members. These exhortations often led to strikes and to mob and vigilante violence.

The conservative business community was alarmed by the increasing volatility and strife, and it banded together into an Employers Association to combat union activities. In 1901 the teamsters and dockworkers combined to launch a citywide strike, which brought San Francisco business to a standstill and cost over $1 million a day in lost revenue. The Employers Association fought back with intimidation and violence of its own. Business leaders were enraged by Mayor James Phelan's refusal to bring in state troops to break the back of the strike and pressured him not to run for reelection that year.

Organized labor was also dissatisfied with Mayor Phelan, feeling that he had not done enough to protect strikers from attack. It decided to seek control of the mayor's office by forming its own political organization, the Union Labor Party, and running a labor candidate. An orchestra leader named Eugene Schmitz was selected, and he won the election handily.

The Schmitz administration quickly sank in a morass of graft and corruption. Schmitz was a weak figure who was dominated by a behind-the-scenes manipulator, Abraham Ruef, and his handpicked members of the city's board of supervisors. The scale of venality attracted national attention when *Harper's Weekly* wrote of Ruef's "great political ambition and boundless avarice."[2] Despite the efforts of a growing number of anti–Ruef reformers in business and the media, Schmitz managed to win reelection in 1905.

It seemed unlikely that the relatively privileged Jim Rolph, already a prominent businessman, employer, and leading figure in the Merchant's Exchange, could relate to the problems of the average worker. He must have had friends who were strident antiunionists and who pressured him to adopt an uncompromising attitude toward labor demands. Instead, he went out of his way to become acquainted with labor leaders, and he enjoyed having lunch with workingmen at his own firm. On these occasions, he would sometimes pass around expensive Cuban cigars. Many of his peers scoffed at these gestures.[3]

As civic corruption and ill will between capital and labor deepened, an unprecedented disaster intervened. A great earthquake struck in the early morning of April 18, 1906. It started dozens of fires by breaking gas connections and overturning stoves. Merging into one great inferno, the fire raged for three days and destroyed most of the city. It spread over 500 blocks and destroyed 28,000 homes. Hundreds died in the conflagration.

The crisis provided the crucible in which Rolph's skills as an organizer and his credentials as a humanitarian were nurtured. His neighborhood had been especially hard hit. Said an eyewitness: "South of Market, in the district known as the Mission, there were cheap man-traps folded in like pasteboard, and from these before the rip of the flames blotted out the sound, arose the thin, long scream of mortal agony."[4] On the first day, with thousands of fleeing refugees in need of food, shelter and clothing, Rolph mounted his horse, rode through the Mission, and called an emergency meeting in his barn.[5] "We knew that old San Francisco was gone," he later recalled.[6]

That evening, he and some friends formed the Mission Relief Association, with headquarters in his own house. Many of the men who later comprised his kitchen cabinet, including neighbor and friend Matt Sullivan, were part of this ad hoc volunteer operation. Within 24 hours, supplies and assistance were flowing to victims, and it soon became known as one of the biggest and most efficient relief efforts in the city.[7] Even so, his deeply felt compassion often interfered with his focus on the task at hand. Witnesses said he wanted to rush out and personally console each victim rather than tend to business in his office.

In the confusion, local government had almost ceased to function. Graft prosecutions of city politicians were underway in 1906, calling into question the ability of government to deal with the mass dislocation and suffering. Hence, the relief enterprise required initiative and resourcefulness. Rolph and his colleagues did not wait for any official permission to feed the hungry. They requisitioned whole carloads of food, reasoning that the Mission district contained the largest number of refugees. When challenged, they showed makeshift credentials—official-looking passes, homemade business cards with "Mission Relief" printed on them, and a deputy

Rolph, sixth from left, poses with members of the Mission Relief Association, which he and some friends formed in the wake of the devastating 1906 San Francisco earthquake. Lifelong friend Matt Sullivan is at far right. In a lawless, chaotic environment, the group requisitioned supplies and forged credentials in order to feed the hungry in their area. "Nobody gave us authority," Rolph said. "We took it" (courtesy of the Bancroft Library, University of California, Berkeley).

marshal's badge that Rolph wore. "Nobody gave us authority," he recalled. "We took it."[8]

In the months that followed, the business community, led by the Merchant's Exchange and the Chamber of Commerce, took a leading role in the rebuilding effort. As a rising leader of that community, Rolph grabbed the opportunity. "The work lay before us," he later reflected. "We attacked it." He transformed his relief organization into a civic association that lobbied for an ambitious citywide reconstruction and improvement program.

Many points in the program formed the nucleus of his agenda as mayor five years later. They included the construction of a new city hall and civic center, which had been all but destroyed during the quake; a new municipally owned railway system; and an ambitious project that would bring much-needed water to San Francisco by damming up the Hetch Hetchy Valley in the Sierra Nevada and building an elaborate system of canals. Rolph's leading role in creating this vision of the new San Francisco led to his election, and subsequent reelection, as president of the Merchant's Exchange.

Despite his close association with the city's businessmen, Rolph continued to be known for his strong pro-union stance. At his own company, he hired only union men and, unlike most employers of the era, he honored the closed shop. As head of the Shipowners Association, he fully accepted the principle of collective bargaining and had helped negotiate an unprecedented contract with the Sailors' Union in 1902.[9] When the association decided to support the open shop during a waterfront strike in 1906, Rolph, unwilling to compromise his principles, gave up his membership.

Why did Rolph identify with the working man instead of taking on the elitist perspective of the business community? As a resident of the Mission, a blue-collar neighborhood, he probably had many friends who worked on the docks or in factories. Because he loved and admired his parents, we can suppose that they instilled in him the belief that character, rather than money, power or ancestry, was the true measure of a human being. "I was never a capitalist in heart or in action," he later recalled. "I'd worked since I was a schoolboy. All my sympathy was with the employee."[10]

It began to dawn on many San Franciscans that a popular and successful entrepreneur with strong ties to both business and labor would be a perfect mayor for a community sharply divided by class. They noticed that Rolph had a disarming manner, a way of smoothing over difficulties, and an ability to find common ground. Friends began urging him to run as early as 1907. Two years later the Republican County Committee unanimously made the same suggestion. The *San Francisco Call* wrote that "no man has so many friends, or so much personal influence." However, he declined to run, citing his lack of political experience, the demands of his private life, and, according to one account, the opposition of his family.[11]

In the aftermath of the terrible quake, it seemed impossible that San Francisco might soon emerge from the ashes and become a functioning city once more. But by 1909 so much progress had been made that Rolph, as president of the Merchant's Exchange, and his colleagues decided to sponsor a celebration that would announce San Francisco's revival to the world. Envoys were even dispatched to Europe to invite representatives of the various governments. "We had done in three years what the world predicted would take at least thirty," Rolph later recalled. "We had all worked with prodigious, inspired energy. We wanted the world's confidence. Let them see that we were actually back on the map."[12]

The Portola Festival, as it was called, was a huge success and a personal triumph for Rolph. Foreign ambassadors arrived in force to be dazzled by the beauty of San Francisco Bay and amazed by the full restoration of the city's commerce. Rolph was chairman of the Portola reception committee. The job required him to deliver many formal and informal addresses as emissaries from around the country and other lands streamed into the harbor and arrived by train. All received a generous dose of the Rolph charm. On one occasion, he was asked to represent the mayor in making a call on a German cruiser. The *Chronicle* reported the next day that "many pleasant things were said to the understudy mayor, apropos of the fact that one time recently he had been urged by his many friends to ... become the real mayor."[13]

After Portola, it would become more difficult for Rolph to turn aside appeals for him to play a larger role in city affairs. He and the members of the Portola organizing committee plunged into a new effort to compete with other U.S. cities for the right to stage an even grander event — an international exposition — to be held in several years to celebrate the anticipated opening of the Panama Canal. During this time newspapers began to call Rolph "Sunny Jim," in recognition of his energy, exuberance, and optimism.[14]

In the meantime, the city continued to suffer under weak and dishonest leadership. The Union Labor Party, which had held the mayor's office since 1905, could not even keep labor unrest from increasing. The administration of P.H. McCarthy, who had succeeded Schmitz, was almost as corrupt as its predecessor. A crusading newspaper editor, Fremont Older, had helped to recruit a tenacious special prosecutor, Francis J. Heney, to investigate Abe Ruef and other city officials. The investigations revealed that the mayor's office took bribes "everywhere from everybody and in almost every imaginable way."[15] Though the graft prosecution attained few convictions, the blizzard of negative publicity fatally undermined the political capital of the Union Labor Party.

Rolph's candidacy for mayor in 1911 was engineered by the city's commercial leaders. San Francisco had just won the right — besting New Orleans in a national competition — to host the international exposition Rolph's Portola group had been promoting. The business community understood the economic importance of a successful exposition and intended to recruit one of its own to run for mayor — someone who would guarantee political stability and social harmony while preparing the city to show its best face. They had supported and helped pass a charter amendment in 1910 that established nonpartisan municipal elections and extended the term of mayor from two to four years. Now 50 leading citizens formed an organization called the Municipal Conference, which included Rolph intimates Matt Sullivan and Gavin McNab, and sought to draft Rolph into service.

Everything about Rolph — his background, his family, his looks, his civic agenda, his work in the Mission district, his ability to get things done — seemed to promise political success. Three times he had said no. "But the fourth time, they came with a demand," Rolph recalled later. "They said it was my duty to serve the city I loved. I agreed."[16]

He was persuaded most by the chaotic state of local government. "The graft was deep seated and had endured so long it was almost sanctioned," he said later. "There was rancor and conflict in every post from mayor to street-sweeper."[17] The idea of a nonpartisan campaign squared with his perception that building a great city was a nonpartisan task. "I am not a politician," he reminded people. "I appear before you as just plain Jim Rolph of the Mission, your neighbor."[18] With those words he launched his political career.

From the beginning, inclusiveness was the centerpiece of his appeal. "I will be mayor of the whole city," he emphasized, "and not the mayor for any particular section."[19] Like the Progressives of the era, he pledged to select city officials based on competence, without regard for party or class. He downplayed religious differences; he himself attended many churches and felt at home in all of them. He reminded voters that the shipping business had brought him into harmonious contact with people of every ethnicity. And he promised to bring into being a new city hall and civic center, even though the electorate had voted down a bond issue to finance their construction two years earlier.

Despite Rolph's political inexperience, or perhaps because of it, San Francisco voters responded with enthusiasm to his candidacy. In 1911, Rolph was a handsome, magnetic figure, with clear blue eyes, a ruddy complexion, and a frank, genial expression. He smiled easily, was unruffled by hecklers, and seemed confident and serene. He radiated friendliness, cheerfulness, and goodwill. If his wife, Annie, had earlier opposed his candidacy, she was now constantly by his side. "In a cosmopolitan, urbane environment," historian Carol Hicke wrote, "Rolph appeared as a cosmopolitan, urbane human being."[20]

His campaign was intensely personal. He exuded a "warmth and flash" in his campaign appearances, "something stirring and vital that drew throngs by the thousands."[21] Showing his trademark high energy, he visited many workplaces during the day—"vinegar works, gas plants, tanneries, breweries, laundries"[22]—and attended four or five meetings at night, shaking thousands of hands. He became skilled at singling out people he knew in the crowd and calling them by their first names. Toward the end of his rallies, he would lead the crowd in singing campaign songs.

Most critical to Rolph's chances for electoral success in San Francisco was his ability to portray himself as a friend of the workingman. Many labor leaders were initially skeptical of his commitment to their interests, calling him a silk-stocking aristocrat. They often sent roughnecks to Rolph rallies to intimidate the crowds and challenge the candidate. Every meeting was "electrical with conflict."[23] Rocks and dead cats were tossed at his car. Fistfights broke out daily.

At first Rolph found the confrontations upsetting, but in time he was carried away by the battle. Even his closest friends, it was said, were surprised by the vigor and combativeness of his campaign. He rejected assertions that he was no friend of labor, reminding voters that he was born in an alley in the working-class Mission district. He told an audience of workers how he had once argued for hours against a lockout of the steam schooner sailors by the shipowners.

In the end, he changed many minds and won over a large share of union leaders as well as the rank and file. Labor icon Andrew Furuseth, head of the Sailors' Union of the Pacific, who rarely involved himself in politics, gave a speech endorsing Rolph.[24] Toward the close of the campaign, the "James Rolph Jr. Union Labor special"—a car full of union officials—would appear at every meeting to lend support.[25]

Rolph's charisma and appeal as a mediator between business and labor were decisive in a campaign that featured no serious policy differences between the two candidates. Mayor McCarthy was vulnerable to charges of corruption and favoritism in city hiring. Sensing his weakness, he resorted to insults—calling Rolph "Dummy Jim"—and reminded his labor constituency of his opponent's wealth.

But he could do little to turn the tide. Along with the overwhelming support of the business community, Rolph had the backing of the three largest newspapers in town. In the end, though balloting was generally along class lines, Rolph ran well in most areas of the city and won the election by a margin of 20,000. He even beat McCarthy in his own district. The Rolph era in San Francisco had begun.

3

Moving Through Cheers

The man who moved into the mayor's office in January 1912 was a true citizen-politician. Because he was not well educated and had given little thought to politics in the years before he ran for mayor, Rolph did not have a consistent political philosophy, nor was he linked firmly with any of California's parties. Though a businessman and nominally a Republican, he bragged about his ties to Democrats in the labor movement and to numerous ethnic groups in his diverse community. He was, above all, pragmatic and nonideological — a "freewheeling political rarity who made up his own rules as he went along."[1] Politically, he was "octangular,"[2] sincere in his efforts to represent the interests of all the people.

Rolph came to office during a time when Progressivism was ascendant in California. The most prominent of the California Progressives, Hiram Johnson, had just been elected governor. For the most part, Progressives were Republican reformers — middle-class professionals and businessmen — who wanted to rein in the enormous power of the railroads and other utilities, to rationalize and democratize state and local government, and to reduce the power of political parties by making elections nonpartisan. The movement also had a strong moral component, favoring Prohibition and opposing racetrack gambling.

Rolph shared some — but not all — Progressive values. Like the Progressives, he believed in the role of outside experts in making government more efficient, and he was never hesitant to use the power of government to accomplish big jobs. But he could never agree with the Progressive morality, which was rooted in the southern half of the state, and he later backed away on several occasions from confrontations with powerful utilities. In sum, though not exactly a Progressive himself, Rolph was a perfect candidate for the nonpartisan era that the Progressives had launched.

Rolph's first term as mayor was an unqualified triumph. His agenda was a natural extension of his earlier involvement in rebuilding a shattered city, only now he sought to help San Francisco fulfill the promise of its favorable geography and climate. He caught the mood of the people when he declared that the city "will be to America what Florence is to Italy and Paris is to France."³ He and his staff tirelessly promoted the passage of construction bonds, turned down by the voters in 1909, and they passed by an 11–1 margin in early 1912.

Having secured the necessary funding, he embarked upon a building program that featured road improvements, tunnels, an extension of the streetcar system, and a dramatic new civic center. The dome atop the city hall, as he became fond of saying, was taller than the Capitol Building in Washington. Much of this construction was to prepare the city to host the 1915 Panama Pacific International Exposition.

Though generally probusiness, Rolph fought for a municipal railway line in competition with private interests, because he believed it would enable San Francisco to control and direct its growth. In doing so, he sought to harness the power of the municipal ownership movement, which was gathering momentum at the time with the support of key Progressives. His handling of this

The new mayor of San Francisco. In 1911, Rolph was a handsome, magnetic figure, with clear blue eyes, a ruddy complexion, and a frank, genial expression (San Francisco History Center, San Francisco Public Library).

issue was typical of his style and approach. Encountering intense resistance from the United Railway Company, which operated the city's private railroad, he avoided arguments about whether the city or the private sector should take the lead and focused instead on the practical tasks at hand — to get city cars running along the most heavily traveled routes and then to extend the system to link with the exposition site.

As endless litigation threatened to hold up a resolution, Rolph took his case to the people. Many San Franciscans were skeptical of the cost-effectiveness of a public railway system and questioned the adequacy of the

San Francisco's Civic Center, like most of the city, was destroyed during the 1906 earthquake and fire. As mayor, Rolph rebuilt it. The new city hall, he would later brag, was a few feet taller than the Capitol Building in Washington, D.C. (San Francisco History Center, San Francisco Public Library).

planning efforts behind it. The mayor's strategy was to gloss over the details and to reduce the issue to one of "optimism versus gloom."[4] He asked the voters to approve a $3 million bond issue to pay for it and, with powerful assistance from city media and a visit by Governor Johnson to urge passage, it carried by a 4–1 margin. He had succeeded in translating a complex technical matter into "a warm, human brand of politics ... which united his supporters and disarmed his enemies."[5] When the streetcar lines opened, he personally piloted the cars on their maiden runs, dressed from head to toe in an engineer's garb.

Rolph's strong belief in harmony and tolerance was a tonic for a city rife with social and economic divisions. Seeking to "smother partisanship with his hearty conviviality and effusive love for his city,"[6] he promoted a vision of civic unity based on the pursuit of common goals. It was often said that Rolph governed from the center, which not only was a reference to his politics but to his role as balancer of competing interests.

He had an uncanny ability to defuse tensions. He was once leading a parade at which a radical labor group, backed by Communists, planned to stage a demonstration that many feared would turn violent. Thinking quickly, he sent a police escort to invite them to the parade, took them onto the reviewing stand, and "harangued them on the glories of the California climate."[7] Thrown off stride, they never got around to their intended agenda.

The people of San Francisco loved their new mayor. Electoral success did not affect his generosity, sincerity, or his ability to relate to everyday people and their problems. He adhered to the practice of seeing anyone who wanted to meet with him, even if it meant holding up city business. As he developed as a politician, he began purposely arriving late at civic meetings so that his appearances had maximum impact. This practice also gave him some time to stop in at a random worker's home to inquire about the family's health.[8]

When an army of laid-off building tradesmen seeking assistance marched to San Francisco in the rain, Rolph quickly agreed to meet with as many as could squeeze into his office. Believing that their demands were reasonable, he arranged for soup kitchens to be set up and temporarily turned over a hotel to them. "Whenever the poor and hungry call on me," he said, "I shall receive them."[9] When fair weather returned, he convinced the workers that they could more easily find employment elsewhere, led them in a march to the ferry, and gave them boat fare. The men were said to believe that he had done all he could for them and thus left happy. Stories such as this one increased the mayor's popularity, precisely because his actions were not perceived as political in nature.

Scarcely a day went by without someone noting one of his many acts of compassion and concern. According to a media account, he once took a man lying in the street to the hospital, then changed into a doctor's clothing, took pulses and carried stretchers for four hours. On other occasions, the mayor was not too busy to secure the release from the city pound of a young boy's dog and to put up his own funds for a ballpark for kids with no place to play but the street. "Rolph moved, in those days, through cheers," Ernest Jerome Hopkins recalled.[10]

To his constituents, he often seemed to be everywhere at once. One woman reported boarding the new municipal railway with her infant daughter and finding Rolph at the front of the car, boisterously greeting the passengers. The mayor spontaneously picked up the little girl and, still talking to everyone, held her until the end of the line. Another city resident recalled being taken to the greyhound races by her father and seeing Rolph in the crowd. Beaming, he rose from his seat and, "dressed to perfection, gave a

Three generations of Rolphs appeared at the laying of the cornerstone for the new civic center in 1913. From left, the mayor, holding a trowel; son James III; daughter Annette, wearing a broad-brimmed hat, directly behind James; wife Annie, holding flowers; an unidentified onlooker; and father James Rolph, Sr., with the beard (Nancy Rolph Welch Collection).

rousing speech that made everyone smile."[11] Rolph always knew how to raise the spirits of everyone around him.

In at least one important sense, Rolph's election marked the birth of a new San Francisco—more genteel than the bawdy and often squalid town of the preearthquake days. Ever since the California gold rush, a downtown area called the Barbary Coast had been a mecca of prostitution, drinking and gambling, unmatched anywhere for rapacity and violence. With the rebuilding that took place after 1906, the business community concluded that vice and "mining-camp amusements" were more apt to harm than to benefit the city's image.[12]

Rolph, as we shall see, was certainly no puritan and usually preferred to follow a live-and-let-live policy when dealing with the pleasure industry. But like many other leading citizens, including key religious leaders, he was probably repelled by the "dismal bedlam of obscenity" emanating nightly from "a tumultuous mob of half-drunken men ... greedily inspecting women as if they had been so many wild animals in cages."[13] Under the circumstances, he bowed to the growing pressure for a crackdown. In 1912, the authorities began to implement a plan that would gradually regulate the Barbary Coast out of existence. A year later, William Randolph Hearst's *San Francisco Examiner* accelerated the process by publishing vivid descriptions of the depravity and dangers of the district. In 1917 Rolph's police department shut down the entire area.

Preparing for the Panama-Pacific Exposition was the rationale for nearly all that Rolph did during his first term, including the construction of the new civic center and city hall. The city itself was in a position to provide little but encouragement and guidance in bringing the exposition to life. Private enterprise had to provide much of the financing. The mayor's great accomplishment was to rally the business community behind the project while keeping labor unions quiet and cooperative. Rolph also found time to visit Philadelphia and persuade the mayor and city council to allow the Liberty Bell to be shipped west and put on exhibit at the fair.

Rolph demonstrated early on that conviction, rather than political expediency, drove his nonpartisanship and appeal to organized labor. Many of his appointees were Democrats or labor officials, or both. When a press union went on strike in 1913, the mayor's decision not to suppress strike disorders drew criticism from the Chamber of Commerce. Rolph insisted, in return for his forbearance, that labor pull together with business behind his single-minded goal of making the Pan-Pacific Exposition a triumph for the city.

The exposition was indeed a great triumph — "everything that San Francisco was not and never had been ... a model of cooperative amity"[14]— and it made Rolph "an impresario with San Francisco for a stage."[15] On opening day in February 1915, he led a parade to the grounds. One-third of the city turned out to march or watch.

Over the next several months, he received, befriended, and enthusiastically entertained dignitaries from around the world. "Sparkling with vitality, glowing with good will, he was a jewel of a greeter," waxed a local journalist years later.[16] The guests, in gratitude, presented the mayor with decorations and foreign titles. He also attended a whirlwind of social functions. By one account, he made a thousand speeches, shook 50,000 hands, and consumed a thousand chicken dinners.

The timing of the exposition could not have been more convenient politically. The mayoral campaign of 1915 would take place at the event's height. He had planned to retire after one term, but for a while he maintained a

Rolph, second from right in front row, marches on the opening day of the Pan-Pacific International Exposition in 1915. The exposition was a triumph, "a model of cooperative amity," and it made the mayor "an impresario with San Francisco for a stage" (Nancy Rolph Welch Collection).

sphinx-like silence regarding his intentions.[17] Behind the scenes, business leaders put great pressure on the mayor to run again. Finally, he told his staff that he was "through with public life. I've enjoyed it.... I'm glad I was San Francisco's chief, but now I'm withdrawing — going back to my home, my dogs, my garden." "Ha, ha, you are," one of his secretaries allegedly countered. "You love it when the street sweepers and the newsies call out, 'Hello, mayor.'" No doubt glad to get such a response, he replied: "I guess you're right. I guess I won't retire."[18]

Busy as he was, he decided to spend only three weeks seeking votes. But three weeks were more than enough because he did not have to do all the campaigning himself. The business community, which had profited the most from his administration, threw itself into the mayor's reelection effort. The *Chronicle* backed Rolph "on the basis of his good-humored unwillingness to offend anybody."[19] "I have given San Francisco a clean, competent and constructive administration," the mayor said. "I will wage no campaign. Let my record speak."[20]

That record was one of undeniable and tangible accomplishments — the Geary Street railway line, the Stockton Street tunnel, a high-pressure water system, a new county jail, a new city hall, much of a new civic center, 69 miles of paved streets, the beginning of the Twin Peaks tunnel, and the introduction of a civil service system into city government. It did not even matter that he had few new initiatives to suggest.

Though his main opponent in the 1915 election was a former mayor, the labor leader Eugene Schmitz, Rolph won the election in the primary, receiving more votes than all other candidates combined. The media reported that he ran far ahead "in all the better districts" and made a "tremendous showing" in labor areas. "I never had much doubt of the outcome," he said later. "I think my fellow citizens knew that I loved San Francisco with all my heart, and that I would work to the last pulse for her. I have.... It's been a glorious privilege — a life's work."[21]

4

Friends and Family

As befit his democratic temperament, caring nature, and nearly universal appeal, Rolph had close friends from across the entire political spectrum and from all walks of life. For him, a friendship was not something formed out of convenience or expediency. It was a personal bond requiring mutual loyalty and support.

He had friendships with a group of men in San Francisco who became known as his kitchen cabinet after he was elected mayor. All of them remained close to Rolph throughout his life, and some followed him to Sacramento when he became governor. He relied on these men not only for comradeship but also for political advice and help in winning elections. Some were businessmen and Republicans like himself, but others were Democrats and labor officials. Mutual affection, rather than ideology, was the cement that bound them together.

Chief among these cronies was Matt Sullivan, a childhood pal who later became an attorney, a law partner of Hiram Johnson, and then briefly chief justice of the California Supreme Court. Sullivan was 12 years senior to Rolph and was sometimes called "Uncle Matt" by the media because of this age difference. As boys, they lived on the same block in the Mission district. Sullivan was impressed with young Rolph's knack for playing hard, working hard, and making friends.

Friendships between boys 12 years apart in age are rare. Young Rolph probably looked up to Sullivan as a kind of mentor, elder brother, and role model. When he formed the Mission Relief Association during the earthquake of 1906, Sullivan was a charter member. Later Sullivan was one of several influential citizens who pressured Rolph into running for mayor. After that, he was always at Rolph's side — managing his campaigns, giving advice, and carrying out a variety of sensitive assignments.

Because of his advantage in years, superior education, and extensive legal background, Sullivan was often asked to provide the intellectual foundation for Rolph's political choices. Sometimes, he helped make the choices too. Trained to be rigorous and analytical, Sullivan may have occasionally winced at the mayor's tendency to let his emotions overrule his reason. When Rolph died, he eulogized that his friend was "a man of heart more than head, and whatever his faults were, the reason was that his heart was too big."[1]

Because of Sullivan's strong influence on Rolph, there was much contemporary speculation about his political views. In some circles, he was known as a staunch conservative,[2] but most of his contemporaries believed that he had Progressive leanings. He had worked for Hiram Johnson, the best-known California Progressive. Along with Johnson, he had stepped in to help prosecute Abe Ruef after Francis Heney, the lead prosecutor, was shot during the trial. Beyond that, he occasionally took aim at corporations and other bastions of privilege. He favored public power at the expense of Pacific Gas and Electric, the giant San Francisco utility, and he attacked a scheme to finance a new opera house with private money in exchange for preferential seating for the sponsors. He probably had the same mix of conservative and liberal tendencies as his friend the mayor.

In later years, Rolph's heavy dependence on Sullivan carried the risk of making him appear weak and indecisive. Many times he would tell the media, in response to a policy question, that he had to check with Matt Sullivan before answering. He once said: "I never do anything that I don't contact Sullivan," and it was almost literally true.[3]

Just about as close to the mayor as Sullivan was Theodore Roche, San Francisco's police commissioner and Sullivan's law partner. Roche implemented the mayor's live-and-let-live attitude toward prostitution, gambling and liquor sales. Though Rolph interfered little in law enforcement, he occasionally asked Roche to crack down on vice—for example, in the Barbary Coast area—in order to placate reformers. He showed his loyalty to Roche in 1918 when, enraged by an article critical of the commissioner in the *San Francisco Daily News*, he wrote a scathing letter of complaint to the publisher.

Roche moved to Sacramento with the new governor and took a high administrative post in the state bureaucracy. There the *Sacramento Union* referred to him as Rolph's "right-hand man and power behind the throne." Roche often worked with Sullivan in support of the governor and probably handled his estate in his legal capacity. When Rolph died in June 1934, Roche told the public of the sad state of his finances.

A third member of the kitchen cabinet was Eustace Cullinan, a Progressive attorney who, like Sullivan, had been a boyhood neighbor of Rolph's in the Mission district and had gone on to become a member of the Mission

Relief Association in 1906. Cullinan would betray his Progressive principles in the 1920s by becoming a public relations counsel for Pacific Gas and Electric, while continuing to advise the mayor.

Rounding out the inner circle was attorney and advisor Gavin McNab, a "cagey, Scotch-American backstage operative."[4] His brother, John McNab, was also a strong Rolph supporter. Because Gavin was a prominent member of the state Democratic establishment and John a leading San Francisco Republican, their backing helped to give the Rolph administration bipartisan appeal. Gavin McNab, who died in 1927, was the only one of Rolph's intimates not to survive into his years as governor.

If the kitchen cabinet was Rolph's brain trust, Ed Rainey was his man Friday, personal secretary, and gatekeeper. Rainey had been recruited in 1912 while working as a reporter for the *San Francisco Examiner* and he quickly became an indispensable aide, drafting and signing correspondence, arranging meetings, and telling the mayor where he needed to be and when. "If you wanted anything at city hall, you went to Rainey," said a former state senator. "He ran the shop for Rolph."[5]

Rainey was often left to deal with difficult situations arising from Rolph's good nature. Once the mayor saw a man in rags sleeping on a bench in a park, called Rainey at midnight, and asked him to make sure the man found shelter. Early in his first term, Rolph began holding "kicker's meetings," or gripe sessions, on Monday mornings. He tired

Ed Rainey was the mayor's man Friday, personal secretary and gatekeeper. "If you wanted anything at city hall, you went to Rainey. He ran the shop for Rolph." He often was left to deal with difficult situations arising from Rolph's good nature (San Francisco History Center, San Francisco Public Library).

of them after six weeks and turned them over to Rainey. According to local bordello owner Sally Stanford, Rainey even facilitated Rolph's occasional liaisons. He knew Rolph as well as any man did. Later he followed Rolph to Sacramento and was named state superintendent of banking in 1931.

Of great help to Rolph in fending off charges that he was a probusiness aristocrat was his alliance with Tim Reardon, a former steamfitter and metal tradesman. Reardon, who became a lifelong friend, played a key role in the 1911 campaign by opposing aggressively and vociferously the labor candidate for mayor.

After his victory, Rolph appointed Reardon head of the city public works department. From that key post, Reardon ensured that city employees were loyal to the administration and took an active part in Rolph's reelection bids. According to Jerry Flamm, they were threatened with the loss of

Rolph and his family relax with their pets in front of their San Francisco home. Left to right: son James III, daughter Georgina, the mayor, daughter Annette, and wife Annie. As Eustace Cullinan wrote in the *San Francisco Chronicle* on April 3, 1937, Rolph "loved horses, dogs and people, in just about that order. Horses and dogs never betrayed him" (Nancy Rolph Welch Collection).

their jobs if Rolph lost. Reardon was, in short, a tough and savvy infighter whose close attention to the nitty-gritty of politics allowed the mayor to take the high road during his campaigns. He followed Rolph to Sacramento in 1931 to become a member of the highway commission.

These six men, based in San Francisco, were Rolph's most intimate comrades, but, according to his secretary David Taylor, he also had a "rural kitchen cabinet"—nine or 10 men with whom he fraternized while relaxing at his Santa Clara ranch. Nothing made Rolph happier, according to Taylor, than to sit around with groups of friends discussing appointments.

Of course, Rolph was also close to his family, although their presence in his daily life is less well documented. As a young businessman, he had a standing date each Saturday for lunch with his father and four brothers. In 1914, his brother Bill sent him a note thanking him for a birthday gift of carnations. "You are altogether too good to me," he wrote. "I have been trying to get in to see you and thank you. I feel ashamed of myself for delaying it so long and hope you will forgive me."[6] At Rolph's funeral, brother Will, whom Rolph had rescued from drowning as a child by jumping into a pond, said through tears: "He was always so good to us."[7] Rolph's son, James III, was a spirited and bright youth whom Rolph loved and taught much. As governor, Rolph invited controversy by turning over his insurance business to his son and then sending state business his way.

Though Rolph's family treated him with a mixture of awe and adoration, he probably spent less and less quality time with them from the early 1920s on.[8] Accounts of his whereabouts usually placed him on the job until late at night, often sleeping in his office, or conferring with friends, or attending public events, or — especially as governor — campaigning around the state. Annie, her objections to his career choice having been overruled, became a dutiful political wife, probably living not quite the life she would have chosen while raising the children and carving out an independent role in support of her husband's administration and reelection efforts.

Opposite: Annie Rolph initially opposed her husband's plans to run for mayor of San Francisco but later accepted his career change and became a dutiful political wife (courtesy of the California History Room, California State Library, Sacramento, California).

Part Two
A Civic "Hereditary" Monarchy

5

Second-Term Challenges

The overwhelming success of his exposition, the accompanying public acclaim, and his reelection cakewalk brought Rolph to a summit that presented dangers as well as opportunities. Chief among the dangers was a loss of momentum. He had, after all, accomplished nearly everything he had set out to do. The closing of the exposition removed a rallying cry that had been useful in persuading the city's interest groups to get behind his rebuilding program. And the uneasy truce that had prevailed between capital and labor was beginning to fray, promising a new wave of strikes in the years ahead.

Rolph's belief in a strong, activist city government, which allowed him to vigorously promote the growth and development of the city, was a tool in keeping the municipal peace. It was also one key to his electoral success. A nonpartisan community consensus existed — among business, unions, and the voters who were regularly called upon to approve bond issues — on the need to pursue a common vision of urban greatness.

Roger Lotchin has suggested that this vision was motivated by the need to compete with Los Angeles and other growing western metropolises in a sort of tournament of cities. It gave Rolph a perennial issue to campaign on, an endless list of completed projects to brag about, and a variety of city contracts to grant. As a result, he came "very close to being in the category of Napoleon III and Baron Hausmann ... or of Robert Moses of New York" — in other words, the planner and overseer of his city's material transformation.[1]

The consensus on city growth tended to dampen disagreement on other issues, giving Rolph the municipal harmony he so valued. Businessmen may have opposed public ownership of city services on principle, but lucrative city contracts gave them a stake in this municipal socialism. Public works money also provided jobs, which helped to keep the peace with labor unions. City employees, who made up a significant proportion of the

Mayor Rolph campaigns for reelection in 1915. A master of retail politics, he was "one of the few who could provoke a spontaneous ovation without sending runners ahead to make sure it was spontaneous" (Nancy Rolph Welch Collection).

total work force, were generously paid. Difficult problems, like Prohibition, immigration, industrial relations, race, and nationality, were rarely discussed at board of supervisors meetings.

One of the projects on which a strong consensus existed was the Hetch Hetchy water system. If the construction of the civic center and the staging of the Pan-Pacific Exposition were the crowning glories of his first term, then Hetch Hetchy would provide a focus for the years ahead. It was also a perfect match for the mayor's interests—a large-scale public undertaking of vital importance to the future of San Francisco. As a Rolph legacy, Hetch Hetchy would turn out to be less than a full-scale triumph, but all of the pieces were put in place during his years as mayor.

It had been clear as early as the turn of the century that the city needed a guaranteed source of water to accommodate its rapid growth. Mayor James Phelan had first promoted the plan to build a dam on the Tuolumne River in the Hetch Hetchy Valley of the Sierra Nevada and then construct

5. Second-Term Challenges

an aqueduct to bring the water to San Francisco. When Rolph took office in 1911, however, backers of the project were stalemated. Opponents such as the Sierra Club said the dam would ruin a pristine wilderness and fought a delaying action that remained effective until 1912.

Rolph had supported the Hetch Hetchy project for many years. Once in office, he was willing to take on the private utility companies who controlled water distribution at the time, as well as the Sierra Club. In 1912 he hired the talented Michael O'Shaughnessy as city engineer and charged him with developing a new public works infrastructure for San Francisco — one that would include Hetch Hetchy as well as the mayor's entire program of civic construction. He promised O'Shaughnessy a free hand and no unnecessary political interference.

Immediately after, Rolph, O'Shaughnessy and a host of advocates, including former mayor Phelan, traveled to Washington to ask Congress to approve the project. They prevailed against formidable counterarguments from such prestigious national figures as conservationist John Muir, former president of Harvard Charles Eliot, and the editor of *Century* maga-

In 1912 Rolph hired the talented Michael O'Shaughnessy (left) as city engineer and charged him with developing a new public works infrastructure for San Francisco — one that would include the Hetch Hetchy water project. Here, he and O'Shaughnessy celebrate an intramural baseball victory (San Francisco History Center, San Francisco Public Library).

zine. In 1912 Congress passed the Raker Act, which authorized work to begin.

Construction got under way in 1916, and by 1923 the Hetch Hetchy dam was completed. Even then, much work remained to be done before San Francisco would get any Hetch Hetchy water. The entire project was a complex undertaking — involving not just one but four dams, five reservoirs, a hydroelectric power plant, a hundred miles of pipeline, and over 60 miles of tunnel[2] — and funding would be a constant problem until it was completed. Also, a distribution system had to be purchased before the city could go into the water business. Rolph's task for the next several years was to do the political work necessary to get bond issues passed and to remove any bureaucratic obstacles that arose.

As Hetch Hetchy progressed, Rolph's second term was rapidly overtaken by the domestic fallout from the Great War in Europe. Triggered by an assassination in 1914 in the heart of the continent, the war gathered momentum through a network of entangling alliances that soon brought the whole continent into the struggle. President Woodrow Wilson was determined to keep the United States on the sidelines, but as war jitters grew, nationalists formed a preparedness movement to demand that the country be ready to fight if necessary.

In an atmosphere of growing crisis, unions sensed that they had increased leverage with employers, and they took the opportunity to make fresh demands for better working conditions. On the extreme left wing, especially in San Francisco, a group of anarchists jangled people's nerves by pushing worker's groups toward violence and disorder. These radicals, as well as much of the labor movement, opposed any preparation for war, seeing it as a distraction from their domestic causes and believing that war would benefit only the capitalist class.

Rolph trod carefully into the growing gulf between wealthier, mainly conservative, San Franciscans and the powerful labor organizations and their allies. A series of strikes in 1916 and 1917 helped him burnish his credentials with the city's workers. A longshoremen's walkout in 1916 angered the city's Chamber of Commerce, which declared its support of the open shop and asked Rolph to hire special policemen to protect strikebreakers. Not only did the mayor refuse to do this, but he also ordered the police to search the strikebreakers for concealed weapons. That same year, during a strike by the structural iron workers, he denounced open-shop supporters for resisting what he felt were reasonable concessions to workers, saying: "They would permit unions to exist if they would confine themselves to the function of benevolent societies."[3]

At about the same time, a tragic event took place that caused Rolph to tack sharply to the right. At a July 1916 Preparedness Day parade in San Francisco—a parade that Rolph himself was leading—a bomb exploded in the crowd, killing 10 people. In the wild aftermath, spurred by public outrage and the mayor's promise to put up his own money as a reward for the capture of the bomber, the police quickly took into custody a labor agitator and hothead named Tom Mooney. Mooney's guilt in the affair was questionable, but the bombing called attention to the danger posed to the social order by the radical left. Rolph left no doubt about which side he was on, ordering the police to "go to the root of the anarchist canker in San Francisco and destroy it."[4]

The threat of radicalism did not undermine Rolph's support for organized labor. In 1917 a strike by United Railroad workers led to a bitter confrontation. Again, the mayor used the police to keep strikers from being intimidated, and he even recommended that the city purchase the company so that employees could have better working conditions. When a striker killed a nonunion worker, the probusiness Law and Order Committee charged Rolph with responsibility. In an open letter to the committee's head, the mayor replied: "The world is changing all around you, and you and your kind don't know it any more than the Czar [did]."[5] The statement was both an expression of his convictions and, in a working-class city like San Francisco, politically astute.

In 1917, angered by repeated violations of U.S. neutrality, President Wilson finally led the country into the European war on the side of Britain and France. Many Americans were initially (and naively) enthusiastic about this opportunity for glory and adventure. Bay Area boys signed up in great numbers for service and began to report to nearby training camps.

Rolph was a strong supporter of the war effort. A month after it began, he spent $50,000 for war bonds. Whenever a military contingent departed for Europe, he made a public ceremony out of it. His wife, Annie, was named "fairy godmother" of a California signal corps company.

The mayor took a personal interest in the welfare of the local enlistees. He bought cigarettes and other items, including gold pieces, and took them to the boys himself. When he offered to deliver gifts from their friends in the city, so many were sent to the mayor's office that he had to hire a special car to transport them.[6] While the local soldiers were overseas, Rolph kept in touch with their families. If a breadwinner was killed, he did what he could to relieve any financial hardship, often with his own funds.

At war's end, Rolph and his wife traveled to New York to receive the troop ships. According to a journalist's account, "Heads popped out of every porthole. 'Hello, Jim' burst from hundreds of throats." Several of the troops kept a promise to bring back a machine gun, though they had to disassemble it first. It was "one way to show what we thought of the way he treated us," said a soldier.[7] Once back on the West Coast, Rolph organized and led a huge parade and then formed committees to ensure that demobilized servicemen could find jobs.[8] He provided a red ribbon and poppy for every returning Californian and told the veterans: "If any of you need money, just come up and see me."

Though these actions underlined Rolph's intense patriotism, his kindnesses toward the troops were also shrewd politics. They were an uncontroversial means of securing loyalty from an important part of the electorate — soldiers and their families — while generating positive publicity and reinforcing his reputation as a humanitarian. Whether intended that way or not, they certainly helped to cement his power and influence.

6

Wealth and Generosity

During the war years, Rolph's business successes paralleled his political ones. Without the dramatic increase in his personal wealth, in fact, the generosity for which he was becoming known could not have been so lavish.

Rolph was not obliged to put his shipping career on hold because of his election as mayor. In those days, conflict-of-interest laws did not exist, and politicians were not fastidious about separating public business from personal profit. Though he was already reputed to be a millionaire when he took office, he organized the Rolph Navigation and Coal Company and several other maritime firms during his first two terms. According to aides, he carried out his public responsibilities all day and then returned to his office after midnight to work on private business. He seldom slept more than four hours a night. "He managed on as little sleep as anyone I've ever known or heard of, even Edison," remarked his personal secretary.[1]

Rolph lived increasingly well, despite his campaign claim of being a plain boy from the Mission district. As his personal fortune grew, he invested most of it in real estate. As early as 1902, he purchased 20 acres in the Los Altos hills, on the peninsula south of San Francisco. The *San Francisco Call* reported in 1911 that he had bought 750 acres of forest, canyons, and streams in the Santa Cruz range to add to 750 acres he had bought earlier. By 1921 he owned over 3,300 acres, all but 250 in San Mateo County. A local newspaper joked that he appeared to be in some sort of informal competition to become the largest landowner in the area.

On this land Rolph had two ranches. One of these, on 453 acres, he called his home ranch, and he brought his family there for long weekends and summer holidays throughout his life. A simple five-room cottage was on the property. The Rolph women, it seemed, did not particularly enjoy country life (they were afraid of rattlesnakes), and Annie objected to his spending money to build a nicer house there. In 1916 he added to his holdings a 640-acre spread, where he built a weekend and vacation complex, complete with a 105,000-gallon swimming pool, kennels for his dogs, a picnic area large enough for a thousand people, barns, a building for his gun collection, and a guest house. Several head of cattle and a pond stocked with fish completed the facility. A flagpole was built on the crest of a ridge, but the flag flew only when Rolph was staying there.[2]

He also invested money in his long-time home in San Francisco. Enlarged in 1912, it had seven bedrooms and lush landscaping. Stables were gradually converted to a garage, which at one time housed seven automobiles. The Rolphs had three live-in servants—a cook and two maids.

For every dollar Rolph spent on himself and his family, he gave away many more spontaneously to people in need. His unselfishness and compassion were the subjects of hundreds of stories. "You'll hear them from the widows, the orphans, the hungry men he gave five dollars," the *San Francisco Examiner* declared. "You'll hear them from waiters and cab drivers and presidents of banks and clergymen.... The tales you'll hear about Jim Rolph are the tales most of us would like to hear about ourselves."[3] A local priest once asked the mayor if he could purchase a city building for his poor parish. "Go home, Father," said Rolph. "The building is yours."[4] Then he paid for it himself. It was believed that he gave away most of his salary as mayor.

Rolph's experience in the shipping industry allowed him to exploit the dramatic increase in the value of ships caused by the war in Europe. One of his most lucrative activities was the buying and selling of ships for a quick profit, a practice that required sound judgment and considerable nerve. His big breakthrough was his snap decision to buy a Mexican steamer, listed for sale in the industry's newsletter, for $50,000 and his immediate resale of the vessel to a New York company for twice that amount. This success encouraged him to begin building his own ships, which he was usually able to sell before construction had even begun.

During the war, ships owned by Hind, Rolph and the Rolph Navigation and Coal Company were on the high seas, and some of them met with disaster. Four Rolph vessels were sunk in the Pacific by German raiders and a fifth was severely damaged by a German submarine off the Irish coast. The mayor, as was his style, kept in close touch with his skippers. They and their wives had a standing invitation to dine at the Rolph home on their first night in port.[5] Sometimes the Rolphs played host to four or five captains on the same evening.

With the market for new ships seemingly assured by the war, Rolph invested in a shipyard near Eureka and began laying keels. Then he received a $1.6 million order from the French government for three troop and supply

6. Wealth and Generosity

transports. Filling this order required permission from the U.S. Shipping Board, so he traveled to Washington and negotiated for the necessary authority. Once work was underway, so many of the area's men were employed at the shipyards that the town of Fairhaven, where the yards were located, changed its name to Rolph. The mayor declared that he would start a bank account with $100 for any child born in the town bearing his name.[6] By that time, according to *San Francisco Chronicle* editor Earl Behrens, his personal fortune was estimated at $5 million.[7]

Rolph used his growing wealth to make working conditions at the shipyards as comfortable as possible in this remote and primitive area. He built modern cottages, a hotel, and a dining room, which was designed to serve as a social center for the crew and their families. He also built a three-room school for their children. Later he donated it to the local school district.

When the first of several four-masted barkentines was about to be launched at the new site, Rolph decided to celebrate. He assigned the planning to an assistant, saying: "Don't spare expense. Make it a real party." A complicating factor was that all the supplies he would need, as well as almost all of the people he wanted to invite — including labor leaders, politicians, diplomats, bankers, judges, various power brokers and their wives — were hundreds of miles away in San Francisco. So a 12-car Northwestern Pacific train was chartered to bring to Eureka 125 guests, 25 roasted turkeys, a jazz band, and two baggage cars loaded with additional food and drink.

The event, as described by Jerry Flamm, was a whirlwind of breakfasts, luncheons, banquets and entertainment that "never seemed to let up." It lasted two days and nights, and no one was allowed to spend a penny. When the guests, overwhelmed by his generosity, tried to respond by throwing a small dinner in his honor costing them $5 a plate each, Rolph arranged to repay those who he thought could not afford it.[8] The "unforgettable, traveling fiesta" left all the celebrants completely exhausted. It cost Rolph nearly $25,000 and soon became legendary back in the Bay Area.[9]

7

Strange Interlude — The First Run for Governor

Rolph's building success in politics and business, and the flush of optimism it engendered, led directly to his decision to enter the race for governor of the state in 1918. His campaign that year is an odd footnote in California political history, because Rolph won more votes than any other candidate, yet he was not elected. The strange and disappointing episode nevertheless proved to the mayor that he could compete and win in a statewide election.

His decision to run was made in haste after an evening meeting with his advisors. Expected profits from his ship-building contract with the French government seemed to promise sufficient funds for an intensive campaign. He announced his candidacy only three days before nominating petitions needed to be filed, but his well-oiled staff was growing accustomed to his bursts of enthusiasm and the energetic pursuit of his goals. The necessary signatures were easily collected before the deadline.

The oddity of the 1918 election was a result of an electoral innovation called cross-filing, which was devised by the Progressives who held power in Sacramento at the time. It allowed a candidate to become the nominee of more than one party for the same office. The primary ballot did not identify the candidate's party affiliation. If the voters were not certain to what party a candidate belonged, they would have to base their decision on arguably more relevant factors—for example, competence and qualifications. Cross-filing was designed to make elections more nonpartisan, but its main effect was to reduce the power of the state's political parties, which had increasingly been subject to corruption and machine rule. The unintended results of the 1918 primary have been called "California's cross-filing nightmare."[1]

The system worked best for candidates who were not strongly identified with any party and whose campaign emphasized the politics of personality—in other words, people like Jim Rolph. So he chose to cross-file in 1918. He ran against five men in the Republican primary, including the incumbent governor, William D. Stevens, and two in the Democratic primary, including noted Progressive Francis Heney. Facing such formidable opposition in what were, in effect, two separate elections, with so little time to prepare would surely test his abilities as a campaigner. He immediately bought an automobile and swung into action, hoping to visit every part of the state. Clinging to nonpartisanship, he ran as an American and disparaged any talk of politics.

Rolph's run showed that he had developed, in a few short years as a big-city mayor, both a surprisingly good understanding of the political process and a first-rate campaign organization. The main issue in this wartime election — besides the conduct of the war itself and the treatment of returning soldiers—was the debate over ratification of the Eighteenth Amendment. This would bring Prohibition into effect, forbidding the manufacture and sale of alcoholic beverages.

An urban sophisticate from a city that knew how to have fun, Rolph was firmly in the anti–Prohibition camp. But he needed to win over significant numbers of voters in southern California, where "dry" sentiment was strong. He managed to soft-pedal his well-known position by declaring the issue irrelevant to the election and promising to uphold the amendment if enacted. At the same time, he made a deft play for middle-class voters by coming out for private health and old-age insurance for workers—ideas that, if he were serious, put him decades ahead of his time.

The "official log" of the Rolph campaign, which survives among family memorabilia, attests to the political skill and high energy of the candidate and the unusually thorough advance work of his staff. The main elements of Rolph's public persona and style were already becoming apparent. He always smiled, never mentioned his opponents by name, and avoided specifics. As befit his benevolent nature, he showed courtesy to all. For example, on one occasion while he was finishing a speech, a rival candidate drove up to address the same crowd. Rolph stayed on the stage and warmly introduced the man to the gathering.

Rolph could also be combative when necessary. He had faced down labor agitators at rallies during his mayoral campaigns. Now, angered by a dismissive article about him in the *Los Angeles Times*, he called the newspaper a "disgusting, despicable, putrid sheet." According to the campaign log, the crowd responded by cheering loudly for 55 seconds "by the watch."[2]

His six weeks on the road consisted of a steady succession of very long days. He often retired between three and four in the morning and rose between six and seven. When advance men had not done their jobs (as on July 29, which the log described as a "day of frosts"), Rolph sent San Francisco headquarters some hot messages, and corrective action was taken. As the primary approached, the campaign calculated that in a few short weeks it had covered 4,752 miles, visited 142 towns and cities, and made 99 speeches that were heard by over 82,000 Californians.

In late August, the primaries were held. The results were both surprising and confusing. Rolph, a Republican, had won the Democratic primary, beating Francis Heney, and had finished second to Governor Stevens in the Republican primary. But Rolph could not now run in the general election as the Democratic nominee. A law passed the year before had stipulated that a candidate who did not win the primary of his own party could not run as the nominee of another one. And because the winner of the Democratic primary had been disqualified, no Democrat could run in November.

Rolph's attorneys, Theodore Roche and Matt Sullivan, appealed to the California Supreme Court. Rolph himself angrily called the primary law absurd. But the court ruled that the law was a reasonable exercise of legislative powers. With the legal dispute resolved, Stevens was automatically reelected.

Rolph's impulsive decision had both positive and negative consequences for his political future. On the one hand, the six-week odyssey had given him experience in state-level campaigning that would be valuable in any future run for governor or U.S. senator. On the other hand, his victory in the Democratic primary had been a severe embarrassment to Francis Heney and provoked charges that Rolph had entered the race for the express purpose of eliminating any legitimate Democrat from contention. Rolph's candidacy had in fact resulted in split allegiances among San Francisco's Democrats, with most supporting their mayor and the rest backing Heney. This local split would persist and complicate Rolph's remaining San Francisco reelection campaigns.

With a war in progress, President Wilson viewed any attempt to weaken his party as undermining national unity as well as his administration. Rolph vigorously denied that intention. He cited as evidence his letter to the chairman of the Republican National Committee four months earlier. "As Americans and Republicans," he had written, "we shall with all our strength support President Woodrow Wilson as the nation's leader...."[3] He also pointed out that he had broken with many California Republicans and Progressives by supporting President Wilson's leadership and his idea for a League of Nations. The storm appeared to die down, and Rolph went back to being mayor of San Francisco.

8

Reversal of Fortune

In 1919, returning to San Francisco after greeting demobilized Bay Area servicemen in New York, Rolph brought with him a black cat, which had been a mascot for one of the army divisions. His personal secretary, David Wooster Taylor, later said that the cat lived up to its reputation for bringing bad luck. Its new owner now entered a period of worries unlike any he had had before.

Up at the mayor's northern California shipyards, the transport vessels he was building for the French government were nearing completion. Almost $2 million of his money was tied up in the project. One day, he opened a telegram from the U.S. Shipping Board and found to his amazement that his authorization to sell the steamers to France had been revoked. Without the French sale, he would lose virtually his entire investment. The ships had been designed for military purposes and could not easily be sold on the civilian market.

Several questions about this government action remain unanswered. The war had ended in November 1918. It was likely that the French government no longer needed the ships and had tried to cancel its order. Perhaps the Shipping Board decided not to hold France to the terms of its contract. One rumor held that the Wilson administration cancelled Rolph's contract in retaliation for the mayor's alleged subversion of Democratic chances in the 1918 California gubernatorial election. Rolph himself believed these rumors and made public charges to that effect. The government denied them, citing diplomatic reasons for the contract's cancellation.

Whatever the facts, Rolph, Matt Sullivan, and former San Francisco mayor James Phelan rushed to Washington and tried in vain to get the board to change its mind. While in the capital, Rolph expressed his bitterness at a meeting of mayors and governors taking place there — an inappropriate forum for voicing private business concerns even by the more lax standards of the day. The protests were to no avail.

Rolph tried to make the best of his defeat by converting the French steamers to general use, but he found that the operating costs were too high. He was ultimately forced to auction them off at a fraction of their value and took a $1.5 million loss. By itself, the loss was not catastrophic. Rolph still had substantial assets and now channeled most of them into the Rolph Mail and Steamship Company, which specialized in trade with Central and South America.

But the end of the war brought not only a collapse of the war market in ships but also a depression in the import-export business. Rolph soon became overextended and by 1921 was wondering how to pay off $2 million in bonds he had guaranteed back in 1919. He was forced to mortgage everything he owned except his original family home. The Hind, Rolph Company, the oldest of his enterprises, went into liquidation. He held off the bondholders until 1923 but then they foreclosed. "Rolph — the liberal, open-handed, carefree millionaire, who seemed to make money for the sheer joy of giving it away, was broke!" He later admitted: "In four years, I lost $7 million."[1]

If the collapse of his business empire was a test of character, Rolph seemed to pass with flying colors. He did not appear concerned about his woes; he kept his good cheer and sense of humor. "The loss of fortune has not troubled me greatly or held me back," he said. "I guess I'm not the type that gets sunk." Friends urged him to declare bankruptcy, but he "couldn't admit that all was lost."[2]

9

Third Term — Growing Conservatism and Passivity

Whatever damage the financial disaster did to Rolph's view of the future, it had no effect on his spirits or his ability to campaign and win elections. He could have retired from politics in 1919, after two successful terms as mayor and devoted himself full time to recovering his fortune. Instead he did not hesitate to declare himself a candidate for reelection. The decision is strong evidence that Rolph found the psychic rewards of public office far more satisfying than the financial rewards of running a shipping business.

In any case, Rolph's network of alliances and steady infiltration of city government with loyalists made him virtually unbeatable. He had been mayor so long and had so completely enlisted public opinion behind his massive program of public works that criticizing him was akin to criticizing the city itself. In another finely tuned campaign operation, the candidate's smiling face was everywhere, while Ed Rainey made strategic decisions behind the scenes and Tim Reardon mobilized public works employees to gather intelligence about the opposition and disseminate propaganda. His opponent was former mayor and labor official Eugene Schmitz, but Rolph took the wind out of his sails early by touting his honorary membership in three unions and earning the endorsement of organized labor.

Because Schmitz had been convicted of extortion during his earlier term and removed from office, Rolph emphasized the cleanliness of his administration. "Not a whiff of scandal," he bragged.[1] He had even less difficulty winning than in 1915. Most of the city's newspapers lauded his efficiency and service to the community. He received 65 percent of the vote; Schmitz did not win a single district.

But something fundamental had changed. Perhaps his catastrophic

Rolph listens carefully to a constituent. "He was a charmer, and he liked people, and people could feel it" (Nancy Rolph Welch Collection).

losses were taking their toll in unseen ways. Though his personal popularity was at its height, he was no longer the energetic businessman who had burst upon the local political scene in 1911 with an ambitious reformist agenda, or the dynamo who completed the bulk of that agenda before the end of his first term. His formidable political skills were keeping him in office, but he was having difficulty sustaining the momentum of his spectacular beginning. He was settling into the job, seeking to build on past successes rather than strike out in new directions, and concentrating on a limited number of priorities. He was also being seduced by the roar of the crowd. Four years as mayor had not only made the modest citizen politician the toast of San Francisco but was earning him a reputation in America and abroad as a builder, visionary, and international sophisticate.

As postwar America entered the 1920s, both the Progressive movement and the Democratic Party were in decline, and the national mood was becoming increasingly conservative. Warren Harding, elected president in 1920, headed a business-oriented administration. The public was frightened by the Russian Revolution of 1917 and the coming to power of a Communist government. It also looked with declining favor on labor unions, who many thought had given only lukewarm support to the war effort. Employers had more success in promoting an open shop system, and union membership declined throughout the 1920s.

Consistent with the times and his own pragmatic streak, Rolph tacked in a more conservative direction. He did not take an overtly antilabor position, but expressed weariness with the sharp conflict between business and the unions. He had seen "too many hostile elements arrayed against each other" and said the map of San Francisco had "too many dividing lines." His apparent goal was not to become involved. "Irrespective of my own union labor sympathies," he admitted candidly, "I am desirous above all else to avoid having this administration drawn into industrial disputes."[2]

Amid the general praise for his abilities, Rolph had long been teased—not quite criticized yet—for his skill in avoiding conflict. As early as his first campaign in 1911, he was handling contentious issues by not taking a position and "remaining serenely above it all."[3] A year later a journalist described the new mayor as a "keep-in-the-middle-of-the-road man ... a happy-medium man, an avoid-all-needless-friction man."[4] The mayor's principle of action, another observer concluded, was not to take on his adversaries but instead to have none at all.[5]

Because he was an optimist, Rolph had an abiding belief that people could always sit down and bridge their differences. Crusading types made him uncomfortable, because they forced disagreement in a society that should be happy agreeing on fundamentals and "letting its members seek pleasure and profit each in his own way in the perfect California climate."[6] He wanted everyone to get along. But in valuing harmony for its own sake, Rolph tended increasingly to split the difference on divisive issues in order to reach consensus, rather than risk hostility by leading boldly in one direction or another.

As Rolph's taste for activism declined, he focused on the symbolic role he felt most comfortable in — being the public face of San Francisco. When he provided leadership, as in promoting the Hetch Hetchy project, Rolph was only reflecting a public consensus that already existed rather than trying to form a new one. Increasingly, he was content to facilitate and preside rather than lead. He became, in a positive sense, the "neutral harmonizing force, the vital human amalgam around whom all San Franciscans converged."[7] But the downside was growing passivity and disengagement.

Rolph had always been fond of ceremonial public appearances, but now they seemed to take most of his time. He was always on center stage — shoveling earth, cutting ribbons, greeting visitors — while his trusted aides, advisors, and political supporters kept the city running. He made a point of greeting any person of importance who came to the city and personally attending to many of the details of their visit. He paid no political price for this behavior. The voters smiled at his grandstanding and took pride in his public persona, so it was easy for him to keep doing what he enjoyed most.

The irony was that Rolph was a hard-working mayor, just as later he would be a hard-working governor. He stayed up regularly until late at night and rose early in the morning. But he got into the habit of delegating his administrative chores. Pressing the flesh at ceremonial occasions and reveling in the adulation of the multitudes was certainly more exciting, and perhaps more fulfilling, than the day-to-day business of being mayor.

Even when he was at his desk in his office, Rolph was apt to be engaged in what seemed like unproductive activities. He wrote most of his official correspondence, answered his own phone, and signed all disbursements over $250. He took time to recognize birthdays, anniversaries, and other special occasions. He continued to make himself available to any citizen who wanted to see him. Of course, he would not have called these activities trivial. They were at the heart of his conception of the job.

As time passed, criticism of Rolph's apparent disengagement became more strident. Accounts by purported insiders testified to his shaky understanding of municipal problems. "The Rolph grasp of affairs is weak," confided an associate. "I have seen his attention wander while trying vainly to comprehend a Power Advisory report."[8] City officials thought they detected a streak of intellectual laziness that kept him from devoting the necessary time to mastering complex issues. Rolph's frequent absences more often required the appointment of an acting mayor from among his deputies.[9] Little by little, wrote Ernest Jerome Hopkins in the *New Republic*, Rolph was giving way to the "surrounding gang behind the scenes, while maintaining, ever more artificially, ... the papier-mache front."[10]

9. Third Term—Growing Conservatism and Passivity

Some of this criticism of the mayor was too harsh. No one could so thoroughly dominate a city politically for so long without disappointing or alienating at least a few people. Besides, delegating heavily and relying on others for advice was not necessarily bad. Like the Progressives, Rolph sought input from experts, and then threw the full weight of his office behind their recommendations. Implicit in this approach was a certain humility—a recognition that he did not have all the answers—and a refreshing preference for facts over politics in making decisions. But on the whole, he was beginning to drift.

Also changing was Rolph's attitude toward hiring for jobs with the city. During his first campaign, he had ruled out personal relationships as a basis for municipal recruitment. In fact, he strongly favored the creation of a civil service based on merit and a restriction of patronage appointments. "I shall select the heads of the city's departments regardless of class or party," he promised, "with a single eye toward their fitness."[11] In the next few years, he followed through by hiring smart, knowledgeable people—"advisors and associates that were the pride of the city"[12]—giving them authority and promising them no unnecessary political interference. "The surest way to bring a city into disrepute," he once said, "is by allowing that city to be strangled in the tentacles of political bossism."[13]

While recruiting the city's "best brains"[14] for leading positions, Rolph increasingly rewarded many of his supporters with lesser city jobs and other privileges. Such practice was routine during a time when the concept of a professional civil service was in its infancy and "to the winner went the spoils," but it clashed with his often-proclaimed goal of a merit-based city administration. His warm-heartedness was both his great strength and his Achilles heel, and as the years went along, personal loyalty increasingly trumped competence in choosing subordinates. He carried that belief to Sacramento, where he would pay a heavy price.

Along with his excessive reliance on others, Rolph faced an even-greater vulnerability. His financial problems were making him ever more dependent on the generosity of his friends and associates. He was a popular man who had done many favors. Now, in his hour of personal need, he would have no trouble finding benefactors, but loans and grants might come with strings attached.

Rumors surfaced that he was becoming heavily indebted to Herbert Fleishhacker, a local banker, conservative Republican, and longtime friend.[15] Rolph's alleged links to and dependence on Fleishhacker would remain an issue during his career. Whether or not Fleishhacker kept Rolph's personal balance sheet in the black, evidence suggests that he helped bankroll his last two campaigns in San Francisco, as well as his later campaign for governor.

"Everyone knows that he owns our present mayor, body and soul,"[16] said a local official in 1924.

Rolph probably took money from other wealthy San Franciscans as well. He needed his friends to pull him through, wrote Paul C. Edwards in the *San Francisco News*, "and they did."[17] Despite his financial disaster of 1923, his lifestyle suffered no adverse consequences. He continued to indulge his expensive tastes in clothes and food, and he managed to give an elaborate wedding for his daughter Annette, who was marrying stockbroker John Symes. The media described it as a "scene of beauty almost impossible to describe," with 400 invited guests and more than a thousand others gathered outside.

Money woes continued to preoccupy the mayor after the forfeit of his companies in 1923. He entered the insurance business, which allowed him to keep his head above water. But his income and salary as mayor were far from sufficient to meet his many obligations, especially the $140,000 annual interest on the bond issue he had guaranteed in 1919. Rolph told people he was "out of the woods" by 1927 and had "pretty well" paid back his creditors by the end of the decade, but it is likely that he had to depend on others for financial support until the end of his life.

Influence, not economic dependence, was the key issue. The mayor denied that such largesse affected his decisions, but doubts about his incorruptibility began to grow. "What happens to a public official's own clearness of mind and vision under the sharp spur of private worry?" asked one journalist.[18] More specifically, what if his retreat from civic reform and swing toward conservatism were at least in part due to his unwillingness to jeopardize this financial support?

10

Hetch Hetchy and Municipal Ownership

It was a Progressive article of faith that large cities could best control and direct their growth if they owned and operated their major utilities. Mayor Rolph shared this belief. It had given strength to his sponsorship of the Hetch Hetchy project and motivated his showdown with the United Railway Company over the extension of the municipal rail line. But the private utilities, such as the Pacific Gas and Electric Company, were large, powerful and influential. If the mayor wished to seek higher office at some point, the support, or at least the neutrality, of these companies might be crucial to his success. So his commitment to public ownership began to be seen as a bellwether of his political self-confidence.

During his first and second terms, Rolph was clearly in the public ownership camp. He was riding high in those years and could still afford to voice the idealism that had brought him to the mayor's office in the first place. "I will keep up the fight for the rights of the people to the use of their own streets," he said of the municipal railway in 1915. In 1917 he publicly accused PG&E of trying to wreck "my public ownership program."[1]

But some of his best friends were conservative businessmen who had become opponents of public ownership. Eustace Cullinan, who lauded Rolph in 1918 for his fidelity to the public interest in dealing firmly with corporations, was now an attorney for the power industry. And Gavin McNab was reported to be behind a scheme to sell one of the private railroad companies to the city at such an inflated price that the city would have insufficient resources to run it properly, causing it to fail.

The flagship public project was still Hetch Hetchy. Continuing to unfold 11 years after congressional authorization, it was proving to be a large and complex undertaking. Even the first phase — a huge dam on the Tuolumne River (later named for city engineer Michael O'Shaughnessy) — was the most ambitious public work attempted in California to that time, and required three years to build.² By October 1924, the money from the original bond issue for the project had been used up. The mayor took the case for new construction bonds to the voters, and the bonds passed.

An important by-product of the Hetch Hetchy project was the generation of a huge amount of hydroelectric power at the new dam — enough power, in fact, to provide up to 80 percent of the city's needs. But this apparent boon raised a policy question — an emotional and divisive one among civic leaders and public power ideologues. Should the city distribute the power itself, as it intended to do with the Hetch Hetchy water, or sell it off to a private power company?

In 1923, the city's board of supervisors came out for municipal distribution. In the long run, it was felt, municipal control would reduce both electric rates and taxes and still be highly profitable to the city. Cheap public power was aiding the rapid expansion of archrival Los Angeles. Rolph, who was running for reelection to a fourth term, strongly backed the board.

The problem was money. The city had enough to build the power plant at the dam, but as Hetch Hetchy ran into cost overruns, it could not afford to build its own power distribution system. And unless this was done in a hurry, the power would come online before the city had any means of getting it to San Francisco. Transmission lines had been built as far as Newark, on the eastern coast of San Francisco Bay. The only short-term options the city had were to buy the existing power lines that ran from Newark to San Francisco, operated by PG&E, or, if no agreement could be reached in time, sell the transmission rights to the company in exchange for a share of the revenue.

At first, Rolph continued to oppose selling the power to the corporation. He vetoed a board of supervisors resolution that would have allowed the city to deal temporarily with local water agencies and accused its backers of intending to cave in to PG&E. "We cannot do business with the power companies or turn the people's properties over to them," he warned. "Unless we are unanimous, the corporations will triumph."³

But as the obstacles to city control became clearer, Rolph's allegiance to the cause of public ownership seemed to waver. He had to be careful not to alienate financial benefactor Herbert Fleishhacker, who was known to be an opponent of public power. John Francis Neylan, a prominent lawyer, Progressive, and publisher of William Randolph Hearst's *San Francisco Call*, viewed the situation with alarm. "Fleishhacker can force Rolph into bankruptcy," he wrote Hearst, and he had "tremendous reach in the Board of Supervisors."⁴ Neylan, through his newspaper, sought to bring the mayor into line. He wrote editorials advocating negotiations with PG&E to purchase its distribution network and, if that failed, immediate construction of a city system, whatever sacrifice that might entail.

The mayoral election of 1923 took place in the midst of the public power dispute. Though he considered stepping down from public life in 1923 in order to devote himself to financial recovery, Rolph gave in to strong pressure to run again. In the midst of his reelection drive, his 20-year-old son, James Rolph III, drove his car off a highway near Berkeley and lay near death for more than 16 hours. The elder Rolph suspended his campaign until the boy was out of danger.

Once the crisis had passed, Rolph confidently resumed his campaign, amusing the voters by belittling his opponent, Supervisor L. B. McSheehy. "My opponent says we need change," he declared. "What kind of change? Small change or short change? If you have a good dollar, would you change it for a counterfeit?"[5]

But privately Rolph felt the need to shore up his support and sought the endorsement of the Hearst papers. Neylan and Hearst hoped Rolph would move in their direction on public power in order to get it. Though the mayor insisted that a city-owned power distribution system would be unaffordable, he agreed to appoint a citizens advisory panel on the subject. This was not the kind of strong leadership Neylan was hoping for, and he told Hearst that Rolph was far from an ideal candidate from their perspective.

But Neylan realized that none of Rolph's declared opponents could beat him. The *Call* reluctantly backed him on the eve of the election. "Twelve years of unquestioned progress" was how the paper described Rolph's three terms in office, and it praised the mayor's courage, intelligence and vision. Neylan's misgivings grew when the *Chronicle*, which had been against public power and anti–Rolph, switched sides and supported the mayor.

Once safely reelected, Rolph continued to edge toward coming to terms with PG&E, especially after both of the solutions preferred by public power supporters ran into serious setbacks. The city could not buy out PG&E's distribution system because the company would not agree to the city's price. Then Rolph backed a 1924 attempt to pass bonds that would finance a city-owned system, but it failed to get enough support for passage.

When the bond issue failed, Rolph decided to reverse course. He made what he explained as a practical decision — to turn over the power to PG&E temporarily while working in the long term for municipal distribution. He would accept the power company's offer of $2 million for the distribution rights, a sum previously thought to be too low. He argued that without PG&E involvement, the power would be wasted and the people would get

In 1924 Mayor Rolph angered municipal ownership proponents by accepting a $2 million offer from the Pacific Gas and Electric Company to transmit power generated by the Hetch Hetchy project. Without the deal, he said, the public would get "sweet speeches" instead of electricity. Many San Franciscans, including this cartoonist, approved of the mayor's pragmatic approach (Nancy Rolph Welch Collection).

"sweet speeches" instead of electricity.[6] A contract with PG&E might be a setback for public power advocates, but the mayor thought that the short-term benefits were worth it.

The decision enraged many people and damaged what remained of Rolph's Progressive credentials, provoking cries that he had sold out to powerful corporate interests. The *Examiner* and *Daily News* charged that unnamed city officials had been bribed. One city councilman accused the mayor of paying lip service to municipal ownership with high-sounding but ultimately meaningless phrases.

Some criticized the involvement of Ralph McLeran, a prominent member of the board of supervisors. He was a building contractor by trade and had just been hired to work on a new wing of Herbert Fleishhacker's bank. It was also learned that he was renting three floors of another building to PG&E. Despite this glaring conflict of interest, McLaren guided through the board the measure that authorized Rolph to sell Hetch Hetchy power to the company.

Rolph's decision was evidence of his ability to assess the balance of forces on a particular issue and to opt for what worked rather than agonize over the proper approach. Ideology had never determined his actions. The *Chronicle* commended him for his honest common sense and said he deserved the gratitude of every reasonable citizen. City engineer O'Shaughnessy, who was most familiar with the technical details and had given careful thought to the city's options, viewed the agreement with PG&E as fundamentally sound. (Nine years later, reflecting on the whole Hetch Hetchy experience, he pointed out that "even those most bitterly opposed to the plan of power consignment have not seen fit to cancel the contract.")[7]

Critics insisted that Rolph was not showing disinterested pragmatism but rather was responding to pressure from PG&E and other anti-public power forces. They pointed to the apparent role of Rolph intimate Eustace Cullinan, who had derided what he called the public ownership fanatics. PG&E, he felt, was capable of handling the power more easily and cheaply than the city. One columnist charged that the company had hired Cullinan expressly to kill public ownership.[8]

The dispute roiled city politics for the next several months until the members of the board of supervisors stood for reelection in 1925. With Neylan's help, all nine supervisors who had opposed Rolph's deal with PG&E were returned to office and those who backed the mayor were defeated. Rolph had to admit that he had lost the battle of public opinion. "The will of the people has been otherwise," he conceded.[9]

Whether or not Rolph had been criticized fairly, his apparent retreat on public power fed two suspicions—that he did not know his own mind until someone made it up for him, and that he had lost his appetite for battle. After coming to terms with PG&E, he pledged to work toward full municipal ownership of electric power, but his interest in the issue dwindled. Another bond issue was put before the public in 1928, but the mayor failed to push forcefully for it, and it was rejected. The decision to put power temporarily in PG&E's hands had given the company a foothold it never lost.

Rolph's handling of the electricity distribution issue showed that he had completed his evolution from idealistic citizen-politician to pragmatic political professional. He had learned to adapt to the prevailing power structure and to find a middle way that would not unduly upset either the private sector or the public.

More ominously, Rolph may have been unable to view the power situation apart from his own political and personal future. He had already passed up two chances to return to his business career. He was now a few years shy of 60 — perhaps too late to start over. He seemed committed irrevocably to the life of public service he had so auspiciously begun back in 1911, wherever it might lead. In order to pursue that life without significant resources of his own, he needed other people's money and plenty of votes.

11

Overdoing the Good Life

As his money problems deepened and his administrative activism declined, Rolph may have experienced something akin to a midlife crisis. During his last run for mayor in 1927, rumors began to circulate that he was drinking heavily and enjoying a vigorous night life. He was often said to be in Los Angeles frequenting glamorous nightclubs. These charges prompted Matt Sullivan, who was again his campaign manager, to deride the "foul-mouthed calumniators" who were trying to besmirch the candidate's reputation. "No profligate," insisted Sullivan, "can work 18 hours daily, as Mayor Rolph does. No profligate can address large gatherings of his fellow citizens ten times a day, coherently, sensibly and with the power of reasoning displayed by Mayor Rolph."[1]

Rolph was 58 years old in 1927. He had always been a robust, energetic man and did not appear to have any underlying health problems, but he had a tendency to work late, eat at irregular intervals, and sleep only three or four hours a night. Still, he had been seriously ill on only one known occasion. In 1916, he experienced a "breakdown" that required several weeks of "complete rest" in a local sanatorium.[2] Following the 1918 election, he had a bout of appendicitis.

Though his health remained good throughout the 1920s, his effectiveness in office was probably reduced by a combination of overwork and overindulgence in food and drink. Rolph's daily diet was far too rich even by the standards of the day. Rolph loved to eat and enjoyed lavish meals in nice restaurants. According to journalist Earl Behrens, he "ate things a younger man would shun."[3] At the other extreme, he often forgot about food when busy until well into the evening and then went to a local oyster house for a midnight dinner.[4] As late as his 1915 campaign for reelection, he was relatively slim, but by the 1920s, newspaper photos showed a dramatically different physical appearance. Though still handsome and animated, he had become portly, almost pear shaped. Irregular eating habits, insufficient exercise, and fattening foods were the undoubted cause.

We know from his personal papers that in 1928, Rolph believed himself to be in good health:

> My blood pressure this morning was 148; my pulse was 78–80. My urine has been tested and there is nothing wrong with it; my liver is working perfect; my stomach is in fine shape and my appetite is good. Doctor Gallwey said that if I will just cut out the night work as much as possible and not stay around here until four or five o'clock in the morning signing bonds, I will live to be a hundred years old.

In this document, he denied that he was a smoker, and that was probably true. He was known to enjoy an occasional cigar, but, according to his personal secretary, he gave up tobacco sometime in the early 1920s.

Like a majority of his fellow San Franciscans, Rolph enjoyed alcoholic beverages. He made little effort to enforce the Prohibition laws of the day — in fact, he actively undermined them when he deemed it necessary. The 1920 Democratic National Convention was held in San Francisco, and the mayor was determined to show the delegates a good time. Dispatching staffers to hospitals and coroner's offices for supplies, he sent quart bottles of bourbon to the visitors' rooms, with no bill attached. According to humorist H. L. Mencken, the flow of booze seemed to be unlimited. "Day by day, they swam in delight," he later wrote. Afterward, a "noisy public inquiry" into Rolph's disregard for legality took place, but he "didn't deign to notice."[5]

Whether Rolph himself drank to excess was strenuously debated by his associates and the media. Writer and later gubernatorial candidate Upton Sinclair, who was a "health nut" and, in any case, had little in common with the mayor, charged derisively that Rolph was "drinking himself into paresis."[6]

According to Jerry Flamm, Rolph's drinking was an embarrassment to his family and friends and worsened his health, especially during his final term. He occasionally appeared wobbly in public, said Flamm, slurred his words, and turned tomato red. One of his drivers told Flamm that Rolph's personal assistant, Ed Rainey, once sent him out to find the mayor, saying "Jimmy's disappeared again, and we have to have him back for a meeting in a couple of days." According to the driver, he was usually holed up with cronies having a party. "Christ," added the driver, "he drank like hell."[7] Another reporter said that Rolph was once so drunk he fell off his horse during a parade.[8]

Rolph denied such reports in categorical terms. Appended in his own hand to the summary of his visit to Doctor Gallwey in 1928 were the words, "I do not smoke and do not drink." His personal secretary, James Wooster

Taylor, admitted that Rolph enjoyed an occasional highball during his mayoral years but believed that his naturally ruddy complexion was often mistaken for a sign of intoxication. Because the mayor kept such late hours, Taylor added, he would sometimes catch quick naps while being driven from place to place, adding to the impression that he was under the influence. Still, the preponderance of evidence suggests that Rolph, at least during his San Francisco years, at times imbibed to excess.

Despite what appeared to be — and probably was — a strong and mutually supportive marriage, Rolph enjoyed the company of other women. San Francisco was a pleasure-seeking and permissive town, and his extracurricular activities were probably not out of the ordinary for that time and place. Their relevance lies in what they may reveal about his personal happiness during the 1920s and in the extent to which they were a distraction from his work.

During those years, famous men did not have to worry about reading of their extramarital affairs in the newspapers. Coverage of such activities by reporters was off limits. A large number of reminiscences and rumors, however, attests to Rolph's wandering eye. One writer recalled that his prowess with the ladies was "legendary."[9] Crony Gavin McNab was reported to have said, tongue in cheek: "This man is wasting his God-given gifts taking any time out at all from these duties to perform as mayor."[10] An *Examiner* columnist recalled: "He should have been a bachelor, because he was that kind of guy. He loved everybody."[11]

Rolph regularly frequented the city's bordellos during the 1920s and was well known to their proprietresses. One of these, Sally Stanford, later wrote of their first meeting. "You're a pretty one," the mayor said, and began negotiating for her time. "I smiled and pointed out that I was the madam, not the merchandise. He was obviously disappointed, and looking back, I know I should have sampled a little for myself."[12] He later befriended Stanford and advised her to conduct her business with class and style. In appreciation of his live-and-let-live attitude toward prostitution, she hung his picture over the cash register. On more than one occasion, Rolph appeared at the annual policeman's ball on the arm of one of the city's leading madams.[13]

In general, Rolph conducted himself with discretion. He had a night life, Flamm reported, but was not conspicuous. During his final term, however, he was often seen in the company of noted actresses who were visiting from Hollywood. Publicly, he was merely doing his job as he defined it — receiving and escorting prominent visitors to the city — but one of the actresses may have also been his mistress. Jimmy McFadden, a reporter for the *Examiner*, recalled that Rolph "went for the beautiful movie stars, but that's human.... He was quite a ladies' man. He's supposed to have had a romance with ... Anita Page. She was up here a lot, and he was down there a lot."[14]

The effect of Rolph's associations on his marriage and family can only be guessed at. Annie Rolph, like most political wives, avoided the spotlight and was unfailingly supportive of her husband in public. It had earlier been rumored that she opposed her husband's foray into politics, but she had apparently laid her concerns to rest. "I think a woman's place is by her husband's side," she said in an interview early in his tenure. "It would seem strange to me not to help him as much as I should in his work—I have always done so." But she believed herself a full partner in his political life. "As a rule, a woman has many qualities that her husband lacks.... They very often, in consequence, make a greater success working together than either of them would make alone."[15] It might be inferred that Annie Rolph was a bright, self-confident woman who expressed her opinions freely.

Anecdotal evidence suggests that Annie had a strong sense of duty. Shortly after her husband was first elected mayor, she and two of her children were in a traffic accident on their way to the scheduled groundbreaking for the Pan-Pacific Exposition, at which President William Taft was to appear. Their car flipped over, and both children sustained minor injuries. But after determining that none of them required hospitalization, she insisted that they attend the event as planned. "We always just picked ourselves up and went on to wherever we were going," said daughter Annette years later. "My mother would not hear about whether anybody had aches or pains. You went."[16]

Because she felt a duty to be supportive of her husband's career, Annie Rolph would not think of exposing his peccadilloes, though she certainly knew about them. Sally Stanford wrote that she once met Rolph at a hotel grill and he seemed preoccupied. He said his wife had hired a private detective to tail him, and the detective's report had mentioned four trysts with four different women in the same day. Mrs. Rolph was said to have sent Gavin McNab a copy of the report with a note saying that if something was not done about it, "their candidate for governor in the next election might be a bachelor."[17]

What, if anything, did Rolph's extracurricular activities have to do with his performance in office? If, in fact, he became addicted to a pleasure-seeking lifestyle, his escapades were evidence of a worrisome lack of discipline. The mayor applied himself best during political campaigns, but once he was reelected, he grew restless—perhaps even bored. The recognition, the deference, and the adulation of being a three- or four-term mayor was intoxicating, but the nuts and bolts of city administration were difficult, contentious, and all too familiar. He could do passably well by devoting 50 percent of his effort to being mayor of San Francisco, but what if he were elected to a much tougher job under much more adverse conditions?

12

A Strong Finish

Rolph ran for a final term as mayor in 1927. The race was hard fought and bitter. If he had been growing even a little tired of being mayor of San Francisco, the tone of the campaign probably intensified that feeling. In a moment of frustration, he told his driver, "I can't understand why this man wants to run against me.... I want to get out of here. I'd like to get 20 years as mayor; then I'd like to forget it."[1]

According to Flamm, some city officials also thought it was time for Rolph to move on. Anonymous letters about his "apartment house escapades and maudlin frolics" turned up. A member of a prominent city family said that "the local wheels wanted to get rid of him, because of his carrying on with booze, babes and all the rest."[2]

Rolph may have been losing enthusiasm for his mayoral duties, but that did not diminish his resolve to win the 1927 election. He launched his bid for a fifth term in October with characteristic energy, combativeness, and skill. It seems likely that he saw the election as a personal challenge that had to be met, as well as an opportunity to renew his lease on an office that brought him much ego gratification. Whatever his motives, the battle showed the maturity and unmatched sophistication of the Rolph campaign apparatus. He and his staff tested and perfected techniques and strategies in 1927 that would be successfully applied on the state level three years later.

The last candidate to try to unseat the mayor was James Power, a former member of the city's board of supervisors who had long opposed Rolph's policies. But Power was widely viewed as fronting for an influential city official and former Hiram Johnson associate, Tom Finn, who was running for reelection as sheriff. Once allies, Rolph and Finn had parted ways during the gubernatorial primary of 1918, when San Francisco Republicans agonized over whether to support incumbent Governor Stevens or their own mayor. Finn took Stevens' side and had been somewhat estranged from Rolph ever since, though he had continued to support the mayor for reelection every four years.

As sheriff, Finn ran a powerful city patronage machine and was an ally of Governor C.C. Young, who often sought Finn's advice when making state-level appointments. According to Flamm, Finn was a scrupulously honest man whose influence was built on relationships rather than favors and who helped many less-well-off people in the city over the years. But Rolph considered personal disloyalty a cardinal sin. He would not be content merely to win reelection as mayor; he also intended to dislodge Finn from the sheriff's office. Crony Tim Reardon, head of the department of public works, prevailed upon a subordinate, a man named Fitzgerald, to run against Finn.[3]

The Rolph camp was alarmed by the apparent strength of the Finn-Power campaign. Political columnist Earl Behrens warned that Finn and his allies had been preparing this challenge to the mayor for two years and were even getting financial help from outside the city. Behrens rated the Rolph volunteers far below those of the Finn-Power group in practical political efficiency. The Finn organization, he concluded, was the western equivalent of New York's famous political machine, Tammany Hall.[4] Everyone in Finn's "entangling net of obligation," said the *Chronicle*, had been pressed into service on his behalf.[5] Adding to his momentum, Power picked up endorsements from the Union Labor Party and the county Republican Party early in the race.

Though it was in the minority among San Francisco's several newspapers, the *Daily News* also backed the challenger. The paper admitted that Rolph was a likable man who had been a "fairly good mayor" for the first eight years, but now he was neglecting his duties. It concluded that he had had too many terms, and it was time for a change.[6]

Power lost no time in attacking Rolph where he seemed vulnerable. The Hetch Hetchy project, Power declared, had been afflicted with "inexplicable and needless delay."[7] Playing on reports of Rolph's growing disengagement from civic affairs, he noted the mayor's frequent absences from important board of supervisors meetings and charged that Gavin McNab and Tim Reardon were the real bosses of San Francisco. He also reminded the voters of Rolph's broken promise on the sale of power to PG&E. The *Daily News* estimated that the city was losing $6 million each year because of the PG&E contract. In a jab at Rolph's indecisiveness about the power issue, Power promised: "I will not be a vacillating mayor."[8]

In seeking reelection, however, Rolph had many things going for him. In 1927 San Francisco was nearing the end of a long period of dramatic growth and increasing prosperity. As mayor, he could and did take credit for guiding that growth. He reminded people that much economic progress, including a widespread increase in wages and a higher standard of living, had taken place on his watch. The city was notably safe, thanks to the work of the police department in keeping out organized crime. Life was so good for most people that labor continued to support Rolph, which tended to mitigate often-heard charges that the mayor was a tool of the business community.

The physical appearance of the city had undergone profound changes since his first term — a new civic center, railway lines, bridges, tunnels, roads, and schools. Rolph realized that the city's growth was an enormous electoral asset, and he played it to the hilt. "My sympathy is always with the builder," he told the crowds. "His monuments are the creation of his hands, always working, never ceasing because of the cackle of his critics. I have endeavored in my administration to be a builder.... It is always easy to criticize, but it is hard to achieve."[9] The force of his argument was apparent in the *Chronicle*'s observation that "what San Francisco is today has been made under the Rolph administration. To slander one is to slander the other."[10]

The leading San Francisco newspapers — the *Chronicle* and *Examiner* — enthusiastically backed the mayor's reelection bid, although the reasons were primarily negative. The *Chronicle*, which had not always supported the Rolph administration, became convinced that a victory for Power and "boss" Finn would be a disaster for the city. We have disagreed with Rolph many times, the paper editorialized, and he has made mistakes — "what mother's son has not?" — but we will support him "in imminent peril of tyranny."[11]

Rolph's plan of attack against Finn took its cue from the *Chronicle*'s coverage, centering on the sheriff's reputation as a political boss and dispenser of patronage. Rolph forces publicly charged that Finn was reaching, through his puppet Power, for control of the entire city. Of course, the mayor himself was vulnerable to the charge of cronyism, but he sought to keep Finn and Power on the defensive. He reminded voters that he had won the election of 1911 largely on the strength of his condemnation of the corrupt city politics of the century's first decade. Finn, he warned, might bring those times back.

In every rally, Rolph claimed to be against bossism and for clean government. "Bossism exists by the spoils system," he declared, insisting that his administration had been "clean and free from even a hint of graft or dishonesty."[12] But it was not enough, he told voters, to return him to the mayor's office. "A vote for me is half a vote. You must vote for Fitzgerald [for sheriff] too."[13]

As usual, Rolph had the edge in rhetoric, color and sheer popular appeal. Despite having been a fixture around town for more than 15 years, he still drew huge, overflowing crowds to his campaign rallies. He reminded his audiences that as "captain of the good ship San Francisco," he had been "on the bridge" for 16 years, and he was not going to turn it over to either of those "pirates."[14] To counteract the endorsement of Power by the party of organized labor, he pointed out that he was the only candidate with a union card. Modesty continued to be his hallmark: "I do the best I know how," he said humbly, "and will continue to do so."[15]

The Rolph forces exploited their finely tuned grassroots organization. The mayor's official family denied the existence of a Rolph machine, but, as one of his cronies said, the whole city was his machine.[16] For 15 years, the mayor and his staff had meticulously cultivated its residents and attended to their needs. Most days he attended civic meetings and appeared before groups. In a typical campaign speech, he reminded people in the Richmond area of his early days in that part of the city, then referred to local neighborhoods and streets, mentioned individual homes and shopping areas, and then — aided by excellent staff work and his own prodigious memory — spoke knowledgeably on the issues of most concern to his audience.

Countless individual kindnesses had built a large body of Rolph loyalists, who sprang to his defense as opponents insinuated he had overstayed his welcome. A local paper wrote: "We hear feeble protests that Jim 'has been there long enough,' but has he? No man in the West is better known than Rolph and few are better liked by the population.... He has been efficient, trustworthy, honest, progressive, tireless, independent, and certainly has failed to make a fortune out of his labors." Rolph clubs, which had formed over the years throughout the city, sponsored so-called debates and discussion groups as the election approached.

Rolph found many ways to cash in on his enormous investment in goodwill and love for his constituents. In September, for example, his campaign asked the publisher of the *Pacific Coast Hotel Weekly*, a newspaper for the local innkeeping industry, if he would be willing to place a political advertisement in his magazine. The publisher wrote back: "Our paper is very neutral as to politics. We never publish political news, but send it to us just the same and once in a while I will make an exception because of my friendship for the mayor, whom I esteem very highly."[17]

Rolph supporters were not above what might today be considered dirty tricks. In their effort to help elect Fitzgerald sheriff, bail bond workers allied with the mayor bought tickets from betting establishments that picked Fitzgerald to win. Then they distributed the tickets to the public. Recipients, seeing a chance to make a profit at no cost, urged their families and friends to vote for Fitzgerald.[18] Other Rolph allies went down to the saloons and flophouses, tore dollar bills in half, and gave the half-bills out to the street people who seemed most likely to vote. "If Rolph wins," they told the vagrants, "you get the other half." This stunt, according to one source, produced several hundred votes.[19]

Campaign organizers orchestrated campaign events, particularly endorsements, to achieve the optimum result. In the final two weeks before the election, several influential public figures endorsed Rolph. Former mayor James Phelan urged voters to "repel the selfish and corrupt hands which seek to violate and invade the city."[20] John McNab, a leading figure in San Francisco for many years as well as a Rolph ally, called the administration a "model of Progressive cleanliness and magnificent accomplishment."[21] The visiting mayor of Portland, Oregon, dropped by a local radio station to give Rolph a plug.

Rolph had learned well a lesson that would elude many politicians over the next 70 years—the importance of staying on message. Each of his speeches featured two themes—his personal incorruptibility and his accomplishments as a builder. (He liked to say that he led a "clean, constructive administration.") At the same time, he sowed concern about Sheriff Finn's alleged plot to take over the city. Message discipline included the use of identical phrases that seemed especially effective. When John McNab warned the voters not to wreck the "whole magnificent structure" of the Rolph administration by electing Power, Rolph borrowed that exact phrase in subsequent self-congratulatory speeches.

None of this would have mattered without the candidate's high energy and willingness to mix it up. "Mayor Rolph has shown a 'go-getter' ability in this canvass that puts him in a class by himself," marveled the *Examiner*. He has been meeting thousands of people a day "without a wilt in him."[22] One evening in late October, he made six separate speeches. Sometimes, his opponent shared the same platform with him. Under those circumstances, Rolph did not shrink from confrontation. He could be very combative person to person, said the *Chronicle*.

Once again, public ownership was an issue in the 1927 campaign. Bond issues to support public distribution of Hetch Hetchy power and for extension of the city's municipal railroad line were on the ballot, and an advisory vote was scheduled on whether the proposed Oakland Bay Bridge would be publicly or privately built. Once again Rolph found himself scrambling to get William Randolph Hearst's endorsement. He had recognized the influence of Hearst and his newspapers and the power of John Francis Neylan's pen when most of his allies on the board of supervisors were defeated for reelection in 1925.

12. A Strong Finish

Neylan saw the election as another opportunity to get Rolph back into line on the issues he felt strongly about. Using Hearst's *Examiner* to make his points, he pointed out that the Rolph campaign had falsely linked Finn and Power to a bribery scandal. Neylan also attacked city engineer O'Shaughnessy for extravagance and delay on Hetch Hetchy, and ran a series of editorials praising the board of supervisors for "throwing off executive dominance."[23]

The editor's jabs had their desired effect. "My office has been infected with candidates for public office," Neylan wrote Hearst. "Mayor Rolph and his friends have been the most persistent. He has been to see me three or four times." Neylan was pleased with the public comments Rolph made after those visits. He told Hearst that the mayor was now "screaming the Hearst program at the top of his lungs and championing Progressivism as if he had invented it." He recommended that the *Examiner* give Rolph its formal support, even though Hearst had earlier issued orders forbidding the endorsement of individual candidates for public office in his newspapers.

By now, Neylan had considerable influence with Hearst, and the publisher agreed to allow the endorsement. Rolph had just appealed for the passage of bonds to complete the final link in the chain that would bring public power to the city. "We support the mayor," said the *Examiner* on the eve of the election, "because he is not afraid to offend the private power magnates who hope to maintain control over the power output of the Hetch Hetchy project."[24] The *Chronicle*, whose support of Rolph was based at least in part on his acquiescence to private power distribution, felt betrayed but could not retract its endorsement at the last minute.

During the final week, Rolph forces sought to cover all the necessary bases. With the media and their cameras following along, the mayor reviewed a line of police, then donned train conductor gear and piloted the first railway car to travel one of the city's new lines. He made a special radio appeal to women, "the very foundation of civil society," in which he praised their role in family life, and asked for the votes of all "home-loving people."[25] Rolph aides played on what they believed to be women's concern for fair play: "They're attacking your Jimmy," said one. "Those bosses, that we drove out, they now want to crush your Jimmy."[26]

Rolph and his spokesmen reminded those who had not voted in a while to familiarize themselves in advance with the voting machines so that their ballots would not be nullified. Hearing that the weather on election day might be inclement, Rolph campaign headquarters offered to provide transportation for those who might be tempted to stay at home.

Of course, Power and Finn counterattacked throughout the campaign, but they either failed to persuade or came across as defensive. Power weakly criticized the mayor for not taking the initiative to attract new industries to the city and for lacking vision. Finn sought to deflect Rolph's bossism charges by saying, "If Mayor Rolph tells all he knows about bossism, it will be a revelation."[27]

As election day approached, Governor Young wrote an open letter to his ally Finn testifying to his good qualities and denying that Finn ever sought to influence state appointments, though "this does not mean I do not welcome your suggestions."[28] The mayor, apparently still thinking he might lose, closed the campaign by saying that, should the worst happen, he would "get together the remnants of a shattered fortune and devote the remainder of life exclusively to private interests."[29]

The election results relegated this plan to the shelf. The final tally was 90,000 votes for Rolph and 60,000 for Power. It was an overwhelming victory. Even more astounding, Finn was defeated for reelection as sheriff, a repudiation for which the mayor had been pushing in his campaign speeches.

On public ownership, both Rolph and Neylan appeared to get what they wanted. Rolph won over the Hearst people by backing the power bonds, but he did not do so strenuously enough to prevent them from being defeated, thus preserving good relations with his anti-public power benefactors and supporters. Neylan considered the results of the 1927 election a qualified victory for Progressivism. A majority had voted for the power and railroad bonds, though not enough to secure their passage, and the advisory vote on the Bay Bridge was for public ownership and operation.

Rolph might have been happier and lived longer had he been forced to return to private life. The campaign blitz of 1927 had saddled him with additional debt. His reelection meant that the time available for working himself out of his financial predicament would continue to be limited. All the same, he pushed himself relentlessly as he moved into his fifth term. In November 1928, his doctor announced that he was suffering from a severe cold and fatigue and would require a full week of rest. He had been working night and day, the doctor reported, plus "attempting in a measure to give consideration to his own private affairs."[30]

Rolph's liquidated shipping company apparently still faced considerable debt. In 1929 he received a bleak note from his "affectionate partner," George Hind:

> I can't seem to forget our business troubles—things generally have not gone very well with us lately. I wake up at night and keep thinking about it all and sometimes think what is the use of ... working and worrying. The last year has been a way to get money to keep things going and am afraid we are going to have our hands full in this regard for some time to come.[31]

Mayor Rolph, right, welcomed Gov. C.C. Young (left) to San Francisco in the late 1920s. The competent but uncharismatic Young later seethed as Rolph unseated him in the 1930 gubernatorial primary. The man in the center is unidentified (courtesy of the California History Room, California State Library, Sacramento, California).

Rolph took the sting out of his money problems by testing the limits of his perquisites as mayor. Shortly after his victory, he presented a list of needs to the city finance committee. According to one writer, these included an official airplane, a broadcasting station, a new official launch "with sufficient mahogany and polished brass to impress a visiting admiral, and with a big enough cabin to prevent frock coats and silk hats of welcoming committees from being dampened by the spray," two new limousines, an increase in the mayor's contingency fund, which he was allowed to spend without an accounting, an elegant renovation of his offices, an extra stenographer, and a filing clerk for night duty.[32] In July 1928, in a demonstration of his growing confidence, he conferred for an hour with Herbert Hoover, who had just been nominated for president, and then monopolized the press conference that followed.

Rolph also did not hesitate to avail himself of public services for private purposes. Stories circulated in 1929 that city employees and equipment had been utilized in making nearly all the improvements on his ranch. It came to light that repairs to a private road on Rolph property were made using a tractor, steamroller and sand machine owned by the Department of Public Works. The department head justified the action, saying that the equipment in question was obsolete and that employees who did the road work did so only on Sundays.[33]

Several mayors in other towns chose to make a joke of the affair and volunteered to lend their own equipment to Rolph if San Francisco would not.[34] But in a different time and a different environment, Rolph's tendency to blur the distinction between public and private resources would not be looked upon with a smile and a shrug of the shoulders.

In the policy arena, the Rolph administration continued to focus upon a single task during the final term: the physical expansion of the city. In setting forth his policy agenda, he identified as priorities the construction of highways, schools, playgrounds, bridges and an airport, along with the acquisition of facilities to transmit power. Major milestones were reached a year into his last term, when the voters approved the purchase of the Spring Valley Water Company—considered crucial to the success of the Hetch Hetchy project—and a $35 million bond issue for the Golden Gate Bridge.

Part Three
Moving On to Sacramento

13

The 1930 Campaign for Governor

As 1930 began, Rolph's self-confidence and sense of possibility were high. He had a first-rate campaign organization. He knew he would be a formidable candidate for governor. He had proved to be a successful vote-getter in the 1918 gubernatorial election. He was an icon in San Francisco. The only question was whether he could find enough support outside the Bay Area to prevail against strong opposition. But he had done a lot of traveling around the state in 1928 in support of Hoover's presidential candidacy and had been pleased with his reception.[1]

Rolph began receiving encouragement in early 1930 to make the run. A local supporter sent him a statistical rundown of the 1918 elections across the state, showing how well he had matched up against then Governor Stevens. A Los Angeles publisher wrote that Rolph had run a few years too soon in 1918: "The liberal element wants you.... The Southland knows you better today, and you can and will win." Rolph replied that he was "very pleased with your optimistic view of my candidacy."

The flattery directed Rolph's way in 1930 probably increased his resolve to test his strength in a statewide election. Typical were the comments of one Richard McKinley:

> You have the background. You have proven your sanity. You have proven your ability. You have proven your honesty. You have proven your cleanliness of character.... And you also know that you could not be mayor of San Francisco if you were too damn good.... We like you because we know that you are not perfect and you don't pretend to be any such thing. We like you because you are in many respects what we would like to be ourselves.

In May, his staff began providing him with position papers on issues that were sure to come up during the campaign.

And so Rolph decided to make the race. On one level, he was nobly

89

opting for public service over private gain. On another, he was pursuing ego gratification of a kind and quality he had not known as a shipping executive. He could hobnob with famous people, enjoy the adoration of the masses, and still live comfortably as governor. It would be like being mayor, only more fun. The only missing piece in the master plan was his vision. What would a Rolph administration look like? Where would he try to take the state?

The main obstacle on his road to Sacramento was the Republican primary. Whoever won the primary was almost certain to win the general election in this heavily Republican state. He would have to face a seasoned politician, incumbent Governor C.C. Young, as well as former Lieutenant Governor, now Los Angeles district attorney, Buron Fitts.

C.C. Young had significant advantages even beyond his status as the incumbent. He had been one of the best-prepared chief executives in the state's history. He was a former teacher, author, businessman, a three-time speaker of the Assembly and twice lieutenant governor before his election as governor. Admirers said that he could have taken over any of the state's huge departments and directed it competently within weeks. Young had never lost an election, he had the support of most of the state's newspapers, and had done an excellent job as governor. Through prudent stewardship of the state's resources, he had amassed a $29 million surplus. Drawing upon his broad administrative experience, he had also instituted a long-term planning process and reorganized the state government.

Young's problem was that, like many candidates before the age of television, he had little charisma and was uncomfortable in the spotlight, especially in contrast to the media-savvy mayor of San Francisco. He was "basically a friendly man who talked easily with associates," noted gubernatorial historian H. Brett Melendy, but he "appeared austere and reserved to the public."[2] The *Oakland Tribune*, while praising his competence, called his manner "not spectacular."[3] He was also a cautious and often vacillating administrator, as is sometimes true of well-informed people who see many shades of gray. A final strike against Young was the fact that four consecutive governors since Hiram Johnson had been ousted after only one term in office. The state, in those days, changed governors "as airily as a nouveau riche matron throwing away her dinner dress after one wearing."[4]

Buron Fitts, though clearly an underdog, had the support of the *Los Angeles Times*, which editorialized vigorously on his behalf. He positioned himself as the southern candidate — the man who would rectify the "organized injustice" that denied the rapidly growing southern half of the state its rightful share of power in Sacramento. Rolph, said the *Times*, "knows nothing of the south and cares less." He is "steeped in and dedicated to the outworn myth of the north's 'preeminent rights' in state affairs."[5]

Fitts' southern strategy, of course, would not earn him many votes in the north, but he hoped that Rolph and Young (whose home was in Berkeley) would split the northern vote, leaving him the victor. To distinguish himself further, Fitts took a more conservative stance on spending issues than either of his opponents. Despite the large surplus Young had built up, Fitts denounced what he called the orgy of spending going on in Sacramento.

As for Rolph, he seemed very much like a long shot. He was the only candidate without experience on the state level. His opponents and the media quickly seized on his "woeful knowledge of state affairs" as a campaign issue. The *San Diego Union* wrote that Rolph, "while personally a charming man deservedly popular—can hardly be called a state leader."[6] Noted writer Upton Sinclair, who went on to become the Democratic nominee for governor in 1934, summarized Rolph's qualifications for high office as "a smile, an excellent knowledge of good liquor, [and] the ability to wear shiny boots and a gardenia and to ride a horse backwards at county fairs."[7]

But Rolph had one undeniable qualification—he was the long-time chief executive of a major American city. As the campaign unfolded, he hammered home the message that his administrative experience in San Francisco was directly transferable to the governor's mansion. "What has been accomplished in San Francisco can be accomplished in and for the state," he said in a July speech. "I think, in that respect, I can serve the state of California as efficiently as it has been my good fortune to serve the city of which I have been mayor for almost twenty years."[8]

Rolph's opponents counterattacked by questioning the notion that his mayoralty had been a successful one. Fitts charged that his administration had been "mediocre in the extreme."[9] The *Los Angeles Times* pointed out that the municipal railroad of which Rolph was so proud was operating at a loss and that the Hetch Hetchy project, for all its scale and importance, was far over budget and still incomplete. As the *Times* wrote, "$117,000,000 in bond issues since 1910—and still no water!"[10] The *San Francisco Examiner*, while not directly opposing Rolph, also noted the mayor's vulnerability. "He has pointed with pride to Hetch Hetchy," it noted. "It may be the sort of pride that goes before a fall."[11]

To the extent that issues had a role in the campaign, they seemed to favor Young or Fitts, particularly in the more populous south. By 1930, whether or not to continue the Prohibition experiment was on the minds of many. Rolph, in tune with his constituents in tolerant San Francisco and in line with his own personal convictions, was an unabashed "wet," but Los

Angeles was a conservative place and Governor Young was an outspoken "dry." The tension between the northern and southern halves of the state caused newspapers like the *Times* and the *San Diego Union* to urge "giv[ing] the south its due" by electing Fitts.

But Rolph had learned years ago not to let his opponents trap him into running an issues campaign. He stuck to his tried and true formula for political success—bonding with the voters and avoiding specifics. He "conducted his usual picturesque canvass,"[12] attending fiestas, milking cows, kissing babies, and riding white stallions in civic parades, while decked out in his custom-made boots with a fresh gardenia in his lapel.[13] The *Nation* wrote that Rolph's style suggested the "glamour, the professional geniality, and the circus monkeyshines of modern royalty."[14]

Until 1930, personality had not mattered much in state and national elections, because most voters had been unable to see or hear the candidates. Now, radio and newsreels carried an office-seeker's voice and image into thousands of homes, and the airplane and automobile allowed face-to-face interaction with the public on a scale never before possible. Rolph even made a short campaign film — a novelty in those times and far from the polished productions candidates would make in later years. In it, he raised only one subject — his pride and pleasure at having visited every corner of the state. Though he seemed unused to talking into a camera from a studio and floundered a bit in his delivery, his firm, deep voice and apparent lack of a script conveyed strength and sincerity.

Since the mayor had a decided edge in charisma over his opponents, he rightly sensed that the more exposure he had to the public, the better his chances were. So he spent heavily on transportation and committed himself to visiting every county in the state — an unprecedented feat. To do this, he needed solid financial backing and physical stamina. He had both. Though he had lost most of his fortune, his wealthy friends bankrolled his travels—and, as the *San Francisco Chronicle* put it, "the inexhaustible energy of the man was proverbial."[15] Alarmed by his media blitz, Governor Young all but conceded his disadvantage, warning voters not to make a change "just because of the personality of one man over another."[16]

Rolph did more than just show up for his rallies. He made every appearance a special event. He often arrived in costume, a gimmick that other candidates probably felt was beneath their dignity. Drawing from his successful mayoral campaigns, he dressed like the ordinary people he was courting or in clothing that emphasized his love of California history. According to Jerry Flamm, he took five complete costumes on the campaign trail—that of aviator, dairy worker, miner, cowboy and Spanish don.[17] As his personal secretary, David Wooster Taylor, noted, the candidate was "at his best—genial, expansive, magnetic—and faultlessly garbed."[18]

Rolph wound up covering 28,000 miles by chartered airplane. He also traveled in a limousine and often slept in it. This allowed him to visit places like Alpine County, which had never seen a gubernatorial candidate. In one tiny hamlet, Rolph impressed the local citizens by taking part in a milking contest, appropriately dressed as usual, and was rewarded with all nine local votes in the election. He also allowed his campaign managers to enter a contestant on his behalf in the Angel's Camp jumping frog contest. He had his own band, which constantly played his personal theme, "Smiles." "It wasn't military," a voter said, "but it had the same effect on you as a war song."[19]

Rolph rarely spoke in a partisan manner, preferring to articulate themes of unity and goodwill. His appeal had always been based on his ability to bring people together, so he studiously avoided controversy and simply asked all Californians to rally behind his candidacy. Early in his career, he had mastered what would become standard political practice several generations later—the calm, smiling repetition of general themes. For example, he pledged to have a forward-looking administration with a humane touch. Sometimes he would set forth his belief in the philosophy of building and his desire to pass it along to the whole state. Even his backers said they were not voting for him because of any particular policy agenda but rather "because of his sheer, overwhelming humanity."[20]

On the stump, the mayor was careful to tailor his presentation to local interests. "I know that the people are proud to have the virtues of their little hamlets and of their fair-sized cities extolled," he wrote to a friend, "and it is a part of my campaign practice to have information regarding the origin of the name, the principal industry, and the things nearest and dearest to the hearts of the local communities in which I intend to appear."[21]

Typical of his style was a speech to the Beverly Hills Kiwanis club in June. After linking himself by friendship with several prominent Beverly Hills citizens, he made optimistic predictions for California, "destined to be the greatest state in the country." Instead of dwelling on the struggle between north and south for political influence in Sacramento, Rolph spoke of increasing the bond of friendship between San Francisco and Los Angeles.[22] "We are Californians," he reminded the electorate, as though that were self-evidently a mark of distinction, and called for a restoration of faith in the state's future.[23]

On one important issue, however, Rolph saw a clear-cut political advantage in taking a position. Governor Young had been bragging about the $29 million surplus that had been so carefully accumulated over the course of his term. Rolph pounced on this boast as a sign of poor administrative ability and declared that at least some of the money should have been spent on unemployment relief.

The charge enraged Young. He replied by calling the mayor ignorant of economic principles. The surplus, he pointed out, was a reservoir to be held pending a revision in the tax system. Fitts seemed even more tight-fisted than Young, denouncing the orgy of spending in the state capital.[24] But the mayor's stand had an instinctive appeal to the economic victims of the 1929 crash, and made his opponents look far removed from the problems of ordinary people.

Rolph had always been good at reaching out to liberals in his party — after all, he had won the Democratic primary for governor in 1918. Long a supporter of organized labor and the closed shop, he was honored by representatives of 42 labor organizations at a campaign appearance in Los Angeles in July. His opponents tried to turn his sympathy for the problems of the workingman into a liability. On August 20, the *Los Angeles Times*, calling him "union card Jimmy," warned that Rolph would unionize state government if he were elected. But his stand on the budget surplus probably reinforced the impression that this Republican was sympathetic with the worsening plight of California's labor force.

Though none of the candidates talked much about Prohibition during their campaigns, here again Rolph positioned himself well. Young and Fitts had been battling for endorsements from key temperance organizations. In the end, the Anti-Saloon League backed Young, and the Woman's Christian Temperance Union supported Fitts, while Rolph simply pronounced himself a liberal on the subject.[25] With Prohibition increasingly seen as a failure in need of repeal, Rolph was regarded as more in tune with public sentiment.

Five campaigns for mayor had taught Rolph a few things about retail politics and grassroots organization. Good staff work resulted in the organization of Rolph for Governor clubs all around the state. On July 23, as an example, the *San Francisco Examiner* noted the formation of Veterans for Rolph and the Young Men's Rolph-for-Governor League. The candidate knew that the local barber was often well informed on which way the political winds were blowing. "When he was campaigning," said a friend, "he'd get shaved three or four times a day."[26]

Rolph was admittedly on the wrong side of key issues important to southern California — being a "wet," prolabor, and a northerner — and so was unlikely to carry the area. But many influential southerners supported his candidacy from the beginning. A city official in Santa Monica sent along a list of ways Rolph could win their hearts and minds. A leading Los Angeles attorney wrote to say that "until the announcement of your name, there [was] no one [in] whom I could take the slightest interest. He might not win southern California, but a strong second-place showing could push him over the top.

Governor Young watched with increasing dismay as his chances for reelection slipped away in the wake of Rolph's glad-handing, monkeyshines, and superficial comments on the tough issues Young had mastered during his long and distinguished political career. The governor showed that he was overly sensitive to public criticism, going "from pained resignation, to elaborate sarcasm, to something bordering closely on extremely bad temper" as the campaign progressed.[27]

His growing anger gave his attacks on Rolph a bitter and dismissive edge that may have alienated some voters. "I can scarcely believe that a candidate for governor would propose such a thing," he said of Rolph's plan to spend some of the surplus on relief. Doing this "for the fun of spending money is ... utterly foolish from a sound business standpoint."[28] The Young campaign also asserted that Rolph could not serve competently as governor while "Hollywooding and spectacularly absenting himself from the gubernatorial office," as he had from the mayor's office.[29]

Rolph seemed to get a bad break when his hometown *San Francisco Chronicle*, which had supported him as mayor since the early 1920s, came out strongly behind Young. The governor has been "notably zealous, tireless and effective," praised the *Chronicle*. "He knows what to do. He knows when to do it. He knows how to do it. He does it." The paper called his first term a "triumph of expert knowledge, hard and unremitting toil, zeal for the public good, and efficient organization of the forces of state government."[30] Rolph needed strong Bay Area support, and he had to hope that *Chronicle* readers would ignore the newspaper's advice.

Though they were running in a Republican primary election, where evidence of loyalty to party principles might seem to be important, neither Rolph nor Young sought to escape their reputations for pragmatism. Young campaigned and governed more as a technocrat than an ideologue, and Rolph's strong ties to both camps had long rendered him unclassifiable politically. Fitts saw the weak Republican affiliations of his opponents as an opportunity to stake out the territory of party loyalist for himself, which gained him the endorsement of the San Francisco party central committee. Rolph's forfeiture of the dyed-in-the-wool conservative vote made him even more dependent on the politics of personality for electoral success.

As the election approached, the *Los Angeles Times* called it one of the most dramatic finishes in the state's turbulent political history. On Republican primary day, everything broke perfectly for Rolph. He won San Francisco

Rolph and his wife, Annie, vote in the gubernatorial election of 1930. The candidate covered 28,000 miles by chartered airplane. In hundreds of speeches, he mastered what would years later become standard political practice — the calm, smiling repetition of general themes. The election was a triumph of personality (San Francisco History Center, San Francisco Public Library).

by a huge majority, while finishing second in Los Angeles to Fitts. Rolph received 377,390 votes — only 36 percent of the total cast — but he finished first, beating Governor Young by about 20,000. Fitts came in a strong third.

Looking back at the 1930 race from a distance, it seems remarkable that a city mayor, however popular, could have mounted a serious challenge to a sitting, successful governor in a primary election, let alone beaten him. Yet it happened. The politics of personality had triumphed.

The California Republican establishment quickly showed that it valued unity above recriminations. Governor Young issued a statement backing Rolph in the general election, and Fitts did the same. Young even invited Rolph to be his guest of honor on Governor's Day at the California State Fair. At its convention in September, the state party pledged a united front to Rolph, and President Hoover sent a wire extending his earnest support.³¹ The party's "dries" consoled themselves with the fact that one of their own — Frank Merriam of Long Beach — had won the nomination for lieutenant governor.

The general election was largely a foregone conclusion, especially since the Democrats were deeply split on the Prohibition question. The night before the election, San Francisco held a huge party to honor the governor to be. It featured bands, theatrical acts, fireworks, speeches and radio coverage. The next day, Rolph buried Democrat Milton K. Young, receiving nearly a million votes, or three-quarters of all the votes cast. Humorist Will Rogers remarked: "Thank goodness we won't be reformed during this administration at least."³²

14

Great Expectations

As Governor-elect Rolph reveled in his victory and prepared to go to Sacramento, the state was sliding ever deeper into the social and economic abyss that came to be known as the Great Depression. It all began, of course, with the stock market crash of October 1929, when a third of the market's value was erased within several days. But the economy seemed to stabilize after that, and the general assumption was that the country was merely experiencing a routine dip in the business cycle. As David M. Kennedy has written, "Policymakers were not only unprepared to visualize the decade that lay ahead of them; they were almost equally unable to see what was going on around them."[1]

Most Californians did not see a crisis coming, either. Even the normally prescient Hearst was the last man to believe in the Depression, according to John Neylan. He ordered his papers in the state to avoid using the word, to stop complaining, and to look ahead.[2] Conservatives in the legislature continued to argue for the kind of tight-fisted spending policies that had been in vogue throughout the 1920s. As a candidate, Rolph had seemed more in tune with actual conditions when he came out for using some of the budget surplus for unemployment relief.

The reason for the widespread lack of concern about the economy was that 1930 was not an especially bad year in California. Because it was not as heavily industrialized as many states, the Depression arrived relatively late. By April, six months after the stock market crash, prices had recovered somewhat. A few indicators, like unemployment, were worrisome, but others, like wages, were not unduly so. The failure rate of banks across the country following the crash of October 1929 was 36 percent, but in California it was only 8 percent. In April 1931, the *Sacramento Union* editorialized that the worst of the downturn was over. Rolph could not be blamed for believing as he took over in January that the state needed only a spirit of confidence.[3] In this conviction, he was no less farsighted than the national

Republican leadership in Washington, which had until this point resisted strong federal action to address the downturn.

More menacing to California's future, in the opinion of most citizens, were the influx of migrants into the state and the growth of radicalism. Rootless drifters, refugees from middle America's Dust Bowl, jeopardized the prosperity of the state's long-time residents because the newcomers needed jobs desperately and were willing to work for a pittance.

California's agriculture was organized into large-scale enterprises, which author Carey McWilliams called factories in the field.[4] White landowners clashed with a mostly Mexican rural underclass whose members were enlisted in huge numbers at harvest time for backbreaking labor. These field hands were organized by groups like the Communist-led Cannery and Agricultural Workers Industrial Union, which struck regularly beginning in 1930 for higher wages and better working conditions. Most people did not recognize that the violence, threats of violence, and tension between the growers and the harvesters were symptoms of a much larger problem — an economy that was rapidly spiraling downward.

Whatever problems loomed on the horizon, they all seemed manageable to the Rolph entourage, which rolled into the state capital just after New Year's Day in 1931 bursting with optimism and enthusiasm. The new governor expected a smooth ride ahead — similar to his successful 20 years at the helm of the San Francisco city government. The lopsidedness of the election meant that Rolph had a clear mandate to govern. He had made no

Flush from his 1930 victory, Governor Rolph expected a smooth ride ahead, similar to his 20 successful years at the helm of the San Francisco city government. But he miscalculated the magnitude of the challenge in store for him (courtesy of the California History Room, California State Library, Sacramento, California).

specific promises during his campaign and thus had ample room to develop a set of policies that reflected his own values and goals.

Accolades greeted his arrival in the capital, though some of them were backhanded. *The Nation* judged that the election of a man who provided radiation rather than leadership might have a calming effect on what had always been a highly partisan atmosphere.[5] Because voters had been energized at least in part by the question of whether to continue the national experiment with Prohibition, William Randolph Hearst celebrated the Rolph victory as a small but promising sign of public distaste for it.[6] A pundit wrote that Rolph was a liberal governor for a liberal state. This was not quite true, but it suggested that the former mayor was a good match for his new responsibilities.

Sober, small-town Sacramento had not seen anything like the inaugural festivities that Rolph and his staff organized. Rolph loved pomp, parades, multi-gun salutes, balls, and ceremony, all of which had been staples of his tenure in the lively city by the bay. Now the inaugural ball, which had not been held in the capitol since 1903, was revived.[7] The celebration lasted three full days. The *Sacramento Union* proclaimed the inaugural a huge success, and expressed the hope that it would become a model for future inaugurals.[8]

But even before he was sworn into office, Rolph had made a major mistake. The event raised the eyebrows of local politicians and state bureaucrats, who grumbled that the times were wrong for such a public display of excess. Progressives, in particular, were repelled by the pomposity and glitz, which the last several governors had considered unnecessary. Rolph escaped open criticism because he was thought to harbor Progressive tendencies, but one contemporary observer called the lavish inaugural a backward step of 32 years politically.[9] It was the first indication that the governor-elect might be seriously out of step with his new environment.

That environment was radically different from the one he left in San Francisco. Most significantly, it was the home of the California legislature and the state bureaucracy — two institutions that would have a strong impact on his ability to govern. Like the U.S. Congress, the legislature was divided into a lower house — the Assembly — which was apportioned on the basis of population, and an upper house — the Senate — whose makeup was determined by geography.

At that time, the legislature met in full session only once every two years, for no more than 120 days after the governor's inaugural address and again for the same period two years later. The atmosphere was markedly clubby, especially in the 40-man Senate, many of whose members had been serving for a decade or more and knew each other and the Sacramento political

14. Great Expectations

Three California governors — past, present and future — think their private thoughts at the 1931 inaugural. Rolph, at right with his wife, Annie, prepares to take the oath of office. C.C. Young, center, appears to reflect on his failed reelection campaign. Lieutenant Governor-elect Frank Merriam, with papers, would announce his decision to run for governor in 1934 only a few weeks later (*Sacramento Bee* Collection, Sacramento Archives and Museum Collection Center).

process well. Their average length of service contrasted sharply with the string of one-term governors who had followed Hiram Johnson. They tended to be especially wary of chief executives with little experience in state politics.

But the office of the governor had several important advantages in dealing with the lawmakers. Because senators and assemblymen were poorly paid ($1,200 per year), they were obliged to spend most of their time in other professions. Their staff resources were lamentably small, especially in comparison to today's modern legislative apparatus. Poor coordination and lack of expertise handicapped the legislature in dealing with state needs. The growing complexity of the state budget finally led during the next administration to the hiring of a professional budget analyst to provide in-house assistance.

The governor, by contrast, oversaw a large bureaucracy, divided into many departments that supervised the full range of state activities—from transportation and public works to industrial relations and agriculture. He was empowered to appoint most of the state's department heads, though he was expected to select people who had a background appropriate to the job. Civil service protections extended to the ranks below the top level. The most powerful state official was the director of finance, who drew up the administration's budget and approved all state agency programs. In addition to commanding so much professional expertise, two other advantages for the governor were continuity of effort, since he was always on the job, and the ability to command public attention.

The relative strength of his position, if properly exercised, put the governor in the driver's seat. He was expected to organize the legislature—that is, set an agenda and provide guidance on priorities—during its infrequent sessions. He also had the obligation to put together and propose a state budget, using the resources of his finance department. The constitution had granted him two other important weapons in asserting his political control—the right to call a special legislative session on a subject and at a time of his choosing, and the right to veto bills with which he disagreed. Vetoes could be overridden by a two-thirds vote of both houses, but overrides had been rare in the history of the state.[10]

Legislators listened for clues to Rolph's approach to his new duties when he stepped to the rostrum on January 6 to deliver his inaugural address—a lengthy and detailed presentation of his views on the key issues facing state government. It set an appropriately modest tone for a governor with no experience in state politics. Rolph asked for the legislature's help and said that he came to his new tasks with much diffidence. As befitted a man who prized harmony, he also asked for a period of tranquility and tolerance, and counseled against the "ferocity for righteousness which brings about turmoil and strife to no end."[11]

Then he turned to the state's recent economic problems. The budget surplus amassed by the Young administration had grown from $29 million to $30 million during and after the gubernatorial campaign. Rolph repeated his conviction that the state should spend some of that money to help people through the current crisis and to alleviate suffering, though "within strict standards of economy and efficiency." He reminded his audience that "any economy which denies to the state's unfortunates the comforts due to human beings is a false economy," and added that "the poor, the stricken and the unfortunate shall have a first claim on the consideration of my administration."[12]

While acknowledging the seriousness of the current economic situation, Rolph was upbeat about the future. For example, he saw no need to

14. Great Expectations

Rolph takes the oath of office in January 1931 as two members of his kitchen cabinet, Matt Sullivan (second from right in front row) and Tim Reardon (face partially hidden by judge's hand), look on. State treasurer Charles Johnson, who would soon complain that the state was "in the hands of inexperienced men," is at left behind Reardon (*Sacramento Bee* Collection, Sacramento Archives and Museum Collection Center).

seek additional revenue, though he had outlined a number of new spending priorities. He expressed what he termed justified optimism that the Depression was coming to an end, that the banking system was sound, and that business was on the eve of an upswing. Rolph looked forward to a time during his tenure when "the flow of revenues into the state treasury will again become normal, and the surplus can be replenished."[13]

The new governor raised other issues that foreshadowed actions he would take in the months ahead. He came out strongly for prison reform and for the rehabilitation of criminals, believing that there must be some spark of human good within them. He said he would work hard on California's water problems, declaring that it was a government responsibility to deal with the uneven distribution of water resources across the state. In line with his strong support of unions, he voiced his sympathy for the just aspirations of labor. And he asked the legislature to authorize more money for the governor's office — to cover, for example, an official car.[14]

The *Sacramento Union* wrote a guardedly upbeat assessment of Rolph's speech, but also put its finger on what would prove to be the main fallacy underlying his budget assumptions. The governor's policy, it pointed out, was to spend part of the surplus and trust in more prosperous times ahead to replenish it; but what if prosperity failed to materialize?

Still, the newspaper pronounced Rolph's beginning most auspicious and predicted that his energetic preparation for office would give him an unusual grasp of the affairs of state confronting him. His flair for showmanship and his ability to hold the public eye seemed likely to be good for the state rather than to prove a distraction. Rolph, it predicted, will be the most colorful chief executive in a generation and will benefit the state because of his ability to get attention wherever he goes.[15]

Rolph's inaugural speech revealed an approach to the governorship that seemed pragmatic and compassionate. As a Republican, he understood the concerns of the business establishment about strict standards of economy and efficiency, but as a supporter of unions and a man of the people, he could be expected to be sympathetic to the problems of the poor. In other words, the same formula that had worked so well in polarized San Francisco might be just as effective with California's increasingly contentious interest groups. In a typically Rolphian touch, the governor announced that he would meet personally with a jobless army that had arrived in town.[16]

If only he had followed up the speech with more concrete action. Shortly after the inaugural activities had ended, so did Rolph's honeymoon. In fact, he hardly had a honeymoon at all. Only a few weeks into his term, many state leaders were already worried that the new regime was seriously off track. What precipitated the sudden reversal, and why did it happen so quickly?

It began with a series of seemingly minor issues that, taken collectively, cast doubt on Rolph's seriousness of purpose. First came an uproar over a body called the Governor's Council. Governor Young had created this council — which was nothing more than a regular meeting between the governor and his department heads that allowed an exchange of information and views but which was apparently a novelty at the time. In late January, Rolph let it be known that he had no use for the council and intended to abolish it. The *San Francisco News* criticized the decision, saying that Rolph was nullifying the greatest advance in state government since Hiram Johnson's term.[17]

But the Governor's Council apparently had not worked all that well in practice. The *Sacramento Union* pointed out that the reports presented by Young's department heads had been self-serving and that the meetings themselves had been harmony affairs. Instead of abolishing the group, the newspaper encouraged Rolph to try to turn the meetings into candid, problem-solving sessions.[18] Finally, on January 29, the administration announced that it would not disband the council. But it was too late to correct the impression that an inexperienced governor was not interested in learning more about the operations of his own government.

At about the same time, Rolph's well-tended reputation for integrity came under challenge. New state officials were required to be bonded, or insured for any financial loss they might cause the taxpayers. Rolph's insurance company—Rolph, Landis and Ellis—was in the business of issuing such bonds. In late January, it was learned that the governor had sent out solicitation letters to state officials in need of bonds and that 17 Rolph appointees had already signed up with the company. The *San Francisco News* charged that Rolph was trying to turn this highly profitable business into a family bonding monopoly.

On February 1, the *Union* reported that the Survey Underwriters of Northern California were investigating the governor for using his position to influence the posting of bonds. Rolph's letter of solicitation was reprinted in the press, though he quickly denied having seen the letter he signed. He also insisted that he had resigned from the company upon becoming governor, but he admitted that his son was a partner. His own resignation had meant that he had done nothing illegal under then current law, but the incident fueled a perception that Rolph's agenda went beyond serving the public.

More important than either the Governor's Council debacle or the bonding scandal were three issues that took center stage at the very beginning of Rolph's term and remained there throughout the stormy three years that followed. The first was the quality of his appointments to high office. The second was his relationship with the legislature. And the third was his nearly constant travel around the state.

15

The Appointment Wars

When Rolph assumed the governorship, he noticed that the terms of many state government department heads appointed by Governor Young did not end with Young's departure — in fact, some appointees had been named to their jobs on the eve of the election. Feeling that these lame ducks might try to block his programs, he arranged for the introduction of legislation that would require all of Young's appointees to step down and future appointees to serve at the pleasure of the governor. At the same time, he introduced a government reorganization plan that would create a number of new department head positions for him to fill.

Rolph's attempt to reshape the state government in order to find room for his supporters was predictable in light of his past conduct, but it damaged his chances for early success. Announced on January 23, his plans quickly met with strong opposition. Legislators regarded the department heads as substantive specialists, not political appointees, and sought to protect the independence and professionalism of the state bureaucracy. In a typical reaction, the *Sacramento Union* chastised him for knuckling under to old cronies. Laws cannot be scrapped, it said, just to benefit such people.

But Rolph was determined to use the power of appointment to surround himself with familiar faces. Not only did he want to find positions for former campaign workers, but as time went along he would seek to reduce his feelings of isolation in the executive mansion by naming as many members of his kitchen cabinet as possible to administrative posts in Sacramento.

Personal loyalty was the Rolph litmus test when it came to jobs. An aide to Governor Earl Warren told a story years later about a superior court judge vacancy that Rolph had to fill. According to the aide, Rolph was speaking to a publisher friend, who happened to say something like: "They tell me that such-and-such a lawyer wants to be a judge." Rolph allegedly replied: "Is he our kind of people?" "Yes, Governor," was the answer. The lawyer got the job.[1]

15. The Appointment Wars

An early example of "our kind of people" was a local campaign manager whom Rolph sought to place in the public health bureaucracy. As a result of the effort, the governor became embroiled in a nasty public dispute with an entrenched state bureaucrat — the president of the board of public health, George Ebright — who considered Rolph's nominee unqualified and announced his opposition.

Ebright and Rolph went back a long way. The Ebright family had owned a resort where Rolph vacationed as a teenager, and Ebright had been one of several citizens who had launched the original Rolph-for-mayor campaign in 1911. But in 1930 Ebright had just been named to a post in the Young administration. Because he owed his job to Young, he had opposed Rolph's run for governor. Understandable though Ebright's attitude might have been, his disloyalty infuriated Rolph. He attacked Ebright publicly and intemperately for blocking the appointment:

> Dr. Ebright, notwithstanding the long years of friendship existing among our families, put himself out of the way in the last campaign to bitterly assail me in my candidacy for the office of governor, but I said nothing.... If he will just remember, I was elected to the office of governor of California by a million people.[2]

Rolph even tried to fire Ebright but was forced to back down when a staff aide pointed out that his term was not due to expire until 1934 and that he was untouchable until then.

The governor's comments seemed out of character for a man known as a harmonizer and unifier, and they made him look vindictive. But then he went even further. On February 17 Rolph described Governor Young's last-minute installation of Ebright as "a deathbed appointment by an outgoing administration solely to discredit me and my administration." At the same time, he asked for an investigation of rumors of an antiadministration plot in the state's Department of Agriculture.[3] This demonstration of anger, frustration, and even paranoia showed that Rolph was used to getting his way in personnel matters.

His attitude rubbed a number of Sacramento officials the wrong way. They mounted a war against Rolph's staffing plans that raged throughout the spring and summer, and even beyond. One front in this war was the Department of Agriculture, where the governor wanted to install the former horticultural commissioner of San Francisco as chief. The State Agricultural Board strongly opposed the move, calling Rolph's appointee unqualified and incompetent. During several stormy meetings, neither side backed down, and in a July climax to "one of the most heated disputes in the history of the farm industry," Rolph finally rammed his selection through.[4] The appointment "pleased the San Francisco gang no doubt," said the *Sacramento Union*, but the farmers would not soon forget.[5]

Rolph also aimed to name one of his closest associates from San Francisco, Theodore Roche, as head of the Department of Motor Vehicles. Since the DMV was then part of the Public Works Department, he prevailed upon the Assembly to make it an independent agency and raise the salary of its chief. Roche took over in August. This battle only heightened criticism of the governor's personnel practices, although the *Sacramento Union* praised Roche as an "able lawyer and extremely lucid thinker."[6]

One of Rolph's more colorful appointments was Rheba Crawford Splivalo, the wife of a health food store owner and a very picturesque person. Named to head the Department of Social Welfare, she impressed one of her new subordinates as "completely ruthless." She told the subordinate frankly that she "intended to administer the department with a view toward political advantage for the governor." One of her first acts was to send a letter to an aged welfare recipient implying that Rolph had personally interceded to place him on the pension rolls.[7]

Later in his term, Rolph appointed close friend Tim Reardon, who had brought the San Francisco public works department into line behind the mayor's reelection bids, to head the state's Industrial Relations Department. When this happened, John Francis Neylan, the Progressive-minded head of Hearst's *San Francisco Examiner*, raised an alarm in a letter to his boss. Reardon, he wrote, was a political handyman for Rolph and totally unfit for his new position.

Rolph's staffing missteps were assessed by the *Sacramento Union* as early as February 3 in a strikingly prescient column. Noting that troubles were piling up for the governor after only a month in office, the paper's political columnist pointed to two weaknesses that could spell more trouble ahead: his unfamiliarity with state affairs and his inability to say no. The writer believed that better advisers would warn Rolph against trying to turn the state government inside out in order to benefit friends who thought they were entitled to good jobs. He concluded:

> Rolph is a worker and puts in long hours [but] he tries to see everyone and do too much. He must quit trying to tear the state machinery apart to make jobs for friends, who are scarcely worthy of the effort required. He mustn't use his influence to get business for his family or anyone else.... He must think of the taxpayers and the voters and not the San Francisco gang, which seems to regard his election as a bonanza.[8]

16

Rolph and the Legislature

To be a successful governor, Rolph needed a good relationship with the state Assembly and Senate. As mayor, he had instinctively looked for common ground with the city council and the board of supervisors, and he campaigned for governor as a unifier, so he seemed well equipped to launch a charm offensive on the lawmakers.

Several days after his inauguration, Rolph seemed to do just that. He visited the legislature and delivered informal addresses to both houses. Among his comments were these:

> It is not the purpose of the Governor to interfere with the problems which you have been elected to carry into effect. It is not the purpose of the Governor to interfere with the formation of your committees or to interfere with your work.... You have noticed that I have not endeavored in any way, shape or form to interfere, or to show, as has been done in other states and elsewhere, that the Governor's hand is shown in the activities of the Senate or Assembly.... You have seen no politics in this administration.[1]

Rolph's awkward and probably off-the-cuff remarks were intended to show deference and a willingness to compromise, but they raised eyebrows around a town that knew how rancorous and undisciplined the legislature could be. Not only was the state facing leaner times, thus intensifying the struggle for resources, but hostility between the northern and southern halves of the state was approaching its apogee in a fight over electoral reapportionment. It seemed to many state leaders that Rolph needed to follow up on the ideas in his well-received inaugural address and give the legislature some direction.

As early as February 3, by which time the Assembly and Senate were in midsession recess, the legislature was running wild. As the lawmakers were about to reconvene at the end of the month, the *Sacramento Union* predicted that the absence of a definite administration program and lack of firm guidance would complicate the situation.

Rolph's opening speech to the Senate had contained important, and largely overlooked, clues about his view of the governorship and himself. In surprising and seemingly extemporaneous comments, he elaborated on his supposed distaste for the political process. "I want every one of you to feel there is no politics in the governor's office," he exclaimed, "because I am no politician, and I know nothing about politics." His legacy in San Francisco, he professed, was a limited one. "The only reason that I have succeeded, if I have succeeded, is because I attend to business, because I have something to show the people through public buildings which have been built. The best kind of politics is to do something that the people like us to do."[2] Earlier that day, he had told the Assembly the same thing: "I am not a politician but a builder."

Why would the state's most consummate politician say he knew nothing about politics? His comments suggest that he was already worried about the prospect for bitter, partisan divisions over policy issues. He seemed to be hoping that he and the legislature could quickly come to agreement about what needed to be done and then he would simply guide these tasks through to completion.

But surely Rolph did not expect to spend his time overseeing building projects. He had been elected to a position with a complex set of policy challenges, all of which — building programs among them — would be controversial and require political give and take. He would not be able to preside over a harmonious group of like-minded people. He would not be able to avoid conflict.

Yet right from the start, Rolph seemed determined to do so. One of the most divisive issues before the legislature in 1931 was reapportionment. The lawmakers were meeting in their first session since the 1930 census, which documented enormous population gains by southern California. A realignment of electoral districts was necessary — one that would shift the political center of gravity from the North to the South — but the North would not yield its advantage without a struggle. The South had been unable to elect Buron Fitts, who ran for governor largely on a platform of giving southern California its due. If southerners wanted to press for their rights, they would have to do so through their representatives in the legislature.

Soon after convening, the Assembly split into two hostile camps over the selection of a speaker. A southerner — Walter Little — ran against a San Franciscan — Edgar C. Levey. Rolph took a hands-off attitude toward this fight. Levey emerged the winner, and a *Union* editorial remarked that keeping his distance was "the smart thing for an incoming governor to do."[3] But the bitter struggle among the legislators engendered much ill will. As January gave way to February, according to a contemporary analysis, the feelings of resentment and hostility had hardened into permanent estrangements.[4] Ultimately, the census data could not be ignored. A bill was passed and sent to the governor in April containing a new redistricting plan that tipped the balance of power southward.

What was Governor Rolph's role in the reapportionment fight? In his inaugural address, he had called the issue a hard question and expressed the naïve hope that the legislature would solve it "without regard to sectional, individual, or party interests." Once the battle was joined, true to his promise to abjure politics, he refused to get involved. He declared his neutrality in the contest for speaker, perhaps because neither candidate had supported him in the gubernatorial primary. By the session's first recess, he had taken no open part in the search for a solution.[5]

As positions hardened, many legislators looked to the governor for leadership. But he did not seem to have any clear idea of how to shape a compromise and showed no inclination to interfere with what he felt was a legislative responsibility.[6] When the bill was sent to him in April, he quietly accepted the political result and signed it. He then made a gesture to the northerners by supporting an attempt to put the issue before the voters in the form of a referendum, but the effort failed for lack of financial support. Rolph had missed an early chance to make a mark as a conciliator. Even worse, with the legislature going "its own blundering way"[7] on reapportionment, it would be hard to bring members together on the serious issues that lay ahead.

The most important of these was the budget. Though Rolph had already declared his willingness to use some of the budget surplus to address the state's worsening unemployment and relief problems, political pressure on the administration during 1931 was on the side of reining in spending, rather than increasing it. A group of legislators calling themselves the economy bloc wanted to slash appropriations for state agencies that they considered bloated and wasteful.

As the legislature moved toward its mandatory mid–May adjournment date, clashes on the budget and on spending bills grew in intensity. Rolph's policy of not interfering with Senate and Assembly business left the two bodies without agreed-upon priorities, which encouraged individual legislators to push for their own parochial measures, regardless of the impact on the overall bottom line. The *Union* warned the governor in a May 5 editorial that unless he exercised his veto power, the crush of unnecessary spending bills would overwhelm the surplus.

With the session reaching its climax, tensions burst into public view. State treasurer Charles Johnson, a member of Rolph's own administration but a long-time state bureaucrat, charged that California was in the hands of inexperienced men and called the legislature "the most disorganized I have ever seen." Johnson also attacked Rolland Vandegrift, Rolph's director of finance, for his alleged ignorance of state financial affairs[8]

Johnson's assault was widely regarded as motivated by ambition. The treasurer was said to be preparing his own gubernatorial run in 1934. But he was mostly right about the legislative session. It adjourned on May 18 in what the *Union* called wild disorder, with individual senators reportedly sobbing in frustration over the lack of adequate time to carefully consider last-minute legislation.[9] Many bills were jammed through at the last minute, with senators hardly knowing what they were voting on. All told, the solons engaged in an orgy of bill passing—approving more than 900 measures that were mainly designed to benefit local interests. In sum, according to the *Union*, "the forty-ninth legislature began weakly and ended in a riot."[10]

Rolph had until June 19—the end of the bill-signing period—to decide which bills to sign and which to veto. Finance director Vandegrift promised that at least $15 million of the original $29 million surplus would be left when all was said and done, but the *Union* predicted that pork-barrel spending, if not contained by the governor, would reduce the surplus to $12 million. Because Vandegrift wanted the surplus maintained at the $15 million level, he spent the next several weeks pressuring Rolph to hold the line, and he was not above making a public protest when the governor seemed ready to sign bills Vandegrift thought were a waste of money. On June 1 he warned against the mounting cost of government, and on June 8, in a meeting that the *Union* described as stormy, Rolph signed a flood control bill over Vandegrift's protest.

This bill-signing period provided a revealing glimpse into Rolph's operating style. As related by one Leland Cutler, a delegation of San Franciscans was urging the governor to sign an appropriation—at that time making its way through a committee of the legislature—for the construction of a livestock pavilion (later known famously as the Cow Palace). Rolph turned to Vandegrift for his opinion. Put on the spot, the finance director gave the easy answer in such company, saying he would advise Rolph to sign it, but adding that it would probably not get through the committee. The bill did get through the committee and was passed by the legislature, but Vandegrift then reversed himself and recommended a veto as an economy measure. When Cutler and his group protested during a crowded hearing on the bill, Rolph said:

> Regardless of the merits, I remember very well the discussion between Mr. Vandegrift and [Cutler] in my office.... They shook hands on Mr. Vandegrift's promise.... If Mr. Vandegrift knew as much about politics as I do, he wouldn't have made that promise, but he did. The bill is before me, and the honor of the state of California is at stake. I will sign the bill.

16. Rolph and the Legislature

In June 1931 Rolph barricaded himself behind closed doors to consider the hundreds of bills passed by a rudderless state legislature. When he emerged, he had signed 1,220 of them (*Sacramento Bee* Collection, Sacramento Archives and Museum Collection Center).

He did this, apparently with all the flourish and drama he could muster, and "cheers shook the ceiling."[11]

Of course, Rolph may have been secretly glad to have an excuse to sign an appropriation benefiting his hometown. But his action was also consistent with the priority he had always placed on personal fairness and square dealing over policy concerns. His phrase "regardless of the merits" was a telling one. According to the *Union*'s account, Rolph felt that the integrity of his administration was at stake.

On June 19, Rolph returned from a long trip around the state and, with only a few hours to go in the bill-signing period, barricaded himself behind closed doors to consider the hundreds of bills on his desk.[12] When he emerged, he had signed 1,220 new laws into effect (a record, according to the *Union*) and had vetoed 96 bills. The result of this legislation and of several special appropriations was to reduce the surplus to $13.2 million — leaving more than Johnson had feared, but considerably less than Vandegrift and other economy-minded officials had hoped.

Over the next several months, some columnists and legislators complained about this drain on state resources, and continued calls were heard for retrenchment and cutbacks in Sacramento. But the budgetary outcome was not out of line for a state undergoing an economic slowdown and declining revenues. It was certainly legitimate to draw down the surplus as times became tougher. Spending state money stimulated the economy and probably lessened the unemployment problem, albeit marginally.

Unfortunately, the spending did not reflect a coherent approach to meeting California's pressing needs. Instead, the money was spread scattershot around the state in a process that favored special interests. And because Rolph and his administration still believed that recovery was imminent, they saw no need at this point to consider additional sources of revenue — i.e., new taxes. This unwarranted optimism (which was, in fairness, widely shared) guaranteed that the state would sooner or later run large deficits.

Why had Rolph been traveling around the state in June instead of leaving himself time to pore over the avalanche of freshly passed legislation on his desk? This question went to the heart of his concept of the governorship.

17

The Permanent Campaign

From the beginning of his term, Rolph showed far more interest in traveling and meeting people than in working at his desk in the Capitol. The new governor defined his office broadly — it was anywhere he happened to be. And that place was not likely to be Sacramento. He enjoyed attending gatherings other governors would not have thought worth their time. The need to be in perpetual motion — attending ceremonies and fairs, making speeches, and stopping off in San Francisco to get advice from his old brain trust — would become a permanent fixture of his approach to governing.

His travel schedule for two weeks in February set a pattern that would be repeated scores of times in the years to come. On a Wednesday, a few days after the bonding scandal broke, the governor attended a dinner in Piedmont. He moved on to a horse show in Oakland the next day. He returned to Sacramento Friday morning, went to San Francisco that afternoon, and was back in Sacramento in time to board a plane to El Centro for the Imperial County Winter Fair. He remained in Los Angeles until Sunday, when he dedicated an Elks lodge building there. On Tuesday he traveled to Glendale to address the Chamber of Commerce, after which he flew back to the capital. The next week found him at his ranch in the Bay Area, a lunch in Riverside, a flower show in Encinitas, an orange show in San Bernardino, a dedication in Long Beach, and a citrus fair in Sonoma before returning to Sacramento for the reconvening of the legislature on February 24.

Rolph was determined to fulfill a pledge made during the campaign to visit every county during his first year in office, as he had during the campaign itself. The only way to cover all that ground in a reasonable time was by plane. Air travel was far from routine in the early 1930s, but Rolph loved to fly. One of his first requests of the legislature was for a private plane. The legislature said no, but Rolph found ways to fly anyhow. Soon the press was

One of the first elected officials to conduct a permanent campaign, Rolph courted voters (and their friends) throughout his term (courtesy of the California History Room, California State Library, Sacramento, California).

referring to him as "California's flying governor." By October he had circled the state three times and logged 3,300 miles by air alone.[1]

This use (or misuse) of his time irritated and baffled his contemporaries and made him the butt of considerable sarcasm. As early as March, a state senator wisecracked that Rolph "might be found in his office if there are no circuses in town."[2] Columnists, particularly in antiadministration newspapers, suggested that in such uncertain times it was unbecoming for Rolph to be flitting hither and yon and enjoying frivolities such as state fairs and building dedications. A governor who makes too many public appearances, said the *Sacramento Union*'s political commentator, soon ceases to be an attraction. "If anyone in California hasn't seen Rolph since he became governor," he concluded, "it isn't the governor's fault."[3] Such trips were also taxing: upon his return from one in October, he had to spend two weeks in the hospital with a severe cold and physical exhaustion.

Rolph defended his peripatetic behavior by saying that it was the only way to find out what the voters wanted done. And he had always believed

17. The Permanent Campaign

that public officials should be visible. But these explanations do not go far enough. He had spent the primary and general election of 1930 getting to know what was on people's minds—now it was time to go to work. By choosing to stay involved in activities that provided a high comfort level, he may have been revealing a lack of confidence in his ability to handle a complex set of administrative challenges. Alternatively, Rolph might have been an early believer in what today is called the permanent campaign. He may have seen it as laying the groundwork for his 1934 reelection bid.

His travels had a significant downside. Frequent absences from Sacramento left little time for building relationships and alliances with key politicians around Sacramento and for communicating the governor's larger purposes, whatever those were. Under these conditions, his decisions and instructions were bound to be rushed and ill-considered. Even worse, the danger grew that state bureaucrats, left with little guidance, would be forced to improvise and would fall into turf battles with other government agencies. The Governor's Council, which he had tried to abolish early in his term, continued to languish, its communications function "lost in the whir of an airplane propeller."[4]

In August 1931, with the legislature adjourned and the capital on vacation, an episode took place that illustrated the governor's tendency to act without thinking or consulting others. On the 7th the Sacramento press announced that Rolph had declared a state holiday—one that would encompass the days between Friday, September 4, which was Admission Day, and Wednesday, September 9, which was Labor Day—so that people could attend the state fair without having to worry about going to work. Before anyone could seek clarification, Rolph went off to hunt sagehens with the governor of Nevada. As the *Union* said, "the state pinched its collective self to see if it heard correctly."[5]

By the next day, the banking and retail sectors, which in their declining state could ill afford additional business holidays, had erupted in protest. Many enterprises said they would ignore the proclamation if Rolph followed through with it. The *Union* editorialized that "only governors have time to ramble about the state attending fiestas, beauty shows and whatnot."[6] People who had to work for a living seemed mostly appalled by the idea.[7]

On August 9, returning to Sacramento from his hunting trip, Rolph backpedaled. Calling the furor a tempest in a teapot, he announced he was delaying any action on the proposed holiday. At the same time, he defended the idea, pointing out that only two days of work would be lost, since Friday and Wednesday were holidays anyway. In the end, he assured the public he would not sign an act that most people opposed, saying: "I want to be safe and sound and keep my feet on the ground."[8]

Was Rolph serious about the state holiday? His friends argued it was a joke that got out of hand. When the governor was told that Admissions Day and Labor Day were so close together, he was supposed to have said: "Well, why not make holidays of all the intervening days?" and then went off on vacation with a smile on his face.[9] But it seems more likely that he was attracted to the idea as a way of alleviating public distress, and then did not have time to think it through before leaving town.

* * * * * * * * * * *

As the summer of 1931 came to an end, Rolph felt, despite all these missteps, that he had made a solid beginning. His advocacy of some modest building programs had helped to get them through the legislature. He had fine-tuned the structure of several state government agencies. And he had set up committees to make recommendations on such key issues as water resources and unemployment. He was most proud, as he told an interviewer, of his attempts to put heart into state government, of the fact that "his office has been open to, and his time at the disposal of, all who choose to come."[10]

The reality was, however, that in a few short months, Rolph's future ability to govern had been seriously compromised. The legislature was learning not to look to him for leadership. The state bureaucracy perceived that he was more interested in continuing his election campaign than in understanding policy, and that he was willing to demean state agencies by assigning ill-qualified political allies to head them. He was developing a reputation for extravagance and excess that was unbecoming during an economic downturn. In short, his commitment to the public welfare was already being questioned.

At the end of the summer, whether he realized it or not, Rolph was in a hole he would not easily be able to dig himself out of. His only hope of righting the ship was to adapt to his environment and engage the issues. Surely he was capable — but was he willing?

Part Four
The Long, Downhill Slide

18

The Depression Worsens

The third winter of the Depression. In towns and cities across the country, haggard men in shabby overcoats, collars turned up against the chill wind, newspapers plugging the holes in their shoes, lined up glumly for handouts at soup kitchens. Tens of thousands of displaced workers took to the roads, thumbs up, hitching west, huddled in boxcars, heading south, drifting north, east, wherever the highways and railways led, wherever there might be a job.[1]

Unemployment increased to alarming levels throughout California in 1931. Approximately 700,000 employable people — about 28 percent of the total work force — were without jobs.[2] Most of these unfortunates lived in the major urban centers; Los Angeles County alone accounted for half of the jobless. With so much disposable income lost, specialty agricultural crops, such as citrus fruit and grapes, underwent a major decline. The economy was locked into a deadly downward spiral.

The situation raised an obvious question: What should the government in Sacramento be doing about it? Neither the state nor the country had ever known unemployment of this magnitude, and no mechanism was in place to deal with it. Rolph was a compassionate man, but what could be accomplished without driving the state into debt? Ultimately, he made the worst possible choice — he dithered.

In late August, he floated the idea of a special session of the legislature to deal with unemployment. At the same time, he appointed a commission, headed by an old San Francisco friend, Archbishop Edward Hanna, to study the problem. Both moves were widely praised. A few weeks later, however, he had second thoughts about the special session. Such sessions had been unruly in the past, were difficult to handle, and often ended up losing their focus. As the governor hesitated, the legislature formed its own committee to formulate an emergency relief plan. At the end of September, the committee seemed ready to recommend a sales tax as a means of raising the necessary revenue for a relief or jobs program.

Lieutenant Governor Merriam and a leading state senator, John Inman, now pressed Rolph to convene a special session without delay, so that it could consider the legislative committee's suggestions. But Rolph was waiting for a report from the Hanna commission, which was said to be working on a more comprehensive program of relief. He declined to call the legislature back until he could see the outlines of a plan that would yield real results. On October 1, digging in his heels further, he declared that he would not be pressured, and he even called efforts to convene a special session politically motivated.[3] In frustration, Inman remarked that "while we are fiddling, Rome is burning."[4]

By then, it was clear that Rolph was leaning against direct state action. He probably knew that the most likely outcome of a special session would be a tax increase, which he was not willing to support. Most of October went by while the legislative committee and the Hanna commission pursued their separate agendas. Meanwhile, Rolph sent his finance director, Rolland Vandegrift, to several eastern states to find out how his counterparts were handling the problem. Vandegrift heightened the governor's doubts by reporting back that most of them viewed unemployment as a local rather than a state concern.

But the main reason nothing was accomplished in October was that Rolph was rarely in Sacramento. Trying to make good on his campaign pledge to visit every county during his first year in office, he circled the state three times in three weeks. That month he covered 3,300 miles by plane, train and automobile. The only rest he was able to get, according to the press, was while propped up in the back of a plane or car. On the 26th, with a severe cold and physically exhausted, he was ordered to bed and then to a hospital by his doctor. He remained there for over a week. On November 6, feeling better despite having lost 11 pounds, he returned to the capital for a day and then resumed his visits to county seats.

To Merriam, Inman and other state leaders concerned about the worsening economic picture, Rolph's manic rush through the state must have seemed bizarre in the extreme. When he finally concluded his journey, he continued to oppose legislative action even though his travels must have shown him a high level of distress. In December, when lawmakers from the South publicly requested a special session, Rolph sent Vandegrift to Los Angeles to assure them that his commission was doing whatever was necessary. By then, Inman and other opposition lawmakers believed that it was too late to act in time to help people get through the winter anyhow.

David Taylor, one of Rolph's secretaries, insisted that the governor devoted "endless hours and sleepless nights"[5] to the issues of unemployment and relief. And he did take a significant step in November that did not require legislative involvement. He established a State Labor Camp

Governor Rolph, with wife Annie, enjoys a respite from worries about his difficult first year (Nancy Rolph Welch Collection).

Committee to study the feasibility of setting up public works relief camps for the urban unemployed. The committee quickly staffed out a plan of action, which the governor approved. By December, the first work camp began operation. Twenty-eight of these camps had been established by July 1932, providing work for more than 1,000 men.[6]

The labor camps represented a rudimentary but creative approach to an unprecedented problem. The men did manual labor for six hours a day and received food and housing, but no pay, in return. Municipal and state governments shared clothing expenses. Living conditions were described as rugged, but the workforce was well fed. After Franklin Roosevelt was elected president in 1933, the California camps served as a model for the establishment of the Civilian Conservation Corps.

Though he skillfully implemented the labor camp initiative, Rolph missed a chance to engage in some joint problem solving with key legislative leaders in late 1931. Did he distrust the intentions of Merriam, who was already planning to run for governor in 1934? Did he think the legislature would show him up if it took action?

Senator Inman had not been friendly to the Rolph people and was thought to be an ally of the former governor—part of the C.C. Young crowd.[7] We do not know if Rolph already had reason to distrust Inman, but his unresponsiveness to the senator's pleadings for a special session probably helped to poison their relationship from that point forward. And by accusing Merriam and Inman of playing politics, Rolph may have been unnecessarily combative. At this early stage in his term, he already saw the legislature, as well as the lieutenant governor, as adversaries rather than as potential partners.

19

Capital Punishment and the Mooney Case

The period between November 1931 and April 1932 was dominated by a controversy that would force the governor to choose between his fabled compassion and his long-felt disdain for the state's radical movements. His actions in the Tom Mooney case would show both the primacy of political calculation in his thinking and the flaws in his operating style that would eventually undermine public confidence in his ability to lead.

During the 1920s and 1930s, capital punishment — specifically, death by hanging — was the ultimate penalty in California for the most serious crimes. The public, then as now, generally supported it, but governors, who had the option of pardoning or commuting the sentences of prisoners on death row, often struggled with these life-or-death decisions.

Rolph came to office with a long record as a humane and compassionate public official. From the beginning of his term, he showed that he had every intention of giving convicted murderers the benefit of the doubt. During the 1931 legislative session, a bill was passed that would make capital punishment marginally more humane by replacing hanging with the gas chamber. In June, Rolph vetoed the bill, saying he was not so much interested in the manner of killing men as in saving them. "Where there might be some error," he added, "I will have a heart."[1]

Rolph spent considerable time and took great care in studying the capital cases that reached his desk during the spring and early summer of 1931. By late June, according to the *Sacramento Union*, his six pardons and four commutations put him well ahead of any previous governor's pace. Once, when he could not take either action in good conscience, he instead ordered a bottle of whisky sent to the prisoner.[2] On any scheduled execution date, Rolph suffered along with the condemned. He wore a black suit to the office and, as the sentence was being carried out, he stopped whatever he was doing at the time and observed a moment of silence.

Rolph was often criticized for overturning the decisions of boards of experts created to handle appeals and for letting his heart rule his head, but the *Union* conceded that "we must sincerely admire his humanity" even when disagreeing on the merits. In June, Rolph made a visit to the prison at Folsom — something no chief executive had done. "I want you fellows to know that I am your governor," he told the convicts. "I have your interests at heart." His words were greeted with both tears and cheers.[3]

Toward the end of 1931, Rolph received an appeal that gave him his greatest opportunity yet to show the state's face of forgiveness. It was from Tom Mooney, the radical labor agitator who had been convicted of planting a bomb at San Francisco's military preparedness parade in 1916. Though

Convicted Preparedness Day bomber Tom Mooney with his mother, left, and wife. When Mooney appealed to Rolph for a pardon in 1932, the facts of the case had long since ceased to matter. Liberals considered his incarceration a blight on the American system of jurisprudence (San Francisco History Center, San Francisco Public Library).

Mooney was an unsavory character who had been charged with possessing explosives in the past, he was only a minor figure among the many anarchists, socialists and other believers in fundamental social change on the far left. His guilt in the affair was far from certain. The main witnesses against him were widely believed to have perjured themselves under heavy pressure from city police. His death sentence was commuted to life imprisonment in 1918.

In the years that followed, Mooney's continued incarceration was perceived in many countries, and around the United States, as a blight on the American system of jurisprudence. Still, a succession of conservative California governors, for a variety of reasons, had refused to set Mooney free. They wanted to see justice done but were aware of public anxiety about Reds and radicals, and any decision on a pardon seemed bound to alienate one or another bloc of voters.

Many people, including the California Supreme Court, continued to believe that Mooney was guilty. Governor Young, who had conducted his own thorough review of the case, asked the court to study it and recommend a course of action to him. By a 6–1 margin, the justices advised against a pardon. Mooney's associations with other radicals, it argued, were the best evidence of his guilt. The *New York Evening World* called the decision "a disgrace to American civilization."[4]

Now Mooney turned to Governor Rolph for justice. But, as Mooney well knew, Rolph was bound to be less objective than any of his predecessors. As mayor of San Francisco, he had led the parade where the bomb had been planted. In fact, rumors persisted at the time that he had been the target of the bombing. Shocked and angry, he had persuaded the city council to raise the reward for capture of the bomber from $1,000 to $5,000, even if he had to pay the difference himself. He had personally overseen the investigation that resulted in Mooney's trial and conviction. And he could scarcely deny being emotionally invested in the outcome. When Mooney backers visited Governor Rolph in 1931 to discuss the appeal, he exploded: "Who killed them? Who killed them? Somebody killed them. I was there. I saw the blood and brains scattered about. I called the hospital. I led the parade; the people followed me, their leader. I led the parade. Who killed them?"[5]

In truth, the facts of the case had long since ceased to matter. Every year, it seemed, new information and testimony of varying reliability came to light, until it was no longer clear whose recollections could be believed. Besides, the bitterness and emotion of the long-running dispute had thoroughly politicized the issue. In such a climate, many people would interpret a Rolph pardon not as proof of Mooney's innocence but as the governor knuckling under to a noisy and influential lobby.

As the whole Mooney mess once again came to rest on Rolph's shoulders, a wild card entered the picture in the person of New York City mayor Jimmy Walker. Walker and Rolph had been great friends while Rolph was mayor of San Francisco—indeed, many voters saw similarities in their extroverted styles and winning personalities, and they were often photographed together.

In November 1931, Walker announced dramatically that he was coming to Sacramento at the behest of labor leaders all over the country to plead Mooney's case before the only person who could pardon him. Further, he was bringing with him a formidable legal team headed by a noted New York attorney.[6] On hearing the news, Rolph commented mildly that he did not know what Walker had to offer on the case but that he was always glad to see his old friend. He asked Matt Sullivan, Theodore Roche and Gavin McNab to be present, though Roche declined because of his leading role in the original police investigation. Rolph recognized that the public nature of the controversy required him to be well prepared, so he spent several days studying the record before Walker arrived.

The announcement of the Walker mission brought criticism in both New York and California. The *New York Times* raised questions about Walker's familiarity with the bulky testimony and suggested that his trip smacked of politics.[7] The *San Francisco Chronicle* speculated that the mayor had "perhaps read a headline or two or seen a banner in a radical parade, or at most been buttonholed by some special pleader." It summarized the trip as a "hippodrome stunt."[8]

The governor could not have been pleased with the media circus surrounding the events of the next few days. Walker arrived in the state on November 27, went immediately to see Mooney's mother, with whom he was photographed, and then visited Mooney himself in prison. His brief chat with Mooney convinced him all the more of his innocence. "Not in that face was there the capacity for such an atrocious crime," Walker told the media. Rolph advisor Matt Sullivan ridiculed Walker's "psychic exoneration,"[9] and many California newspapers bristled at his interference. The *San Francisco Examiner* urged him to go home and mind his own business.

On December 1, attired in black morning dress and speaking in a voice made hoarse by a bad cold, the mayor of New York held forth on Mooney's behalf. "At times his voice was low, suave and persuasive," reported the *New York Times*. "At others, he threw it across the twenty-five feet separating him from the governor and his legal advisors with passionate force." Occasionally he became dramatic and emotional. Referencing the wish of Mooney's mother not to die before her son was released, Walker said: "One night [the sun] will go down on a day when mother Mooney will not be here. Oh, God,

19. Capital Punishment and the Mooney Case 129

The governor welcomes his old friend, New York mayor Jimmy Walker, to California in late 1931. Walker made an impassioned plea for the pardon of Tom Mooney, but Rolph crony Matt Sullivan ridiculed Walker's "psychic exoneration" of the convicted bomber (Nancy Rolph Welch Collection).

don't let it happen!"[10] Walker's legal team pounded home its case to Rolph and his associates for more than four hours, concluding with written pleas for mercy from, of all people, the district attorney, the judge, and the jury in the case.[11] It was a most effective bombardment, said the *Sacramento Union*.

Whatever his private thoughts about being placed under such enormous public pressure by a man he regarded as a friend, Rolph agreed to study the evidence Walker had presented. Longtime Rolph watchers, believing that "sympathy is the outstanding ingredient in Rolph's character,"[12] predicted that he would give in and, at a minimum, commute Mooney's sentence, if not pardon him outright. Saying no had always been difficult for the governor. True, it would take some courage for him to rebuke members of his San Francisco machine, but most commentators saw leniency as a clear political plus for the governor, as well as the right thing to do.

The best predictor of Rolph's ultimate action, however, was his public delegation of the decision to his best friend and closest political advisor. On December 3, he announced that he had "turned the whole matter over to Matt Sullivan's judgment, and I shall be guided by his recommendation." This was a remarkable statement. All public officials delegate decisions to experts and specialists, but they rarely say so out loud. In this case, it did not seem possible, or even desirable, for Rolph to distance himself from the Mooney decision. Mayor Walker had forced the governor to become personally and visibly involved. And the matter had a political context that only Rolph could think through.

One explanation for putting Sullivan in charge is that Rolph did not want to pardon or release Mooney under any conditions. Assuming he knew that Sullivan felt the same way, he could distance himself from any political damage resulting from a denial of the appeal. The governor had revealed a closed mind toward Mooney in the past. According to historian Kevin Starr, Rolph charged on one occasion that the campaign to pardon Mooney was a Communist conspiracy.[13] And the governor's personal secretary, David Taylor, claims his boss once said at a press conference: "I'll tell you boys ... I studied the case forwards and backwards—saw it through. Mr. Mooney will never be pardoned or let out as long as I am governor."[14] Mooney's backers were also pessimistic. One of them remarked: "He is only liberal on Prohibition so far as we know."[15]

While mayor of San Francisco, Rolph had resisted the efforts of others to convince him of Mooney's innocence. According to *The New Republic*, several opponents of the Mooney prosecution, including noted newspaper editor Fremont Older, once arranged for Rolph to hear a confession of coaching from one of the lead witnesses in the case. Apparently lured there under a pretext, Rolph soon realized he was trapped in a very distasteful situation.

> Rolph is a kindly man and has a constitutional antipathy for nasty messes. The famous smile froze. Older sat between him and the door. He was forced to listen to the full recital.... The recital ended, and Mr. Older moved back toward his desk. Without a word the Mayor shot through the door. Nothing was done about the revelations.[16]

In delegating the case to Sullivan, Rolph probably hoped to have the decision seen as based upon facts rather than politics. Though conservative, Sullivan was a former judge and was regarded in many quarters as impartial. Some contemporary observers even believed he had Progressive tendencies and might be in the pro–Mooney camp.[17] But his personal involvement in the case as a member of the San Francisco investigative team, like that of the governor himself, probably prevented him from being genuinely objective.[18] Other intimates of Rolph were anti–Mooney as well. Banker Herbert Fleishhacker, a key financial supporter of the governor's, pronounced Mooney an "S.O.B." and said Rolph should keep him where he was.[19] A Rolph legal advisor, assigned to help Sullivan, told an associate that Mooney would rot in jail before his release.[20]

Though the odds of a pardon or commutation appeared long, Rolph's reputation as a humanitarian and a maverick kept people guessing—and Mooney supporters hoping. The latter pointed to Rolph's by then 81 pardons, commutations and reprieves; Governor Young had granted only 28 in a full four-year term. The *New York Daily News* reported in late February 1932 that Rolph had decided on a pardon.

In the meantime, the pressure grew. The Judiciary Committee of the U.S. House of Representatives on February 23 failed by only one vote to adopt a resolution urging the governor to pardon Mooney. About 20,000 letters poured into the governor's office, most urging a pardon. The *Sacramento Union* reported that his assistants had formed a protective wall around Rolph but that appeals from men in high places were still leaking through. Writers Theodore Dreiser, Sinclair Lewis and Upton Sinclair made pilgrimages to Mooney's cell at San Quentin. And Mooney's mother made a national tour in February 1932 to publicize her son's case.[21]

Finally, on April 21, Rolph convened the news media to present the Sullivan report. Rolph timed the event to occur only moments before he was scheduled to leave for a national governors conference in Virginia. In an "arena atmosphere" and in front of a bank of "talkie cameras," the governor, visibly nervous but speaking in what the wire services described as a firm and measured voice, announced that no new evidence justified Mooney's pardon or release. He refused to take questions and bristled when

Rolph and Matt Sullivan meet the press to announce the Tom Mooney decision. Rolph accepted Sullivan's recommendation not to pardon Mooney, thus becoming the fourth governor to uphold his conviction. He refused to take questions and bristled when asked how long he had personally spent on the case (Nancy Rolph Welch Collection).

asked how long he had personally spent on the case. Without another word, he departed for the East Coast, leaving Matt Sullivan to handle the media barrage that followed.

Far from a sober, lawyerly assessment of the case, the Sullivan report leaned heavily on circumstantial evidence. It laid out Mooney's well-known radical views, his threatening letters to public officials, and his use of explosives in the past. The bombing, it said, reflected Mooney's philosophy of violence. Many observers were more shocked at the report's tone than with the decision itself. It heaped scorn on the Walker mission and the mayor's argument, calling it "forensic hyperbole," and contained florid language about Mooney's "insensate hatred" of the United States and "fanatical desire" for a Communist form of government. "Too implacable, too bitter," sighed the *Union*. The report and decision, it added, cast opprobrium on the state and would dig Rolph's political grave. "We stand disgraced in the eyes of the world."[22]

But most reaction in California was favorable. Former governor Friend Richardson, who had refused an earlier Mooney pardon, congratulated Rolph for his "wise and able decision."[23] The *Los Angeles Times* editorialized that the unanimous conclusion of four consecutive governors "should someday beat down the walls of prejudice erected by propaganda and put an end to the Mooney agitation." Rolph's decision, it said, "must meet the approbation of thinking citizens."[24] Despite his tenderheartedness, said the *San Francisco Chronicle*, Rolph had steadfastly resisted the pressure in denying the pardon. "No one who knows his high character and complete independence" could doubt that that was his sincere conviction.[25] Most Californians, it seemed, were not inclined to waste their sympathy on a committed anarchist.

Opinion outside the state was mildly to scathingly critical. The *New York Times* observed that if enough evidence remained after excluding the tainted information, the Sullivan report should have included it.[26] Upon hearing that several California newspapers had endorsed Rolph's position, the national magazine *Literary Digest* labeled Californians "experts in obsessions and phobias." The *Baltimore Sun* called the Sullivan report a "confused mass of hysterical nonsense"[27]

Was Rolph's handling of the Mooney appeal a political blunder or a shrewd calculation? The pundits may have seen a pardon or commutation as the better political move, but Rolph clearly did not. His constant travel had presumably shown him that a majority of Californians were frightened by agitators on the far left. Communism was making inroads among the growing army of unemployed, as well as among the farm labor population. Rolph wanted to be seen as a bulwark against the instability and chaos represented by Mooney and his ilk, even if he harbored private doubts about Mooney's guilt. Thus, denying the appeal would probably work to his advantage, whether he ran for reelection as governor or, as many commentators were already speculating, decided to make a bid for the U.S. Senate.

Rolph's conduct of the Mooney matter can also be seen as evidence of his slow drift to the right in response to the increasing threat of extremism. He certainly paid a heavy price with the labor movement by taking the stand that he did. But it did not mean that his fabled compassion for criminals was simply a pose. Mooney was not a garden-variety convict. He was a dangerous radical who stood for an overthrow of the existing order. This difference, plus Rolph's own personal and emotional involvement in the crime itself, contributed to the governor's political judgment.

More dangerous to Rolph in the long run were his heavy reliance on and deference to his San Francisco cronies and the weakness of his personal staff. The state legislature and bureaucracy were already critical of his constant solicitation of political advice from his old friends. He needed sources of expertise and advice in Sacramento as well. Someone close to the governor should have been charged with reviewing the tone and content of the Sullivan report to ensure, among other things, that the decision appeared to be based on the facts of the case. Competent staff work, especially in the difficult years to come, could have compensated for Rolph's irregular attention to policy matters. Instead, the lack of it became a chronic problem.

20

1932 — A "Most Troublesome Year"

The news everywhere in early 1932 was bleak. Against the backdrop of economic decline and hardship, the newspapers contained daily accounts of atrocities committed by Japanese troops as they attacked and occupied eastern China. In the spring, the country was transfixed by the kidnapping and subsequent murder of the baby of national hero Charles Lindbergh. People, it seemed, had very little to cheer about.

Though the tales of discord coming from Sacramento were making Californians more ambivalent about their eccentric governor, his irrepressible and reassuring personality wore well when everything else appeared so grim. He even launched a Good Times Campaign in 1932 and pressed corporate leaders to join him.[1] His words of confident optimism were carried by radio, but he also visited small towns in person and listened to local concerns. "He has neglected many important things and made many laughable mistakes, yet the Rolph administration has popularized itself," the *Sacramento Union* noted. "If good will and camera posing count, he is batting 100 percent."[2] The governor knew that the people of California, not the power brokers in the major cities, would decide whether he was reelected in 1934.

But much of the informed public believed that the gap between personality and performance had become too great. On May 4, as the Mooney case was at long last receding into the background, a front-page open letter to the governor in the *Stockton Record* landed on Rolph like a ton of bricks. It was written by the *Record*'s publisher, who had been a campaign manager for C. C. Young in 1930, but it no doubt expressed a widely held view of Rolph and his administration:

> It is time to call a moratorium to leading parades, starting horned-toads in Chillicothe, jumping frogs in Angels, leading grand marches in policeman's or fireman's

balls, flitting about in airplanes, posing before the camera in your night garments ... time to stop bowing and scraping to lovely actresses or carnival queens and get down to straight business.... Play time is about over. It is time for school to begin.... Don't you think it is time now to get down to brass tacks?

For the past year and four months, you have had a good time. Perhaps the people of California, generously minded, don't begrudge you that. But in the present acute condition of things, the public will not much longer permit you to trifle and fool away your time in a thousand and one inconsequential matters. The people demand action.... Remember that while you are up in the air, the people are likewise up in the air. So stay on the ground.

In short, be a real governor of your state instead of a playboy, making a joke of yourself and of the government.[3]

The other Stockton paper, the *Independent*, rejected the *Record*'s criticism of Rolph. "The people of his native state love him," it editorialized, and "pleas for his gracious company will not be denied."[4] And the *Sacramento Union* conceded that, yes, he is a playboy and a hand-shaking governor, but "he does it naturally and unaffectedly. He's always done it and he always will do it."[5]

The danger was that Rolph's laughable mistakes would sooner or later erode public support.[6] The governor had a tendency to go public with ill-formed ideas without taking into account potential opposition. As a result, he found himself frequently backing down. It would be splendid, commented the *Union*, "if he would work as hard as he travels and think before he promises."[7] Rolph also became agitated about alleged deficiencies of state government he heard about during his travels, and once back in the capital he turned Sacramento upside down in a belated effort to remedy them.

Lack of attention to detail — a weakness throughout his last three terms as mayor — also threatened Rolph's credibility as the state's chief executive. His usual approach to solving a problem was to appoint a commission and charge it with making recommendations while he concentrated on courting California's voters. "He slips out from under routine with the same dexterity that a trout slips off a hook in the hands of an amateur fisherman," marveled the *Union*.[8]

A good example of how his superficial understanding of some issues could lead to embarrassment was a civil service controversy that followed the resolution of the Mooney case. Rolph had long believed in the absolute right of a chief executive to hire and fire as he pleased, without regard for civil service protections. At that time, the state was instituting an examination system for hiring and retaining state employees in an effort to remove politics from the state bureaucracy.

In May Rolph expressed disdain for tests that emphasized "a lot of theory" over practical knowledge and common sense.[9] He also began to receive

20. 1932—A "Most Troublesome Year"

Rolph, left, Nevada governor Frederick Balzar, second from left, and an unidentified man, right, listen as pilot Roscoe Turner points out the route they will take in an attempt to break the transcontinental air speed record between Washington, D.C., and Los Angeles. The party was returning from the National Governors Conference in Virginia in April 1932. They fell short, but Rolph called it an exciting lark (Nancy Rolph Welch Collection).

complaints from some veteran employees who said they had been fired after failing the new exam. What irked the governor was that they were being asked to pass a test despite many years of good performance and that some of the test questions seemed irrelevant to the work being performed. In response, he charged the state personnel office with treating longtime workers as "so many sacks or tons of merchandise." In this and other instances, Rolph seemed to enjoy being seen as a defender of fairness in the face of impersonal forces that might harm ordinary people. But as the days passed, no one could find any full-time state official who had actually been fired. The whole affair turned out to be a tempest in a teapot.

Rolph's early handling of the Central Valley water project also exemplified his pattern of careless advance followed by hasty retreat. He had, to his lasting credit, identified water resources as one of the most important issues facing his administration. As envisioned by years of planning, the Central Valley project would divert water from the Sacramento Valley in the north to the often-parched San Joaquin Valley farther south. It would also build a flood-control system for the volatile Sacramento River, which frequently overflowed its banks. The project would be expensive, and the state decided early to seek federal involvement.

A more perfect project for a man who prided himself on being a builder could not be imagined. Rolph staffed it out in his accustomed manner, creating two separate commissions to give him policy advice. One of them was composed of private citizens and headed by Matt Sullivan, and the other was made up of members of the legislature. Because the disposition of water resources was controversial and affected so many parts of the state, Rolph had been urged to call a special session of the legislature to deal with it, but he said he would not do so unless advised to by his commissions.

In April, shortly before the Mooney decision, the legislative commission recommended a special session, and the Sullivan group followed suit in June. Rolph immediately announced that a special legislative session would be convened in the near future. He quickly sent the report of the Sullivan commission to the legislators and invited groups to his office for conferences so that when they convened they would "be agreed upon a plan [and] can adopt a water conservation program in a single day."[10]

Lawmakers reacted with astonishment. A comprehensive water plan for the state, involving millions of dollars in costs and requiring agreement between North and South on allocation and distribution, was bound to be an arduous, time-consuming and partisan process. Senator Inman called the issue too difficult and said a special session wouldn't get anywhere. Rolph backtracked almost immediately, saying "there's no use prejudicing the program by going up against too much opposition."[11]

Rolph soon realized that the state was badly split on water resources. The South stood to gain the most from any program, and the North worried about its water being confiscated. Not wanting to give up on the special session but also fearing embarrassment if he called one and it failed to agree on a plan, Rolph decided to poll the legislature. It voted overwhelmingly against having the session, with Sacramento Valley legislators leading the opposition. In this climate, Rolph again backed down, saying: "I'd be foolish to call a special session and not have the votes."[12] In doing so, he blamed a group of senators headed by Inman for standing in his way.

Rolph had managed to look weak even while showing vision. He was unwilling to gamble on his ability to control a special session and to bring legislators around to his point of view. Instead, he drew criticism by polling

Rolph prepares his car for another exhausting year. He was the first gubernatorial candidate to visit every county in the state. He did it again after he was elected (*Sacramento Bee* Collection, Sacramento Archives and Museum Collection Center).

them via telegraph and mail rather than putting the issues to them directly. Calling public attention to Senator Inman's presumed negative influence seemed unnecessarily antagonistic and carried the risk of further alienating an influential public figure. Rolph was asked whether he had given up on the special session once and for all, but his answer did not show leadership. "I will have to confer with Matt Sullivan and John McNab before I can give a definite answer," he said.[13]

Another major issue that gave Rolph a chance to show leadership was the budget crisis. As early as the beginning of 1932, it had become clear that California was facing a serious revenue shortfall. As we have seen, the $29 million surplus inherited from Governor Young was cut nearly in half in the spring of 1931 when the legislature passed a last-minute flurry of spending bills that Rolph chose not to oppose. With the Depression deepening, Finance Director Vandegrift was continually revising revenue projections downward, which threatened to throw the state into deficit even before the end of the 1931–33 biennium. Difficult and unpopular choices lay immediately ahead — drastic cuts in government expenditures or new taxes, or some of both.

Though a Republican and a businessman, Rolph had always been known as a free spender. In his private life, particularly before financial troubles almost bankrupted him in the early 1920s, he was notably generous with his money. Upon becoming governor, he had irritated some members of the legislature by requesting a sizeable increase in the budget for his own office, including his own private plane. He had been unwilling to impose spending discipline on the legislature during its 1931 session. It did not help when he opened lavish offices in Los Angeles in 1932 to accommodate his frequent visits to the South.

Rolph was sensitive to the public relations problem that his reputation might cause during hard economic times. In an interview with the *Sacramento Union* in January 1932, the always impeccably dressed governor pointed out that he was wearing a year-old suit. "You see, I have to economize too," he said.[14] In February, he signed a largely symbolic ban on the private use of state cars and a freeze on new state services.[15] In March, he pointed out that his administration was spending at a lower per capita rate than in previous years and that any charge of extravagance was false.[16] Then he put Vandegrift to work on options for cutting some $40 million in existing services, hoping to forestall any need for new taxes.

In another impulsive, dramatic gesture whose negative consequences he underestimated, Rolph announced in June a reduction of one day in the state employee's workweek — a measure that would cut each salary by 14 percent and save $2 million. Many in the legislature, as well as the State Employees Association, protested vigorously. Both groups complained that they had not been consulted about the action, and the *Union* reported that the governor's decision had directly followed a meeting in San Francisco of his kitchen cabinet. Senator Inman called it a "sorry gesture to placate public opinion."[17] Declaring himself "captain of the ship but [who] is always glad to hear from the crew," Rolph again backed down.[18]

Rolph kept the California delegation to the Republican convention in June 1932 solidly in line behind President Herbert Hoover's renomination (Nancy Rolph Welch Collection).

While the governor continued to look ineffectual in the arena of state politics, he was afforded the opportunity in June of appearing on a much larger stage. He left for the Republican national convention in Chicago on the 10th and was heard to complain about having to undertake the slow, multiday journey by train instead of flying: "I'd have had a private plane from the last session of the legislature if I hadn't been such a greenhorn."[19] Photographs show him at the head of flag-waving demonstrations for President Hoover on the convention floor. In an illustration of his maverick tendencies, he broke ranks with the party regulars by favoring a plank advocating the outright repeal of Prohibition.

Back in Sacramento after a week of hoopla, Rolph found that he was in danger of losing control over his own state bureaucracy.

21

A Government Divided

By the middle of 1932, deep fissures were developing within Rolph's administration, and between it and the legislature, that would throw his governorship into a crisis lasting well into the next year. His loss of political capital in 1931 left him few options that would have satisfied his critics or led to a resolution of the mounting policy challenges. Still, he would have to find a way to calm the "boiling cauldron"[1] that was Sacramento politics during this period.

The early 1930s were not a good time for a California governor who abhorred conflict. A consensus on key issues had been achievable in San Francisco, but on the larger stage of state politics, harmony might have been an impossible dream. One of Rolph's main problems was the man elected as his second in command—the lieutenant governor. As early as June 1931, the media began to speculate on Frank Merriam's ambitions to run for governor in 1934. In September, Merriam freely admitted his candidacy, saying it was the South's turn to run the state and he was next in line. Thus, he was taking public aim at the man he was supposed to be serving. From that point forward, Rolph could not assume that Merriam had the administration's best interests at heart. In fact, Rolph was reluctant to leave the state at critical times for fear that Merriam, while acting governor, would do something to undermine his position.

Beyond that, the chaotic 1931 legislative session had left a number of lawmakers bitterly opposed to the Rolph administration and disinclined to compromise on policy issues. The economy bloc continued to be appalled by Rolph's perceived extravagance, no matter how much he promised frugality. Individual senators mounted what at times seemed to be personal vendettas against the governor.

State senator John Inman's strong and difficult personality, plus his ties to C.C. Young, had turned him into Rolph's most implacable foe. Inman had been sniping at Rolph's policies since the governor's arrival in the capital, but in the summer of 1932 acrimony between them reached a new level. In July, Rolph publicly accused Inman of trying to block a special session of the legislature on water resources that the governor considered necessary. Soon allegations surfaced in the media that Rolph was providing covert support to Inman's opponent in his fall campaign for reelection. Asked in August to comment on the race, Inman instead changed the subject: "My real opponent, my friends, is James Rolph, Jr., the governor of California."[2] Inman led an effort, in the legislature and elsewhere, to discredit Rolph in every way possible.

Rolph could not even count on support from within his own state bureaucracy. At the same time that his feud with Inman was boiling to the surface, public squabbling began among the governor's department heads. Leaks about policy differences, particularly on budget matters, became more frequent. To a man for whom loyalty was a cardinal virtue, Rolph's inability to get his people in line must have been particularly galling. In one of his increasingly frequent public displays of temper, Rolph reminded his lieutenants in early September that he was captain of the ship and said: "If any of you don't like the way I'm running things, your resignations are in order."[3] A few days later, for emphasis, he directed his subordinates to "pull together or get out."[4]

But an important reason for the discord was the governor's own neglect of his administrative duties. As mayor of San Francisco, Rolph was able to rely on the many members of his political machine on the city payroll to keep things humming while he indulged his need to "play with the people and enjoy their holidays" or to retire to his ranch for recreation. But when he left his state department heads on their own, they bumped into one another. The state treasurer, the controller and director of finance were continually wrangling in public about how best to address the state's impending revenue shortfall. As the *Sacramento Union* put it, "while [Rolph] is [out] building up good will, the boys at home are tearing it down."[5]

State bureaucrats watched as Rolph traveled to the Bay Area as often as once a week for consultations with his kitchen cabinet. Sometimes he made decisions directly afterward, before checking with anyone in the capital. From the point of view of the department heads, Rolph was a governor who needed their help but turned instead to unqualified outsiders.[6]

Meanwhile, Rolph seemed to be growing more irritable and bewildered. His public remarks took on a sharper tone, and the famous sense of humor was less in evidence. A general uneasiness settled over the administration. A visitor to the governor came away feeling sorry for him. Rolph had asked: "What have I done? What's wrong? How can I straighten this out?"[7]

As the summer of 1932 ended, the rancor in the administration intensified. Rumors of a cabinet shakeup began to circulate. Attention was focused on two leading state officials—Walter Garrison, who ran the state Department of Public Works, and Earl Lee Kelly, head of the Department of Highways, who reported to Garrison. Initially the issue was Garrison's grant of permission for an employee of the department to take leave to run for a local political office, a clear violation of the rules, but soon it was clear that Garrison and Kelly were in open combat. Kelly even told the press that he considered Garrison incompetent.[8]

Rolph's frustration was apparent. Returning from a trip to the California gold country, he found things "much worse than I expected," and warned: "I'm on the warpath."[9] Dramatically, in October, he fired Garrison and promoted Kelly to department chief.

Though Rolph received praise in some quarters for acting decisively, Garrison put him back on the defensive by charging that the real reason for his dismissal was that he had resisted pressure from the governor to favor his friends and family in the awarding of contracts. Of course, this was not the first time that the word "spoils" had been associated with Rolph. Senator Inman, seeing an excuse to embarrass him, pounced on Garrison's allegations and threatened to launch a legislative inquiry into the administration's personnel practices.[10]

Recriminations now began to pour forth in the state media, deepening the impression of an administration in disarray. State treasurer Charles Johnson attacked Finance Director Vandegrift for losing state money in the bond market, though the latter had both the authority and the obligation to try to get a return on state funds. Vandegrift, in reply, called Johnson a "cuttlefish" and an "unmitigated juggler of the truth."[11] Defending his finance director, Rolph noted that Johnson had "committed the mistake ... of thinking that when the people elected me, they made him governor."[12] Johnson, expressing his regret at supporting Rolph then, said his "only error in judgment ... was an overestimation of [Rolph's] capacity." The *Sacramento Union* editorialized that the state government seemed to be sitting over a volcano.[13]

Some evidence of improprieties in the hiring of civil servants began to leak out, causing several media outlets to join in the attack on the governor. As the *Union* put it, "just enough flame is visible in the smoke to make it plausible."[14] Rolph said he would investigate reports that jobs in the public works department were sold to the highest bidder. Johnson alleged that Rolph had filled 108 departments with "professional chiselers."[15] The *Union* reported that civil service exams had been waived for 27 political friends of the governor.

The *San Francisco News*, which had been observing Rolph's personnel practices since he was first elected mayor in 1911, now charged the governor with "arrogance and boldness in promoting the spoils system in Sacramento." It singled out the continuing influence of longtime Rolph intimate Tim Reardon as the personification of that system. Altogether, the newspaper considered the recent revelations a "culmination of the undermining of standards of public service that began as soon as he took office."[16]

The pitched battles taking place in Sacramento succeeded in attracting the more measured attention of the *New York Times*. While praising what it called the amazing effectiveness and dexterity of Rolph's response to the bureaucratic warfare, the *Times* noted that the crisis had been a blessing for the governor's many critics and that the worst was surely yet to come. Still, the paper marveled, as new allegations surfaced daily and newsmen struggled to follow the whirl of events, Rolph had, in a display of equanimity, "flown and motored gaily about the state."[17]

As the year's end approached, then, Rolph was on the defensive in three major areas—his personnel policies, his inattention to administrative detail, and the growing fiscal crisis. Of the three, he had the least control over the last, and yet his skill in addressing it would be crucial to his political survival.

22

The Firestorm Over Taxes and Spending

Month by month, California's financial situation had been deteriorating. Rolph's easy optimism about the future, on display throughout 1931, could not be sustained once he "discovered the Depression."[1]

The national economic crisis had put all the states in a difficult bind. The general prosperity of the 1920s had allowed them to provide their citizens with an increasing array of public services. State expenditures for education, highway maintenance, assistance to the aged, and public works grew, and so did the cost of government itself. When the Depression struck, revenues fell sharply, and the states either had to stop providing many of those services or find new sources of income, or both.

By the time Rolph took office, California had in place a program of social legislation that was generous by the standards of the era. Along with funding pensions for civil service retirees, teachers, the aged and the blind, the state's capital outlays had to keep pace with the rapid growth in population. Expenditures increased 15 percent between the 1927–29 and 1929–31 budget cycles (called bienniums), and were projected to increase an additional 10 percent by 1933. But revenues declined precipitously. During the 1931–33 biennium, they sank from $136 million to $108.5 million — against $151 million in proposed spending. The result was a looming budget deficit.

Despite the crunch, California was not ready for new taxes in 1932. Most lawmakers, as well as the governor, wished to solve the problem through greater economy in government rather than by seeking new sources of revenue. But spending cuts would end or reduce programs people had come to count on, and the state bureaucracy, structured for times of plenty, was deeply reluctant to do without its continuing appropriations.[2] Despite the pleadings of the so-called economy bloc, the 1931 legislature, as we have seen, had been unable to reverse the growth in state programs.

The state's tax system had long been deemed unfair and in need of reform. Utility companies did not pay property taxes, but were instead taxed on their gross receipts, which had been declining during the Depression. At the same time, ordinary citizens were chafing under a local property tax burden they considered excessive, because assessed valuations of private property were rising. A 1929 study, commissioned by Governor Young, found that the system had failed on several counts: it no longer raised enough revenue, it did not equalize the tax burden between ordinary citizens and utilities, and it had not given relief to holders of real property, whose tax burden was "approaching the point of confiscation."[3]

Rolph's refusal to consider new taxes after he took office forestalled any discussion of that subject for more than a year. As the revenue picture darkened throughout 1932, however, a property tax relief measure supported by nine statewide associations was placed on the November ballot. It broke new ground by calling for an income tax and a sales tax on selected items, but opponents, led by utility companies and real estate interests, attacked it as amateurish and impractical. It was voted down by a 2–1 margin.

The budget problem took on added urgency after the November election, which sent Franklin D. Roosevelt to the White House. Between then and his inauguration in March 1933, the U.S. banking system shut down almost completely. Against this grim backdrop, California's controller announced in late November that the state government was "broke worse than before." Forecasting an $11 million deficit by the end of the year and $63 million by the end of 1934, he estimated that as much as $50 million in new taxes might be necessary.[4] These alarming figures finally made it clear to everyone that drastic measures were needed.

By the 1930s, California's budget had grown considerably in size and complexity. Finance director Rolland Vandegrift confronted the unenviable task of dealing with this complexity while trying to respond to the governor's political needs. He came under pressure as the crisis intensified. The legislature frequently accused Vandegrift of mismanagement, though he turned out to be an able financial officer and one of Rolph's best cabinet-level appointments. He had been director of research for the California Taxpayers' Association before joining the governor-elect's staff shortly after the general election of 1930. Most important to his credibility, he was not one of Rolph's old San Francisco cronies.[5]

Vandegrift, at Rolph's behest, now plunged into an effort to build a budget for the administration that would recommend the elimination of some government services. The state's tax research bureau also readied a series of policy recommendations for the governor to consider as he prepared

In November 1932, with the Rolph administration seeming to come apart at the seams, the governor and his wife found time to welcome defeated President and Mrs. Herbert Hoover back to California (courtesy of the California History Room, California State Library, Sacramento, California).

his address to the January 1933 legislative session. Unfortunately for Rolph, most state leaders had little confidence in his ability to impose strict fiscal discipline on the government. Veteran political reporter Earl Behrens was only one of several observers who dismissed his efforts, judging that the governor's "free-spending ways were out of line with the tenor of the times."[6]

Rolph had given a speech in August 1932 that further eroded confidence in his fiscal judgment. Concerned by delays in federal payments of claims to a group of California war veterans, he suggested that the state might float a bond issue on their behalf. He argued that it would not cost the state anything in the long run, because California could later be reimbursed by the federal government. But state financial officers gasped when they learned the payout would be $136 million. The veterans association hesitated to take advantage of Rolph's offer, fearing it would weaken their pending federal claims. The media had a field day. It ridiculed what it called another of the governor's magnificent gestures that gave little thought to economic consequences.[7] So Rolph had a credibility problem even before the state's financial woes progressed from serious to critical toward the end of 1932.

In early December, the California tax research bureau issued its report. It confirmed what many politicians had believed for years—that public utilities and banks were undertaxed relative to home owners and most other businesses. After considering his options for several weeks, however, Rolph followed the lead of Finance Director Vandegrift and declared himself opposed to any increase in utility taxes. Using what historian Franklin Hichborn later called a "stock utility argument, repeatedly refuted,"[8] Rolph predicted that utilities would simply pass along a tax increase to customers in the form of higher rates. Whatever the merits of this view, the fact that wealthy corporations like Pacific Gas and Electric and the Bank of America were paying less than their fair share during a time of economic hardship was bound to fuel public anger.

At about the same time, Rolph and Vandegrift took an unpopular position on another budgetary issue—what to do with surplus money in the state highway fund. This fund had grown to many millions of dollars, fattened by a tax on gasoline, but the law specified that it was to be used only for automotive purposes, such as building and maintaining roads. Vandegrift had proposed, and Rolph had agreed, that $8 million in gas tax revenues be used to pay off interest on highway bonds, an expense borne at that time by the state's main source of cash, the general fund. To the administration, such a diversion seemed not only fiscally necessary and sensible but also in the spirit of the law.

But opposition to this idea was surprisingly intense and widespread. According to rumor, former public works director Garrison had lobbied against it from inside the administration until his dismissal in October. Others viewed a gas tax diversion as a budgetary trick and a dangerous first step that could lead to routine raids on the highway fund. Most Californians saw it as shady bookkeeping that solved nothing—like robbing Peter to pay Paul.

Though Rolph closeted himself in the Capitol throughout December to work on a budget message—conspicuously canceling several trips around the state in order to do so—his authority was slipping away. On the taxation issue in particular, other political leaders were beginning to promote their own tax and spending plans rather than waiting for leadership from Rolph.

The details of these plans were fast becoming public. State senator Arthur Breed was advocating a 20-percent reduction in state expenditures across the board and no new taxes. Controller Ray Riley promoted the elimination of

Rolph wears his Spanish don costume at the opening of Santa Barbara's annual fiesta. "It's time to call a moratorium to leading parades," the *Stockton Record* said in 1932. "Play time is about over. It is time for school to begin" (Nancy Rolph Welch Collection).

22. The Firestorm Over Taxes and Spending

all fixed expenses, leaving the legislature in complete control of the budget. The tax research bureau pushed for equalization of tax rates, which would force utilities and banks to pay more, along with new taxes on incomes, beverages, tobacco and luxuries. Senator Inman, aware that Rolph opposed equalization, showed early signs of agreeing with this view. Finance Director Vandegrift, speaking for the Rolph administration, took a middle position that contemplated reductions in the cost of government coupled with undefined new taxes.

* * * * * * * * * * * *

As 1932 came to an end—a "terrible year," said the *Sacramento Union*—nothing but trouble seemed to lie ahead. A fractious legislature would convene in January, with Rolph's leadership much in doubt, and the lawmakers were determined to root out malfeasance and corruption among the governor's inner circle. The newspaper summarized this bleak outlook in an extended article at year's end. Calling 1932 "the most troublesome year in Rolph's public life," it portrayed a governor who was tired, conscious of increasing criticism, and nervous about the future.

The article also acknowledged what could easily have been forgotten in the dismal political environment—that his record had strengths, too. Rolph had pushed from the beginning of his term for a state water plan, and he had spent much time trying to get agreement on its key elements. He had shown his concern about unemployment by setting up a widely praised food distribution program and labor camps to provide work for single men. In a typically Rolphian touch, he had launched a Good Times Campaign in 1932, featuring radio addresses in which he spoke with confident optimism about the state's future.[9] His reputation as a humane chief executive had been enhanced by the 300 pardons, reprieves and commutations he issued in just two years, as compared to just 11 during the entire Young administration.

And he had become the best-known governor in the West. Six cross-country plane trips and extensive travels throughout the state underlined his pledge to be governor of all the people. In spending so much time on the road, he sacrificed sleep and, at times, state business, but, as he pointed out: "If I stay in Sacramento, how can I know what people want? How can I know what their problems are?"[10]

In the new year, Rolph would learn whether any of these pluses might turn his political fortunes around and give him a chance at reelection in 1934. It would take, at a minimum, a well-thought-out, well-received budget message in January.

23

1933 — In the Eye of the Storm

The mood in the capital during the first three months of 1933 was as dark as it was elsewhere in the country. Both abroad and at home, the news was bad. Hitler took power in Germany. Japan quit the League of Nations and continued its aggression on the Asian mainland. In Washington, a state of paralysis afflicted government as Hoover prepared to leave office and Roosevelt waited in the wings for his March inaugural. Most of the nation's banks were closed or closing. When the Roosevelt team arrived in Washington, recalled an advisor, "terror held the country in its grip."[1]

Frequent industrial labor disturbances and farm strikes made California the most chaotic state in the union during this period.[2] Awareness of the state's serious and growing problems led to frustration and bad temper among the elected officials who met in early January to consider possible solutions. In this poisonous atmosphere, Rolph stepped to the rostrum on January 3 to deliver the governor's biannual message, which was broadcast by radio for the first time. The galleries acknowledged his presence with warm applause, but, ominously, the legislators themselves, after a perfunctory greeting, received his words in near complete silence.[3]

Rolph quickly signaled that he would not recommend additional taxes even though "my opponents and critics ... have accused me of being sympathetic to the point of weakness and extravagance with the poor, the needy, the sick and distressed who are public charges." Instead, he would take the extremely repugnant path of advocating a drastic reduction in state expenses. He recommended slashing support to public schools and old-age pensions— moves that would require local governments to pick up the slack. He repeated his support for the gas tax diversion, saying "there is no logical reason ... why the general fund should be called upon to continue to pay such a large annual amount for highway purposes."

Finally, he attacked those who wished to raise utility taxes, accusing them of "cloaking their prodigality by specious assertions that the additional revenue which they demand will be extracted solely from utilities and other industries and will not be paid by the people" through higher rates.[4] At the heart of his argument was the belief that government should use a light hand on the private sector, since "the welfare of business is closely involved with the welfare of all of the population."

Criticism of Rolph's message was widespread. His refusal to consider higher utility taxes while proposing to force local governments to pay more for education and pensions seemed perverse and unjust to many. Even more damaging were allegations in several newspapers that Rolph intimate Eustace Cullinan, an attorney for PG&E, had edited the governor's message.[5] On the same day that Rolph delivered his speech, Senator Inman introduced legislation to increase utility taxes by $12 million per year.

The *Sacramento Union* considered the message nothing short of a disaster, "a marvel of inconsistent thinking, contradictory proposals, and pretended economy." Stirring up the gas tax issue was, in the paper's view, a major blunder. It also challenged Rolph on the main ground he chose to occupy — his claim that keeping his finger on the pulse of the state would help him do the right thing. On the contrary, "flitting about from place to place and lighting like a butterfly has not enriched the governor's knowledge of state affairs." The message "proves beyond the shadow of a doubt that the governor, in spite of two years' experience, is entirely innocent of public trends of thought. He seems too naïve to be real."[6]

In more conservative southern California, however, Rolph's pledge not to raise taxes was well received. The *Los Angeles Times* thought his words accorded with public opinion on the need for drastic budget reductions and even agreed that cuts in the state's share of school costs "called for attention as long as high standards are not impaired."[7] The paper also took Rolph's side against Senator Inman, calling it absurd to think that taxes on utilities would not be paid by consumers.

In the capital, however, matters soon went from worse to much worse. Not only did the legislature seem certain to ignore the Rolph budget, but on January 5 the Senate voted almost unanimously to launch a probe of alleged irregularities and suspected extravagance on the part of the administration. Lieutenant Governor Merriam appointed Inman to head the committee conducting the probe. A Rolph staffer searched the committee roster in vain for potential allies and declared that the governor had been delivered into the hands of the enemy.[8]

Much of the news media and even some legislators perceived the investigation as a partisan effort to discredit the Rolph regime rather than an honest attempt to uncover wrongdoing. The motivations of Inman and Merriam, who had both long sought to undermine the governor, were called into question. One senator called Inman's role a "camouflage for his own [political] intentions"; another said the investigation was premature, since no charges had been filed.[9] The *Union* predicted that the obvious bias of the committee would work in the governor's favor by offending public opinion, while the *Los Angeles Times* lamented the negative effect an investigation would have on the Senate's ability to tackle the real problems faced by the state.[10]

Rolph took the high road by announcing his willingness to cooperate fully. Told of the Senate's action, he said: "I welcome it. They may go as far as they like ... I have nothing to conceal."[11] He also insisted on public testimony, in contrast to Inman's call for some secret sessions.

What sort of allegations would the Senate be investigating? The common ingredient was favoritism. Rolph or his lieutenants, it was charged, tried to put the governor's friends or family members in a position to profit from state-funded programs. Some critics of the investigation felt that even if such charges were proved, they would amount to nothing new. Rolph had long been known to favor cronies and allies in making appointments. Besides, every administration dispensed a certain amount of preferential treatment to insiders. As Inman's group began taking testimony, the question was whether the irregularities, even if demonstrated, merited an expensive and time-consuming official inquiry during a time when legislative attention was needed in many other areas.

Recently deposed public works director Walter Garrison provided details in support of the allegations. He charged Rolph with:

• Ordering him through an intermediary to include an unimproved road running near the governor's ranch near San Mateo in the state's secondary highway network;
• Introducing him to an assemblyman who wanted a state steam shovel contract, saying: "Do what you can for him";
• Telling another assemblyman, when informed of Garrison's refusal to help influence a trucking contract: "See, they will not let me take care of my friends"[12];
• Having his staff solicit campaign contributions from contractors, and from Garrison himself.

Garrison also said he warned Rolph that "he was getting poor advice from friends who were using him for their own political advancement."[13]

The involvement of Rolph family members in state business was also scrutinized. Finance Director Vandegrift had come under fire for leasing a building in San Francisco on behalf of the state for far more than the building was worth. It turned out that a share of the proceeds from a commission on the lease deal went to Rolph's son-in-law John Symes. Further, the insurance firm of James Rolph, III, the governor's oldest son, was shown to have been an agent for several companies that had done considerable business with the state. Unfazed by the disclosure, the younger Rolph caused some discomfort when he testified before the Inman committee that he had shared commissions on insurance contracts with members of the state legislature.

The committee met for a few weeks in January to hear testimony. Then it adjourned, along with the rest of the legislature, for most of February. Vandegrift and young Rolph defended their actions and claimed to have done nothing illegal. The governor and his finance director alternately attacked and ridiculed the committee. On his way to Yosemite Valley for some recreation, Rolph invited Senator Inman to join him, saying "it would do Inman a lot of good to get a couple of laughs."[14] The media was unimpressed with the investigation's initial results and castigated the legislators for neglecting the budget mess to pursue what looked like a political vendetta.

On January 19, Rolph entered St. Francis Hospital in San Francisco with a flulike illness. His doctor said his resistance had been lowered by overwork and lack of sleep, and he would not be back in Sacramento for at least 10 days. Insiders disclosed that the governor had been suffering from a severe cold for several weeks but had refused to go to bed.

Sick in San Francisco, under investigation by the state Senate, and increasingly irrelevant in the great budget debate, Rolph came under attack from a new antagonist in the last days of January. The state Grange, an association of farmers concerned primarily with agricultural policy, announced that it would lead a movement to recall the governor. The farm lobby feared Rolph would advocate higher property taxes that would bankrupt its already hard-pressed members.

But its antipathy toward the governor ran deeper than that. The Grange had been seething since 1931, when Rolph had strong-armed San Franciscan Dudley Moulton into place as head of the state agriculture department. The *Sacramento Union* had warned at the time that "embattled farmers are not pleasant antagonists,"[15] and the paper had been right. The Grange action was a concrete manifestation of the widely felt anger at Rolph's preference for loyalty over competence in making state appointments.

But the recall attempt struck nearly everyone — opponents of the governor as well as supporters — as a bad idea. It is true, commented the *Union*, that Rolph has been poorly advised, has not been attending to business, and has made many bad appointments, but "his batting average has not been low enough" for this.[16] The *Los Angeles Times* accused the head of the Grange of being politically motivated.

Even state Treasurer Charles Johnson and Sen. Arthur Breed, both Rolph critics, announced their opposition to the recall. Johnson predicted that it would cause nothing but controversy and be a distraction from the state's urgent economic problems. Labor and business groups feared it would impair recovery and disturb commerce, while providing no guarantee of improved governance. Faced with a nearly universal lack of enthusiasm, the Grange gave up on the recall idea in mid–February — only three weeks from the date it was first announced.

Meanwhile, the Inman hearings had reconvened in the capital. Their focus changed from Rolph's management of state affairs to the conduct of his appointees. Finance Director Vandegrift, who had defended the gas tax diversion while resisting higher utility taxes, was a frequent target even before the investigation because of questions relating to his investing of surplus state money in the bond market. As finance director, Vandegrift had unlimited authority to make such investments, but in the current economic climate, some losses were inevitable. Inman's panel now charged him with manipulation, speculation, and a raid on the Treasury. Dudley Moulton, a primary target of the Grange recall, came under heavy fire as well.

On February 23 Rolph left his ranch, where he had been recuperating, and returned to the capital. He appeared weaker, thinner, and flushed of face, and he confessed that he had been pretty sick. Word leaked out that his illness had been much more serious than anyone had thought — a heart ailment complicated by an influenza attack.

Nevertheless, he was in a combative mood. He began by ejecting a reporter for the *San Francisco News* from the Capitol Building, saying: "I don't intend to put up with your insults any longer." Then, perhaps emboldened by ebbing public enthusiasm for the investigation and by several media pieces critical of Inman, the governor went on the attack. He called Inman a "crooked grafter" and the "little Caesar of state politics [who] can dish it out but not take it." In reply, the senator called Rolph's remarks libelous.[17]

On the defensive and roiled by internal disagreements on how to proceed, the Inman committee abruptly ended its work on February 25. According to one inside account, Inman had wanted to continue the probe but a majority said no. Inman himself admitted the next day that the complaints he had been investigating primarily concerned agriculture and finance, and Rolph had solved the first of these the day after his return by replacing Moulton.

What had the investigation uncovered? It found ample evidence that the Rolph administration was not a meritocracy. But charges that members of the governor's family had received special opportunities were hardly new. It also showed that state officials, lacking supervision, occasionally exceeded their authority and made mistakes. Some used their involvement in state administration for personal advantage. As a *Union* columnist expressed it, "friends had tried to tell [Rolph] these things before, but he had to catch a plane."[18] Still, in 1933, the judicious use of nepotism and favoritism was not viewed as a flagrant offense. "Politicians don't consider that a sin," said a *Union* columnist. "It's a rotten system, but it is the system."[19]

The committee report, released in late March, mustered no more damaging allegations than had already surfaced in the media, prompting a *Union* editorial to scoff that the Inman hearings had come to nothing.[20] The report was mild compared to the dramatic testimony it was based on, and the only mention of Rolph was a vague paragraph near the end on the duty of the chief executive to inspire respect and confidence. Most of the state's newspapers had regarded the hearings with skepticism from the beginning — politics, pure and simple. All in all, the absence of evidence of serious corruption in the report made it look exactly like what Rolph said it was — a partisan undertaking, "conceived in hatred, written in venom, and tempered only by cowardice."[21]

In a hard-hitting and heavily sarcastic rebuttal, which was read into the Senate record on May 11, Rolph charged the committee with refusing to consider pertinent evidence and feeding false allegations to the press before testimony could be heard. The committee "has shouted about political honesty, but itself has shown no honesty of purpose.... Does the Legislature feel enlightened by such a report?"[22] He conceded that individuals under him had sometimes used poor judgment but none had behaved dishonestly or with intent to defraud. He even turned the tables on the lawmakers by submitting evidence that Inman and a colleague on the committee had been guilty of more egregious ethical lapses than any member of his administration.

Any doubt that Rolph's conflict with the legislature had become personal was removed by his bitter references to individuals on the investigating committee. He attacked Lieutenant Governor Merriam, "an avowed candidate for the governorship," for packing the committee with men who "are, notoriously, inveterate enemies of me and my administration. We did not expect or receive fair treatment from this political cabal." He called one senator "my implacable political enemy" and accused another of living "in the odor of political sanctity." The committee, he said, had produced "political propaganda of the most unscrupulous sort," and its report was entitled to "no weight and no respect."[23]

When the governor was through, the only unanswered charge was favoritism in his appointments to state office, but he dismissed this issue in one withering remark:

> The investigating committee may regard the appointment of relatives or [hiring] recommendations by the governor to heads of departments as political sins; but that can hardly be the opinion of the majority of the legislature in view of the ... number of times that legislators have requested me to recommend friends or relatives for appointments in executive departments.[24]

The Inman investigation tapped a reservoir of anger in Rolph that no previous slight had been able to reach. When the press asked him how he felt, he abandoned diplomatic language and again allowed his unvarnished fury to surface. He complained of being kicked around like a football by the Senate and told reporters: "There isn't one of you who has the guts to stand up and defend me against Inman. You can't fool around with the governor like that. I have no use for the Senate."[25]

The governor's outburst, instead of chastening the Senate, sent it into new paroxysms of fury. On May 12 it subjected Rolph to a scourging unprecedented in California legislative history. One by one, lawmakers stepped forward to utter vitriolic denunciations of the governor, unrestrained by Merriam, the presiding officer. Typical was the comment of Senator Rich, a member of the Inman committee, who said: "Rolph possesses all qualifications for being a governor except ability." Inman added that Rolph's invective against him was part of an elaborate system of administration espionage. "I have never asked quarter in any fight, and this one has just begun," he warned.[26]

The venting of spleens on both sides, however, effectively ended the investigation. Some political observers, in fact, had begun to predict that this latest wake-up call would bring Rolph back to political life. It took a serious illness, said one, to impress upon the governor that his first two years had been a failure — now he will stay at his desk and get some work done.[27] Now he knows there is more to being chief executive than fiestas and folderol, wrote another.[28] It will be a dreary grind to come back — a sober Jim had to replace Sunny Jim — but he could do it if he was serious. Just before a legislative recess, Rolph showed the humanity for which he was famous. He walked into the chamber, shook hands all around, and wished the members a good vacation.[29]

But as the legislature returned its full attention to the fiscal crisis, Rolph would find that the lawmakers were less forgiving. They were determined to act without him.

24

California's Tax Revolution

The acrimony in Sacramento was distracting the legislature from its primary task — solving the state's financial crisis. Action of some kind would have to be taken to bring receipts into balance with expenditures. A consensus was developing that cutting expenditures alone (the Rolph approach) would be too painful and too difficult. With a property tax revolt in full swing, a new source of revenue was needed.

There were two main alternatives to the property tax — the income tax and the sales tax. The sales tax would affect everyone who spent money and thus would spread the burden more widely than the property tax. But it would weigh more heavily on those with lower incomes, who spent a larger percentage of the money they earned. The income tax, on the other hand, especially if progressive, would fall hardest on those people who were relatively well off. So from the beginning, the tax argument had class overtones.

As we have seen, the California legislature was not alone in grappling with the need for new sources of revenue. Under great pressure, state lawmakers all over the country were learning to think more flexibly about taxation. Most states, especially the larger, more urbanized ones, were overwhelmed by the Depression and ended up appealing to the federal government for assistance. The coal mining industry in Pennsylvania, for example, collapsed during the first half of 1932, with unemployment in the coal fields increasing by 87 percent during that period. The state as a whole had over a million unemployed workers, compared to 700,000 in California. Pennsylvania quickly spent its available relief funds and then could do no more on its own.[1]

Kansas, an agricultural state, underwent an economic free-fall as commodity prices dropped between 1930 and 1932. The governor called for cutbacks in state government and pushed for an income tax, but the state's resources were not sufficient to meet the crisis. He had to apply to the

Reconstruction Finance Corporation in Washington for help in late 1932. He was later defeated for reelection — a lesson not lost on Rolph as he contemplated whether or not to support tax increases.

Despite the risk of increased popular discontent, 32 of the 43 state legislatures that convened during 1933 felt the necessity to introduce new taxes.[2] Six of them chose a version of the sales tax. By the end of the 1930s, fully 24 state governments had imposed sales taxes. In raising taxes at a time when people could least afford to pay them, local politicians all over the country must have felt that they were risking political suicide.

The full Rolph budget, previewed during his January 3 address to the legislature and released to the media on January 17, was clearly an attempt to avoid this fate. As an effort to solve the state's financial woes, it seemed to fall short. Though it represented a serious effort to cut state spending, it was not seen as dealing adequately with the revenue side of the problem. The only infusion into the general fund envisioned by the program was the transfer of gas tax money, which was widely viewed as an accounting trick.

By preferring spending cuts to new taxes, however, Rolph was squarely in the mainstream of national economic thinking in the pre–Roosevelt era. Moreover, his approach might have worked. According to a recent analysis, very deep cuts, along with the gas tax transfer, would have eliminated the existing deficit without requiring tax increases.[3] But Californians were not prepared to balance the budget on the backs of retirees and schoolchildren. Nor would they countenance the gas tax transfer, even though Rolph pointed out that 32 other states had adopted a diversion similar to his. It seemed the public preferred a change in the mix of taxes rather than a reduction of outlays.

The budget message had given Rolph his last chance to seize the political initiative and shape the legislative agenda. The consensus in the state media, however, was that his suggestions were dead on arrival at the capitol. The legislature, it appeared, would proceed to develop a plan on its own, pausing only to extract such wisdom as it could find in the governor's words.[4]

After reconvening on February 28, the legislature attempted to raise taxes on the utilities but quickly ran into a formidable industry lobbying campaign against it. The Assembly passed a tax hike anyhow, perhaps influenced by board of equalization figures showing that Pacific Gas and Electric could absorb a $3 million tax increase and still make $8 million in profits over and above what the board considered a fair return. But the Senate, on which the utility companies had stronger influence, voted down a similar bill by a four-vote margin, thus torpedoing the whole effort.

California's legislative deliberations took a back seat during most of

March to the drama being played out in Washington. There, the newly inaugurated president was taking a series of bold actions to rescue the nation's banking system and sending emergency measures to Congress. For weeks, the headlines were dominated by news of the administration's first 100 days. Soon the media began to make unflattering comparisons between the president's dynamism and creativity and the state government's lack of ideas. "You should use Roosevelt as an example," the *Sacramento Union* advised the governor. "You can do it too—the people are waiting for a plan."[5]

All the Rolph administration could do, however, was sit on the sidelines and watch. The governor made several attempts to rededicate himself to the issue, but the poisonous atmosphere created by the Inman investigation ensured that the legislature would ignore anything the administration had to say. Finance director Vandegrift had put months of work into developing a budget, but the lawmakers did not even plan to use it as a starting point. They proceeded along both the budget and revenue tracks on their own.

What came to be called the Riley-Stewart plan evolved from the proposal that had been defeated by the voters in 1932. Ray Riley, the state controller, and Fred Stewart, director of the tax research bureau and a member of the board of equalization, had both been active in advising the legislature on budget and fiscal matters. Considering that Riley-Stewart was later described as a tax revolution, it made its way through the legislative process with relative ease. Introduced on January 26, it passed the Senate without a dissenting vote and then spent two weeks in the Assembly's revenue and taxation committee. It was passed by the Assembly on May 2.

Ironically, the Riley-Stewart plan would widen, rather than close, the revenue gap. Its primary purpose was to provide relief for the property tax payer:

• It would put an end to the state's split system of taxation, which had separated common property and utility property since 1910. The utility companies would no longer pay state taxes on their gross receipts. Instead, their property would be returned to local property tax rolls, just like that of the average home owner. This move helped property owners by broadening the local tax base by about one-sixth but took away a major source of income from the state.

• At the same time, the state would take on $38 million in public school expenses, previously paid by the counties through property taxes.

• The budgets of state and local governments would be limited to 5-percent annual increases.

• The amount of state government cost that could be borne by taxes on real property would be limited to 50 percent.

Riley-Stewart was radical — a leap into the unknown. Under its provisions, the state would surrender millions of dollars in taxes from the utilities while adding significant education costs. Where was the money going to come from?

As Riley-Stewart gained strength through the spring, the prospect of its passage forced the legislature to face the inevitability of new taxes. By the end of April, it came to an agreement that a sales tax would be part of any solution. It deferred a final decision on a complete tax package, however, until after a two-month recess, to begin in mid-May. In the meantime, California voters would be asked to go to the polls in late June to pass judgment on the Riley-Stewart approach. Their decision would guide the legislature when it reconvened in July.

On April 13, while the budget battle raged, the legislature, mindful of the need for additional revenue, passed a bill that would legalize pari-mutuel betting at horse races. Proponents pointed out that, besides allowing the state to tax gambling activity, it would bring badly needed regulation to what was then considered a shady enterprise. Opponents stressed the immorality of gambling and of making the state a partner to it.

No one seriously believed that Rolph would hesitate a second before signing the bill into law. As he had on the Mooney issue, however, Rolph was to confound political observers by acting either out of a hitherto hidden streak of social conservatism or on grounds of pure political expediency. Whatever the reason, or combination of reasons, the result was yet another public relations disaster.

In mid-April, a week after the legislature passed the racetrack gambling bill, Rolph flew to San Simeon to confer with William Randolph Hearst. He and some other wealthy Californians, among them Harry Chandler of the *Los Angeles Times* and Hollywood producer Louis B. Mayer, were said to have investments in Mexican racetracks and to oppose the bill because it would tend to keep racing money in the state. Once he returned to Sacramento, Rolph pronounced himself dubious about legalizing pari-mutuel betting, saying, "there's plenty of sentiment against the bill and not much for it."[6] The *Sacramento Union* commented disapprovingly that making a special trip to consult one individual about his gubernatorial duty would cause the people of California to blush with shame.[7]

On April 28 Rolph astonished official Sacramento by announcing that he was in fact vetoing the bill. It would, he said, bring back "the sordid, baneful, infecting vice of racetrack gambling" if passed. He grounded his decision squarely on moral considerations and pointed out that state voters had twice before expressed themselves as opposed to such gambling — once in 1926 and again in 1932. He conceded that the bill would have produced revenue and brought gambling under some measure of control, but said that such benefits "cannot balance the broken lives, the ruined homes, the welter of crime and sorrow that racetrack betting leaves in its wake."[8]

Putting two and two together, the *Union* saw Hearst's influence behind Rolph's action. The Hearst papers had begun trumpeting the merits of the Central Valley water plan, on which Rolph had placed so much emphasis, shortly after the governor's visit to San Simeon, suggesting a quid pro quo between the two men.[9] The paper also quoted Rolph as telling an unnamed state legislator: "Why, Hearst can give me the nomination."[10] (It was not clear which nomination was being talked about.) The governor's veto message, given on the same day he declared that he had no use for the Senate, left the impression that his anger at the Inman investigation was also a factor in his decision.

The bill's proponents still had the option of submitting the racetrack gambling issue to the public via the initiative process. In his veto message, Rolph freely endorsed this course of action — let the people decide. Sure enough, racetrack gambling joined a variety of tax-related propositions in a referendum to be held on June 27.

The economic stakes were high on the June 27 ballot, primarily because of Proposition One, which put the Riley-Stewart tax plan before the voters. A majority "yes" vote would completely revamp the state's tax structure, while requiring the legislature to impose new levies.

Nearly all of the state's newspapers had reservations about Proposition One, but most of them recognized the need for drastic action and fell in line behind it. Rolph was silent on the issue, however,[11] and Finance Director Vandegrift declared any change unnecessary. "Every sound argument is against it," he argued. "Our present system is working all right."[12] The liberal city of San Francisco, fearing the impact of a sales tax on its blue-collar labor force, formed a bulwark of opposition to the Riley approach. According to the *Union*, the Hearst publishing empire also opposed Proposition One, again raising concerns about whether the Rolph administration was toeing the Hearst line.

Along with the Riley-Stewart referendum, several other important issues on the ballot guaranteed a large turnout on June 27. The voters would:

- Decide for or against the repeal of Prohibition;
- Pass judgment on the legitimacy of diverting gas tax money from the highway fund; and,
- Determine whether state-organized racetrack gambling would be permitted despite the governor's veto.

Though Rolph had been careful to avoid antagonizing southern California by seeming too partisan on the issue of Prohibition, he now cited the economic benefits of a strong alcoholic beverages industry and asked the state to deal the Depression a "smashing wallop" by voting to repeal the great national experiment.[13] The *Union* commented that he should keep quiet, judging that with his stock so low, his public approval of any measure was bound to jeopardize its passage.

The people had little trouble making their decision on June 27. Proposition One prevailed by a 2–1 margin, despite the expected strong opposition from the San Francisco area. Voters also showed their disagreement with the administration's arguments for the gas tax diversion by rejecting it overwhelmingly. Both actions by the electorate cut off key sources of revenue for the state government and thus gave the legislature permission to move in bold new directions when it reconvened on July 17. Finally, Californians reversed their earlier negative verdict on legalized track gambling by nearly a 2–1 ratio, thus overturning Rolph's veto.

The outcome of the balloting was seen as another defeat for the administration. Except for the referendum on Prohibition, in which three out of four voters agreed that it should end, everything the Rolph people wanted was defeated "arbitrarily and relentlessly."[14]

The legislature reconvened in July to make some crucial financial decisions. Perhaps making a virtue out of necessity, Rolph decided not to get involved. "My plan has been turned down," he said. "Let those who can do better make the suggestions and be the leaders. I'll not place obstacles in their way. It's entirely up to the legislature."[15] It was also his political judgment that letting the lawmakers do the dirty work of raising taxes would allow him to position himself as the governor who tried to hold the line. Vandegrift agreed, saying that the legislative debate would be a political butcher shop,[16] but the *Union* bitterly noted that the governor had dodged the job of his own rehabilitation.[17]

Since mid–May, Rolph had been holding hearings on the bills the legislature had passed before going into recess. Most of these bills were economy measures, taken to reduce the need for new taxes. He did not like the mix of cuts represented by the new bills and had decided to veto a large number of them. Rolph had already proved vulnerable to the veto override, however, and he expected skirmishes once the lawmakers reconvened on July 17.[18]

The skirmishes turned out to be another full-scale war. On its first day back, in an unparalleled revolt, the legislature overrode 11 Rolph vetoes—far more than the entire total of overrides since 1850. Two days later, it passed seven more bills over Rolph's attempted rejection. His reaction was uncharacteristically mild. "That's all right," he said. "I'm just sorry they couldn't see the way I see."[19]

Rolph staked what little influence he had left in urging the lawmakers not to override his veto of a bill that reduced the salaries of state employees. Of all the actions taken by the legislature, this one troubled him the most. "There's nothing fair about the bill," he had said in May.[20] Cynics in the capital attributed Rolph's opposition to a provision that would take state hiring out of administration hands and place it in an independent board. But the governor argued in a special message to the legislature that cutting salaries would be out of step with President Roosevelt's recovery program and would leave state workers disadvantaged by inflation. On July 18, by a slim margin, the lawmakers sustained Rolph's veto, allowing him to retain a shred of his fast-disappearing prestige.

Aside from his strong stand on the state salary bill, the governor made no real effort to prevent the legislature from nullifying his actions. On the day of the 11 overrides, two of Rolph's strongest defenders from San Francisco were said to be in the executive office demanding to know why administration aides were not doing anything.[21] The governor himself was planning an escape to a far more congenial task—playing host to the national governors conference at the end of the month. His absences, as always, made life more difficult for those left behind. "He's just as liable to return in a peeve and fire everybody if he feels that some friend of his hasn't been given proper consideration," observed the *Union*'s political columnist.[22]

Though the legislators found temporary unity in overriding Rolph's vetoes, acrimony returned as the subject turned to taxes. With the influence of the governor at a low ebb, the 1933 session was as rudderless as the 1931 session. Lawmakers were divided into two camps—one favoring only a sales tax and the other advocating both an income tax and a sales tax. Tempers flared daily as temperatures in the Capitol's sweltering chambers reached 107 degrees.

Aware that eight other states and many European countries already had a sales tax, legislators began to move in that direction. It was a propitious time for such a tax. Most people considered it less onerous than the property tax. Merchants had become reconciled to it, and many consumers were expecting that relief from property taxes would neutralize its effects. A bill was drawn up using New York's law as a model. Neither the Senate nor the Assembly made an attempt to exempt food from its provisions.

When the session ended on July 26, the legislature had passed a 2½ percent sales tax—a compromise between Senate and Assembly preferences—and the first personal income tax in the state's history. The latter was too low to produce much revenue, but it was widely seen as a socially necessary balance to the sales tax. Even though these new taxes fell slightly short of closing the deficit, the legislature ignored squeals of protest from the Rolph people[23] and repealed the governor's right to levy property taxes to make up the difference. Lieutenant Governor Merriam called the remaining deficit workable and predicted it would encourage additional economy.

Rolph would respond another day. He had left town to fulfill his promise to make that year's national governors conference a real spectacle. Ever since the group had decided to meet in California in 1933, Rolph and his staff had been planning the kind of dramatic reception for which he had long been noted.[24] He had asked the legislature for money to paint the

At the height of his struggle with the legislature over taxes, Rolph, fifth from left, took time out to pose with his fellow state governors at the 1933 governors conference in Sacramento. He staged an elaborate reception for the group that included a mock holdup of their train as it crossed the Nevada-California border. "I want 'em to remember it," he said (courtesy of the California History Room, California State Library, Sacramento, California).

capitol for the occasion but had been turned down. But he had other ideas. As he said in anticipation, "I want 'em to remember it."[25]

They surely would. Late at night on July 22, as the train carrying many of the governors to California crossed the Nevada border at Truckee, a welcoming party that included humorist Will Rogers roused the distinguished visitors with a 19-gun salute, a cannonade of aerial bombs, and a staged holdup of the train by Rolph himself. This was only the beginning of several days of revelry, marching bands, and celebratory speeches, culminating in travel to Los Angeles where the governors were entertained by Hollywood stars. On the day the historic first state income tax was passed by the legislature, Rolph was in Yosemite National Park with his fellow chief executives. He was not one to let professional setbacks interfere with his obligations as a host.

Once the governors had departed, Rolph once again became relevant to the tax debate — he would have to sign or veto both bills. He had little choice but to sign the sales tax into law, but the income tax bill presented a difficult political choice. Vetoing it would antagonize labor and farm organizations, as well as the man on the street. Signing it would alienate conservative members of his constituency, including the Hearst interests, and most of his advisors. No matter whether he decided for the "organized minority or the unorganized mass," said the *Sacramento Union*, it would just be "another nail in his coffin."[26]

Contemporary observers were sure Rolph would sign the income tax bill. As a balance to the sales tax, it seemed eminently fair. It was little more than a token tax, having scant effect on most wage earners and raising only $10 million in increased revenue. And if he vetoed the legislation, he would either have to call the lawmakers back into session to address the remaining budget shortfall or arbitrarily impose unpopular property tax hikes. Yet, as Rolph held hearings on the pros and cons of the income tax bill, he seemed openly hostile to the arguments of its supporters. At one point, he broke into a proponent's presentation to say he was opposed to any new taxes. "That's my program," he said, "no new taxes."[27]

Rolph decided to attempt a political balancing act. He went ahead and signed the sales tax bill — after all, even his finance director, Vandegrift, had concluded as early as June that a sales tax was inevitable — but at the same time he disassociated himself from it. Publicly, he blamed the "wholly unnecessary Riley tax plan" for forcing the state to take extreme measures.[28] "I had nothing to do with the sales tax, except that I signed the bill because the legislature refused to accept my program."[29] Afterward, during a speech at the opening of the 1933 state fair, he called for its repeal or, at a minimum, its modification to exclude food items.

But people blamed him for the sales tax anyway. A week after it went into effect, waitresses were heard telling their customers: "That'll be seventy-five cents for lunch and two cents for Governor Rolph." By August, the saying "a penny for Jimmy" had become the best political joke of the year, and pundits were predicting that Rolph would be tied to the unpopular sales tax as surely as Hoover had been tied to the Depression — and with the same electoral consequence. Critics rubbed it in by saying that the extra penny was needed so the governor could throw another party.

It seemed that Rolph's wisest course of action was to sign the income tax bill to take the sting out of the sales tax and to remove the impression that he favored the rich at the expense of the poor. But on August 11 he again confounded official Sacramento by using a pocket veto. He reminded legislators that no additional taxes of any kind would have been necessary if they had accepted his January recommendations. "I simply refuse, by my signature, to permit the legislature to impose an income tax on top of the sales and gasoline tax," he said.[30]

Again, Rolph was battered in the media. He was called "totally blind to governmental conditions and deaf to the advice of those in touch with popular sentiment,"[31] and, of course, another way would have to be found to balance the budget. Controller Riley saw a hike in the new sales tax as the only practical option, but the tax was already hated across the state and sentiment was even growing to try to repeal it. The state's budget remained awash in red ink, and by 1935 the issue would become not whether to have an income tax, but what the rate would be. Governor Rolph continued to pose as the public's only defender against tax increases, showing that policy was taking a back seat to politics as the 1934 election drew near.

* * * * * * * * * *

How should Rolph's contribution to the tax debate be evaluated? It would be easy to conclude that he was irrelevant to it. But it would be fairer to agree with historian Loren Chan that he made a serious attempt to deal with the crisis. "Within the limits of the political philosophy of his party and the authority of his office," concludes Chan, "the governor did indeed try his best."[32] He sent Finance Director Vandegrift on a trip to eastern states to find out how they were handling the economic downturn. He responded to criticism of his extravagance by coming up with a program of spending cuts that, while painful, would have forced the state government to live within its means. He opposed new taxes. If his travels around the state had shown him anything, it was the cruelty of raising taxes during a time of great hardship.

Rolph's position on the gas tax diversion, in retrospect, seems to have been the correct one. It was hard to argue that interest on highway bonds should have been paid from the general fund while the highway fund was running a surplus, particularly as a fiscal emergency loomed. As one tax authority asked at the time: "After all, who wore [the highways] out, except the highway user?"[33] Yet Rolph was unable to get either the legislature or the public to agree.

His inability to influence the substance of the debate must be blamed primarily on his poor relations with the legislature, strained past the breaking point by months of acrimony. Rolph himself had become the issue. The lawmakers did not resent his ideas so much as his style and approach.

He continued to try, without success, to avoid association with the sales tax, despite the obvious fact that Riley-Stewart left the state in dire need of new revenues. His painstaking effort to deny responsibility for the tax even while he was signing it into law must have struck some people as a ludicrous attempt to have it both ways. And his opposition to the nominal income tax left him open to charges of protecting friends and favoring the wealthy.

His failure, then, was one of imagination and, in line with his history, his grasp of the issues. Mastery of policy nuances had never been his strong suit, and tax issues were complicated to begin with. So he did what he had always done — he relied on other people for advice, and he made a gut-level political calculation. Being on record as supporting any kind of tax increase promised to be a liability in a reelection campaign, as well as to alienate key supporters. Thus he refused to countenance the raising of utility taxes early in the debate. Politics, in fact, seems to have been his paramount consideration. He would shift the blame for taxes, if he could, to the legislature and campaign against the lawmakers in the coming election.

The legislature had elbowed the governor out of the way and pushed through its own tax plan. It was far from perfect. Even on its own terms— as relief for the property tax payer — it did not wholly succeed, according to a contemporary analysis. Still, the passage of the Riley-Stewart program was one of the most important events in the state's financial history. By forcing the state to open the door to new sources of revenue, it provided an engine — unintended at the time — for the later dramatic growth of state government.[34] Its effect was immediate — after declining from $69 million to $50 million between 1931 and 1933, state revenues shot upward to $83 million by 1934. The law was also an early manifestation of the property tax payer revolt that would roil the state again during the 1970s.

25

Embattled, Fatigued and Broke

"No one will ever know the struggles Jim Rolph went through," wrote his personal secretary David Wooster Taylor.[1] Taylor's portrait of life in the executive mansion toward the end of Rolph's term shows a governor who was not only facing pressure from every side but also working himself to death. He was said to be a virtual prisoner in his office, taking an occasional half-hour snooze on his sofa wrapped in an old Indian blanket and then returning to work until the early morning hours.

Weariness settled upon him permanently, wrote Taylor, as he slipped into a routine "that led from inkwell to couch, and back again to inkwell."[2] Of course, it was not so much the press of business that caused this overload but rather his heavy travel schedule, which left him little time for state business. Also to blame was his open-door policy, which, "carried to such an extreme that he insisted on seeing almost every person who came into his office, worked a personal hardship on him."[3] Of course, this practice had been a permanent feature of his governing style since his first years as mayor.

As we have noted, Rolph's final term in San Francisco had been filled with personal distractions. His financial situation was in peril, he socialized vigorously, and he drank to excess. Once he arrived in the capital, public reports on his social life ceased altogether. We do not know if he decided to change his ways, was simply unable to afford the time, or conducted his extracurricular activities with discretion. The press occasionally called him a playboy but did not elaborate.

On the issue of alcohol, Taylor concedes that his boss did drink as mayor, but not as governor, and that many people mistook the symptoms of his physical decline after 1931 for drunkenness. "Unable to sleep, yes. Groggy from weariness, yes," but "any kind of drink would have killed

Rolph jokes with actor Wallace Beery. The governor loved to hobnob with Hollywood celebrities. "In distant states," wrote the *Sacramento Union*, "Rolph merges in with the glamour of California" (Nancy Rolph Welch Collection).

him." Many times, said Taylor, he turned down a drink when he would have wanted one.[4]

By the time Rolph became governor, the effects of 60 years of irregular eating habits, questionable nutrition, and overwork were making themselves felt. Moreover, constant travel led to fatigue and lack of exercise. Though his vigor and enthusiasm were rarely absent for long, his overall health steadily worsened. He was hospitalized for fatigue in May 1932, and was seriously ill with a heart ailment, aggravated by the flu, in January and February 1933.[5]

Pressure and stress led to another crisis in August, just as the furor over his veto of the income tax bill was starting to subside. For weeks he had been racing around the state with little sleep and, according to his doctor, complaining repeatedly of being tired. The governor's growing weariness exploded into public view on August 30, when he was responding to Sacramento media protests of his refusal to grant clemency to a convicted robber. "Some people don't know how to treat a governor," he barked, slamming his fist on his desk. "They browbeat, they criticize. They abuse a governor from the time he comes until time to kick him out. If I was running the city, I'd have some respect for the governor. Every governor who has been here has been hounded to death."[6]

Fatigue and impending illness may have been more to blame for the outburst than anger. Two days later he told aides he thought he had come down with a cold. He felt worse the next day but insisted on going to a press luncheon. After opening the state fair that afternoon, he could no longer pretend nothing was wrong. He was taken to St. Francis hospital in San Francisco with congestion in his lungs and a temperature of 105 degrees. By the next day he was gravely ill with pneumonia. On September 8, while telling the media that the governor was out of immediate danger, his doctor revealed that the attack had nearly cost him his life. To that point Mrs. Rolph had still not been allowed to see her husband. An aide would later say that he had been "almost given up for dead."[7]

After two more days of isolation and intensive care, Rolph's doctors announced that he would spend two weeks at St. Francis. He gradually improved after that, and on September 24 the governor left for Sacramento, whereupon he went immediately to bed. Reporters who saw him later that week thought he seemed tired and his face looked thinner, but anyone who thought a near-death experience would alter his schedule was mistaken. He went back to the irregular hours and late-night paperwork that had been his trademark, though he promised his doctors that he would not work until two or three in the morning unless absolutely necessary.

Another problem that would not go away was Rolph's financial plight. In 1930 he had sold several parcels of land in an effort to keep his head above water. But his $10,000 salary as governor was not nearly enough to take care of the debts that pressed in from every side. The premiums on his life insurance policies alone, which covered his obligations to banks, cost him $25,000 a year. When he was unable to pay the premiums, a family friend stepped in to help.[8]

Taylor paints a bleak portrait of the governor's hand-to-mouth existence in Sacramento, "digging down to his last thin dollar bill" while shopping for his own food. It was a strange experience, Taylor wrote, "often attending brilliant functions, meeting and mingling with persons of position and wealth, without more than a dollar or so in our pockets."[9] Despite this hardship, according to his secretary, the governor was scrupulously honest — he would not even borrow stamps from the government.

It was a testimony to his resilience that he was able to push ahead through the year and even to see a ray of hope in the distance. But more difficult challenges awaited him, and they came at a time when his physical ability to deal with them was much diminished. The first was the building confrontation between California's farm labor population and the state's large growers, which by the fall of 1933 could no longer be ignored.

26

The Farm Labor Crisis

The most vivid historical images from the Depression in California illustrate the wretched lot of migrant farm laborers. The bad times brought more than 300,000 white Americans from the Dust Bowls of the Great Plains to the fields of the Central and Imperial valleys, where they joined an already oppressed Mexican workforce in picking fruit, vegetables, and cotton for large, often corporate, landowners. Reduced demand for the crops and an oversupply of labor drove wages for pickers down below the subsistence level. Before 1930, no one defended the interests of these unfortunate transients, who not only were underpaid but lived amid "filth, squalor, an entire absence of sanitation, and a crowding of human beings into totally inadequate tents or crude structures built of boards, weeds, and anything that was found at hand...."[1]

The Cannery and Agricultural Workers Industrial Union finally organized many of the state's field workers in the early 1930s. Tensions between the union and the state's large growers steadily grew, as the growers felt squeezed between union demands and a steadily shrinking profit margin. In response to a 20-percent cut in wages, cannery employees in the Santa Clara Valley walked off the job in July 1931. Noisy demonstrations by strikers were met by threats of violence from cannery guards, and none of the workers' demands were satisfied. In November 1932, fruit pickers in Vacaville struck, again for higher wages. In response, vigilantes and local police intimidated CAWIU organizers, while public opinion remained unsympathetic to a union leadership comprised largely of Communists and non–Californians. The fruit pickers likewise came away empty handed.

Governor Rolph was certainly aware of the growing ferment in rural areas, but before 1933 he did not publicly acknowledge it in either word or deed. In his long and detailed address to the legislature in January 1933, his comments on agriculture were minimal, and they revealed no particular concern for the rural labor force. Instead, he focused on the "seriousness of the situation confronting our farmers" who have "carried on their work without halting or complaining, although they have much opposition to overcome."[2] Of course, Rolph had spent his entire political life working on urban problems and had always lived in the city. We can imagine that he had the same compassion for the farm workers that he had for all the state's disadvantaged people, but he probably regarded agricultural strikes as a problem for local authorities to handle.

At least 37 strikes took place in California in 1933, the year the Great Depression hit rock bottom. They provoked a strong and sometimes violent reaction from growers as well as the general public. The danger for strikers grew as they and their leaders were roughed up by both local police and vigilante elements. Bunkhouses were dynamited. Laborers were packed into trucks and shipped out of town. Though killings were infrequent, the clash of economic interests produced a volatile and dangerous mix.

Rolph first publicly expressed a position on a strike-related matter during August 1933 walkouts by peach pickers in Merced and Tulare counties, which were frequent battlegrounds. Local authorities requested that Rolph call out the state militia to quell strike demonstrations. His refusal to do so suggested sympathy with worker demands for higher salaries, or perhaps a conviction that state interference would be inappropriate. Instead of sending troops, the governor turned to Tim Reardon, the best friend he had in the labor movement, and asked him to mediate. The action was entirely consistent with Rolph's decision-making style. Reardon's intervention resulted in agreement on a 40-percent raise for the strikers.[3]

A more serious strike, by grape pickers in Lodi, flared up in late September. When it continued into October, despite a campaign of intimidation and arrests by local authorities, several hundred vigilantes, using clubs and fists, drove the strikers out of town. CAWIU leaders protested their treatment in a note to Governor Rolph and asked for state protection, but again he refused to take action.[4]

Finally, a massive confrontation came along that was too explosive for the governor to ignore. It involved workers in the state's cotton fields. At the time, cotton was a major crop, widely planted in the San Joaquin and Imperial Valleys, and California had become the 11th ranking cotton producer in the country. The harvest was a highly labor-intensive operation, requiring back-breaking work, and the CAWIU made its wage demands in October, just as pickers were most needed. But growers were locked into contracts with foreign buyers even before the cotton was harvested, and they felt they had little leeway in wage negotiations with the union. CAWIU leaders considered the pay offered by the growers outrageously low.[5] The work stoppage that followed has been called the "single greatest strike in the history of agricultural labor relations in America."[6]

People on both sides of the conflict were hoping that the state government would intervene. George Creel, the California representative of Roosevelt's National Recovery Administration, charged by the president with encouraging cooperation between capital and labor in hastening economic recovery, thought the strikes set a dangerous precedent and should be stopped. A more liberal state NRA official, Rabbi Irving Reichert, wrote to Rolph in early October concerned about antiunion vigilantism, which he felt would alienate working people in other areas of the economy. In this way, the governor came under pressure to act both for and against the interests of the farm workers.[7]

When he received the Reichert letter, the governor was still recovering from his recent serious illness. As was his custom, he referred the issue to a subordinate — in this case, the state labor commissioner — who attempted to mediate the dispute. The growers were not interested in negotiating, however, and opposed any dealings with the CAWIU, which they denounced as a Communist organization with subversive intent. Their intransigence drew the ire of both state and federal officials.

In any event, little time remained for careful consideration of the problem. In the next week, intimidation, evictions, and violence by growers and their allies broke out on an unprecedented scale, and several strikers were killed on October 10. Local authorities were worried about alienating the influential farm owners and therefore did nothing, or actively abetted the suppression of the picketers. "The lawlessness which I predicted has come to pass," Reichert noted bitterly. "Gangsterism has been substituted for law and order."[8] A public outcry ensued. Growers and local authorities were condemned for their brutality and the state for failing to protect the rights of strikers. Newspapers demanded a quick and effective settlement of the dispute.

As the crisis intensified, Rolph called for immediate arbitration of the matters at issue. Again, he seemed to take the side of the workers. He criticized the "smart-aleck guys" who were intimidating the strikers and taking the law into their own hands, and called for the disarming of growers who were carrying guns. But he continued to refuse to call out the militia, except where local police "prove themselves incompetent by asking for it."[9] He increased the number of highway patrolmen in the affected areas, but these officers tended to side with the growers, viewing the strikers as a lawless mob.

Rolph may have been the victim of biased information arriving from the strike areas. According to one account, the two officials from whom the governor was receiving reports on the situation were strong opponents of farm unionism. They tended to focus on the unruliness of the strike "agitators" and to soft-pedal the tactics of the growers and vigilantes.[10]

On October 12, the governor received a delegation of strikers in Sacramento. He had always responded best to concrete problems and their effects on real people, so the laborers were wise to seek a face-to-face meeting with him. At first, he sat unmoved through a presentation of demands from the representatives of the strikers, but when an old lady rose to share the details of her arduous working day, he snapped to attention. "Of all these people here, you most impressed me with your sincerity. You're the only one who has actually picked cotton. What you have said has shown me what you want done. Rest assured I will do what I can."[11] He immediately agreed to provide relief to all farm workers in need of it, whether or not they were on strike.

Combatants and mediators alike were urging Rolph to call out the National Guard to restore order, but he again passed up strong action. Such demands for direct state intervention involved legal points that had to be studied, he said. Instead, under pressure from George Creel, who was asserting federal jurisdiction in the dispute far in excess of his formal authority,[12] Rolph decided to appoint a fact-finding committee, consisting of one academic and two religious leaders, including Archbishop Hanna. Meeting on October 19th and 20th, the committee took dramatic testimony from strikers on their impoverished lives. The hearing provided a useful forum for the airing of their grievances and succeeded in raising public awareness of their plight. Over the next few days, with NRA assistance and the commission's backing, a modest wage increase was agreed to by both sides, and the strike ended.

Rolph's response to the cotton strike can be assessed in many ways—as weak, as prudent, as political, or as influenced by his physical incapacitation. In fact, it was all of these things. It was weak because he dithered until inaction was no longer an option, and he allowed others to take the initiative, even though he was the only one empowered to act on behalf of the interests of the entire state. It was prudent because he judged that the use of force by the state might incite more violence than it would prevent, would undermine local authorities, and would leave the state open to the charge of taking sides. Instead, he took a measured course that allowed emotions to cool and negotiations to begin.

His response was political because he calculated that most of the state's voters had a visceral dislike for immigrants and a strong antipathy for the Communist ideology of the CAWIU organizers, even though the workers were too caught up in day-to-day survival to think much about ideology. If politics did govern his reaction, the public's sympathy for the strikers might have caught him by surprise.

Rolph's behavior is also consistent with his weakened physical condition. One month before he was called upon to deal with the cotton strike, he had been near death at St. Francis Hospital. He had been out of the hospital for only a week. If he had had more energy and more willpower, he might have been able to inform himself more thoroughly about the strike and its causes and overcome the inertia that can afflict those recovering from serious illnesses. His critics often overlooked the impact of his deteriorating health on his effectiveness.

However Rolph's actions in the crisis are judged, the outcome could have been much worse. His refusal to overreact may have saved lives, and his appointment of a highly effective commission led directly to a settlement between capital and labor that had not been possible before. All in all, he did not show great leadership, but neither did he run from the problem. His performance was adequate under the circumstances.

As October faded into November, Rolph probably thought that 1933 could not possibly bring more intense public pressure or high-profile challenges. Almost unbelievably, the worst was yet to come.

27

Preparing for the 1934 Campaign

Watching Rolph's many troubles unfold in 1933, California's journalists often noted, regretfully at times, that the governor's reelection was still not out of the question. The *Sacramento Union* saw his veto of the track gambling bill as a bid for the support he would need from the Hearst newspapers in 1934. The *Alameda Times-Star* pointed out that the as-yet undeclared candidate had been quietly campaigning for some time. His sponsorship of the Central Valley water conservation plan, as both newspapers noted, was bound to strengthen him in the valley and elsewhere. But the *Times-Star* grumbled that "things have come to a pretty pass if a man so unfitted (sic) for the office should be reelected."[1]

Indeed, the media seemed to adhere simultaneously to two inconsistent beliefs—that Rolph could not possibly win, given his record, and that he just might, given his ability as a campaigner and the apparent lack of strong opposition. Newspapers continued to excoriate his leadership and declared his popularity a thing of the past. "Probably never in the history of California," concluded the *Union* on July 8, "has any administration known so little what it wanted or has been so bungling in dealing with the legislature."[2] The paper urged him to relieve himself of much embarrassment and take himself out of the race.[3]

But Rolph had a surprising number of things going for him. He was the best-known governor in the country, even before the San Jose incident (see pp. 182–186). His magnetic personality, his love of travel, his unpredictability, and his knack for seizing the spotlight had assured him of media coverage far beyond California. "In distant states," wrote the *Union*, "Rolph merges in with the glamour of California," and tourists come "see its wonders, including Hollywood and the governor."[4] A visitor from New Jersey, whom Rolph, as was his custom, did not hesitate to see, said that he had wanted to meet two people in California — Rolph and Will Rogers. "Why, we hear more about you back east than we do about our own governor," he said. Like San Franciscans before them, state voters took a certain amount of pride in Rolph's colorfulness and flair for the dramatic.

By late 1933, President Roosevelt's dynamic and creative first several months in office had gained him national admiration. California newspapers yearned for Roosevelt-style leadership on the state level as well. Whether out of political calculation or genuine respect for his leadership and energy, or both, Rolph had consistently backed FDR's efforts to spur economic recovery. In July, while calling upon California's employers to raise wages to make up for rising prices, he said: "The President ... seems to be doing all the thinking. It's time some of us helped him. He is a great leader and deserves the support of every public official and every employer. This is far above politics. The life of the nation is at stake."[5] A month later, endorsing the president's National Recovery Administration, the governor once again called Roosevelt a great leader, whom "all America should be behind ... heart and soul."[6] This shrewd stance appeared to be, as he had said, above politics, while it enabled him to court the rapidly growing Democratic segment of the California electorate.

Rolph's biggest advantage was the lack of strong competition in either party. Lieutenant Governor Merriam had declared his candidacy but his colorlessness and reputation as a rock-ribbed conservative undermined his chances; the *Union* said he was as dead as an Egyptian mummy.[7] State treasurer Charles Johnson, also considered an old-school Republican, was campaigning hard in mid–1933 but with little effect. Democrats were deeply divided, and no credible candidate had yet emerged. As of October a total of 30 men from all parties had thrown their hats in the ring. The greater the number of lackluster nonentities in the race, the better Rolph's chances would be.

All the same, Rolph had an uphill fight ahead of him. The *Union* called him an anachronism, "an echo of the days when hand-shaking, posing in front of cameras and leading parades constituted a good executive."[8] Life had become a serious business, the *Union* observed, and few people had time to wave flags. Political columnists who had taken soundings around the state reported that the one common belief among voters was that a change of administration was needed in Sacramento. In any case, Californians had not given their governors a second term since they reelected Hiram Johnson in 1916.

Rolph may have been worried that his reputation for mercy and compassion in handling criminals would prove to be a liability in a reelection campaign. By the summer of 1933, he had far exceeded any of his predecessors by using his clemency power 138 times, which included 31 commutations of sentence and nine pardons. The one glaring exception to this pattern of leniency, of course, was his refusal to pardon Tom Mooney in 1932.

In August 1933, another high-profile case demanded the governor's attention. A man named Jack Green had been sentenced to death in Los Angeles for the murder of a policeman during a robbery, though it was his accomplice who actually pulled the trigger. Rolph seemed prepared to allow Green to go to the gallows, reportedly because the Los Angeles police department and district attorney (1930 gubernatorial candidate Buron Fitts) threatened to withhold their political support if he did not.

The *Union* published a front-page editorial accusing Rolph of playing politics with pardons. Several other newspapers appealed to Rolph to reconsider. The next day, a scowling, desk-pounding governor, in one of the most bizarre scenes of his official term, called Green a cold-blooded murderer and denounced his critics. "A few sentimentalists are trying to make a fool out of this governor," he fumed. "I won't be browbeat into commuting this sentence. I'm not afraid of anybody. Not anybody. It's lucky there's a governor with some guts in him."[9]

Two days later, Rolph was near death in a hospital, so his outburst may have been a reflection of his worsening health. In any case, he changed his mind about the Green case as soon as he was better. In mid–September, while still very ill, he had issued a temporary reprieve, allegedly based on new evidence. Then, in January 1934, he removed Green from death row. The governor's public statements suggested that he had looked into the case thoroughly and finally accepted the arguments of Green's defenders. Rolph received congratulations from many quarters for his wise and humane decision, while Fitts and the L.A. police complained bitterly.

Toward the end of the year, however, Rolph took steps to toughen his image. While reviewing the candidacy of a Stockton man for the state prison board in October, he said: "As far as I am concerned, hanging is too good for some convicts. Some of them ought to be hanged. You need a governor like me to keep the hanging law on the books. There are too many killings and murders and robberies and attacks going on."[10]

At the same time, he continued to show an interest in the fate of individual convicts whose cases caught his attention. On October 19 he ordered whiskey given to a condemned man, eliciting criticism from the Woman's Christian Temperance Union but support from most other quarters. In November he visited Folsom for his second meeting with a black man convicted of murder. Said Rolph, he is "lucky to be alive, because I am governor."[11]

Then came the San Jose incident.

28

The San Jose Kidnapping

It is a sad irony that Jim Rolph, who spent much of his term trying to humanize the penal system, who treated convicted criminals with kindness and respect, and who pardoned or reduced the sentences of many men, would become known and condemned around the country for his public approval of a lynching in his home state. This was his last major ordeal as governor and certainly the most damaging, both to his reputation and his health. His granddaughter, Nancy Rolph Welch, believes it ultimately cost him his life.

The so-called San Jose incident could not have come at a worse time. Rolph was trying to recover from the debilitating pneumonia he had experienced in September, but, as usual, he ignored doctors' orders to slow down and take a long vacation. In mid–October the *Sacramento Union*'s political columnist watched him preside over hearings on the Central Valley cotton strikes and wrote: "Gov. Rolph looks far from well. He has aged and failed physically since his last illness." Some aides had said he was snapping back, but the death of a longtime colleague and friend, Daniel O'Brien, affected him greatly, and he went to pieces again.[1]

In mid–November, during this period of heightened physical and emotional vulnerability, an incident took place in San Jose that seemed at first to have only local importance. Brooke Hart, the popular 22-year-old son of a prominent city merchant, mysteriously disappeared. Several days later, ransom notes to the Hart family indicated that the young man had been kidnapped. The kidnappers, two local men, had actually thrown Hart off the San Mateo Bridge shortly after they snatched him, though their requests for ransom money led everyone to believe he was still alive. After about a week, they were caught, confessed to the crime, and were jailed. When fishermen found Brooke Hart's grisly remains, public shock and fury over the murder mounted to an explosive level. An enraged mob attacked the jail where the kidnappers were being held, overcame the police, and then lynched the killers in a nearby park.

28. The San Jose Kidnapping

Outrageous as the Hart murder would have been any time it happened, it struck a raw nerve in all Californians during the early 1930s. The nation was experiencing an epidemic of kidnappings—the most notorious being that of famous flyer Charles Lindbergh's baby in May 1932.[2] The family's prolonged agony and the child's ultimate slaying became a national tragedy, followed daily in the newspapers by millions of people. Kidnapping as a means of extracting money from panicked family members became so commonplace in 1933 that the popular "Moon Mullins" comic strip featured a story line in which a major character was taken and held for ransom.

This type of crime inspired terror in the 1930s the same way that political assassination would in the 1960s, airplane hijacking in the 1970s, and hostage taking in the 1980s, wrote Harry Farrell in his book on the Hart case. "Fear was abroad, borne on a nationwide wave of killing, kidnapping and extortion."[3] The National Governors Conference, hosted by Rolph a few months before the San Jose incident, elevated the issue by urging in its concluding session that kidnappers be prosecuted to the fullest extent of the law. In fact, a son of one of the governors in attendance had been kidnapped and nearly beaten to death.

Against that backdrop, Rolph, who was an emotional and family-centered man to begin with, could be expected to have strong feelings about the Hart boy's disappearance. When the two suspects were jailed, he declared that "this case has been on my mind constantly since it began." After the victim's fate became known, he was heard to mutter "terrible, terrible." He added, presciently: "I imagine the finding of the body will create a renewed flare of indignation."[4] When it appeared that a mob might try to take justice in its own hands, and some people suggested that the National Guard be employed to prevent that from happening, Rolph asked: "Why should I call out troops to protect those two fellows?"[5]

Rolph was by no means alone in wishing to deny state protection to the prisoners. The *San Jose News* editorialized: "If mob violence could ever be justified it would be in a case like this, and we believe the general public will agree with us. There was never a more fiendish crime committed anywhere in the United States."[6] Many felt that a legal presumption of innocence was no longer warranted once the confessions were made. "The guilt of the culprits is unquestioned.... There is no defense or mitigation. The crime was cold blooded, premeditated, fiendish and sordid," wrote the *San Francisco Chronicle*.[7]

Once the lynchings had taken place, Rolph uttered words that delighted some people and shocked many others. Informed of the deaths of the two kidnappers, the governor said approvingly: "This is the best lesson California has ever given the country." He went on to praise "those fine, patriotic

San Jose citizens who know how to handle such a situation."[8] And he resolved that "if anyone is arrested for the good job, I'll pardon them."[9] Criticized for failing to use the militia to prevent the lynching, Rolph responded: "Well, if the people have confidence that troops will not be called out to mow them down when they seek to protect themselves against kidnappers, there is liable to be swifter justice and fewer kidnappings."[10]

Surely Rolph understood that his remarks would be controversial and widely criticized. He must have realized that he was endorsing an illegal act — an act of mob justice. He had spoken deliberately and clearly, so it would have been difficult to claim later that he had been misquoted.[11] But he had no intention of backing away. The next day, he said: "I have not changed my opinion one iota. I stand by my original statement,"[12] but he also took pains to emphasize that he meant his words to apply to only one crime. "We are justified in going to any extreme to stop kidnapping," he said. He recalled the discussion of the issue at the governors conference in July, and he reminded the press that the "kidnapping danger to every child and to every man and woman in this country has been growing greater.... I think the governors of other states will be with me."[13]

With the 1934 gubernatorial campaign about to get underway, Rolph would have been sensitive to the political impact of his stand. Maybe he calculated that most Californians would approve of accelerated justice in the Hart case, particularly since the prisoners had already confessed. As he had shown during the Mooney appeal, Rolph also felt that swift and sure punishment had a deterrent effect on crime. A lynching, abhorrent though it might be, would send a clear message. Reacting to criticism, he said: "That's all right.... We'll at least have the satisfaction of knowing we're making women and children safer."[14] Later: "I'm going to run [the kidnappers] out of California if I can. I propose to make the hearts of the fathers and mothers more contented than they have been since the Lindbergh baby was kidnapped."[15] So Rolph's views on the lynching were more than visceral, though they were that, too — they reflected both a political calculation and the belief that the times required drastic action.

Early reactions from around the state were tinged with the outrage that every citizen felt. The day after the lynching, telegrams and public statements ran 20–1 in Rolph's favor; the next day, they ran 5–1.[16] Some national media supported the governor's position as well. The *Denver Post* called it a fine example for other states.[17] The *Sacramento Bee* pronounced the lynching a "goodly and a righteous and necessary thing."[18] The beloved humorist Will Rogers said: "All Californians I have met are going around proud today." Actor Leo Carrillo wired: "The entire country commends you for your courageous attitude."[19] After Rolph's death, the *New York Times*, which had strongly condemned the governor's remarks when they were made, conceded that "he said what perhaps nine out of ten persons said when they first heard of the lynching."[20]

By the second day, however, a torrent of verbal abuse from around the state and the country had begun to descend on the governor. "Seldom," said the *Baltimore Sun*, "has high office been so shamefully degraded." The *New York Herald Tribune* termed Rolph's remark about California's best lesson to the nation the foolish remark of a cheap politician. Under the headline, "Has Governor Rolph Lost His Mind?" the *San Francisco Chronicle* said: "It may be natural enough for private citizens to approve the San Jose lynching. But not the governor of California. He has a larger responsibility."[21] The national journal *Commonweal* wrote that Rolph "should not only be impeached but incarcerated in an asylum for imbecilic children." A New York pastor suggested that the word lynching be replaced with its modern equivalent, Rolphing.[22]

Adding considerable weight to the chorus of critics, former President Herbert Hoover condemned the governor on November 29. Endorsement of a lynching, he said, "particularly when coming from the chief executive of the state, undermines the very foundation upon which the state and all civilized society are built."[23] Many American political leaders put pressure on President Roosevelt to follow suit, and he finally issued an indirect rebuke: "We do not excuse those in high places or low who condone lynch law."[24]

Rolph periodically met the press as the criticism came in — "not only with equanimity but with every sign of enjoyment," Farrell believes — and read from the telegrams that he claimed were still running 5–1 in his favor. "The mothers are with me," he said.[25] He also spoke of the importance of judicial reforms that would speed up the courts' handling of the most egregious kidnapping cases. Feeling the need to flesh out his views, he wrote these words for the North American Newspaper Alliance: "The first duty of government is to protect its law-abiding citizens, no matter what the methods or the cost. The criminals have armed themselves. They have made war, and so have we."[26]

Rolph would never again face the electorate, and opinion polling was in its infancy, so we will never know whether a majority of the voters approved of his statements. His insistence on the legitimacy of mob justice in extreme circumstances certainly showed the public that his well-known sympathy for criminals extended only so far. In fact, it might have erased his compassionate image altogether. He may have been right in betting that Californians were more outraged by the crime than by the lack of due process.

One of Rolph's intimates, Louis Oneal, was certain that the governor knew exactly what he was doing—he "was not a fly-by-night idiot by a damn sight." His forte was knowing and pleasing people, and he was a winner with the masses. According to this view, the state's "genteel façade masked a broad redneck strain," and his words had given voice to the average Californian.[27]

The *Sacramento Union* considered his stance a purely political calculation. An editorial in December judged that the two Rolphs—the merciful governor and the lynching governor—were both "merely vanes in the wind to catch the currents of popularity."[28] It saw the lynching controversy as more of a plus than a minus for Rolph's reelection chances, because it took to a new level his talent for getting on the front page—indeed, it made him "the most talked-about governor in the history of California."[29] But to the newspaper, the episode was another major embarrassment. "California is crying for a real governor," it editorialized. "Isn't there some worthy man who will take the job?"[30]

29

The Central Valley Water Plan

Though the year brought him many setbacks and disappointments, Rolph had bragging rights to one major accomplishment by the end of 1933 as he thought about whether to seek a second term. The legislative passage and public approval of the Central Valley water program showed what Rolph could do when he knew what he wanted.

It had long been recognized that the state needed a way to transfer surplus water from the northern Sacramento Valley to the fertile but dry expanses of the San Joaquin Valley. In 1933, California was in the fifth year of an eight-year drought, and agricultural interests were increasingly anxious to see progress on a state water plan. But feasibility and cost were the main concerns, particularly as the Depression shrank state revenues.

Despite the Depression, this was an era of massive water reclamation projects and dam building throughout the country. Among the advantages of these public works, recognized by both Hoover and Roosevelt, was that they put idle people back to work. Hoover had pushed appropriations for a dam at Boulder Canyon and made money available to the Colorado River project. His administration came up with the idea of a federal-state partnership on such projects, with the federal government building them and the state operating them, while paying back Washington with interest.

As his backing of the Hetch Hetchy project and the San Francisco municipal railway demonstrated, Rolph believed in the value of large-scale public works where the need was clear. He had pledged at the very beginning of his administration to work hard on California's water problems. He demanded action from the 1931 legislature, threatening to call it back into a special session if none was taken. Private power companies opposed a Central Valley program from the start, because it was apt to create state competition by building dams and generating cheap public power. Lobbying efforts by the utilities at first prevented progress, but Rolph had no intention of giving in to pressure.

In June 1931 the governor had set up a committee of legislators to make recommendations to him on the content of a water resources plan. Two months later, he named a citizens advisory committee, headed by the ubiquitous Matt Sullivan, to complement the legislative effort. In addition, he was determined to find federal funding for the project, which was far too expensive for the state alone to finance.

All through 1932, Rolph kept the pressure on these committees, which were frequently at loggerheads, and threatened periodically to call a special legislative session on water resources to move things along. Encountering strenuous objections to such a session, he gave up the attempt to coerce legislative action during the summer but repeated his belief that, after unemployment, the water problem was the second most important item on his agenda. Making such a comment took courage during a time when severe economic hardship made water a trivial concern to California's urban voters. Realizing the need to educate the public on the water issue, Rolph pledged to stump the state to promote a water program. "They think I travel a lot. I haven't traveled at all [compared] to what I'll do on this thing," he said in July.[1]

Rolph revived the water problem in his speech to the legislature in January 1933, asking it to enact a bill "establishing the fundamental principles of a coordinated plan of state water development." Under constant attack from the Capitol that spring, the governor picked up an unlikely ally when Senator Inman, the head of the committee charged with investigating his administration, began to work hard for legislative approval of a water plan. In May the Senate passed enabling legislation for a Central Valley water project.

But with the budget and revenue crises on everyone's mind, the key to a water plan that voters could get behind was enough federal money to take the cost of a program out of the debate. Rolph wired Roosevelt in March requesting federal assistance, and in July he sent a representative to Washington to try to bring the water project into the president's national recovery program. The aide returned with guidance on how to draft a plan that would qualify for federal assistance — the primary requirement for which was a strong clause affirming public ownership of power generated by the program. Acceptance by federal authorities would guarantee 30 percent sponsorship by Washington.

In July 1933, the Central Valley water plan was passed by the legislature, thus inaugurating a huge experiment in public ownership of power and distribution of water. The bill's sponsors had come up with a program that would not cost the taxpayers a penny—the bonds issued to finance it would be paid off in revenue from the project itself, and the federal government would take care of the rest. Successful passage was deemed a personal victory for the governor, and it fulfilled a campaign promise he had made to Central Valley farmers in 1930.

The power companies still had several cards to play. A special election was needed to provide final authority for the water project, and if they could persuade Rolph to delay calling an election until 1934, the availability of federal grant money would lapse, thus torpedoing the entire effort. But Rolph served notice upon signing the bill that he would not knuckle under to pressure. In one of his strongest public statements as governor, he said: "I will not stand for any sideshows on this serious matter. If any special interests try to block this measure or delay it in any way, I am prepared to fight them to the last ditch of my executive authority."[2] After hesitating long enough to get advice from Matt Sullivan, he called the referendum for December. The *Sacramento Union*, lately a bitter Rolph critic, called the decision very brave and the project the "greatest monument that any governor has built to the memory of his administration."[3]

Though scheduling the referendum was an important step, most prognosticators felt that strong opposition from the power companies and the indifference of people—especially in southern California—who perceived no benefit from the water plan guaranteed its defeat at the polls. Still, supporters took heart when they saw Senator Inman and Rolph putting their shoulders to the wheel together and planning a massive voter education effort. "I'll certainly never allow personalities to interfere with the public interest," the governor promised.[4] For his part, Inman sprang to Rolph's defense when a critic charged that Rolph's interest in the project was purely political. "I oppose the Rolph administration too, but [he] is entitled to the appreciation of the state for refusing to bow to the power monopoly."[5]

During the referendum campaign, Inman worked tirelessly on behalf of the water plan, and Rolph chipped in at critical times with strongly supportive public remarks. The governor was preoccupied with the San Jose kidnapping case for about two weeks, but he appeared in Los Angeles on December 16 to assail the power companies and to tell voters that the water program was actually a life-and-death matter.[6] "Here is a remedy made to order for recovery," he said the next day, "and all you people have to do is to go to the polls ... and vote yes."[7]

In his enthusiasm for the cause of ratification, Rolph again revealed his inability to grasp the concept—or the value—of an apolitical civil service. He believed that all state employees were obliged to support the water plan; anyone who did not was a traitor and "ought to resign and work for

Surrounded by usually hostile legislators, Rolph signs the landmark Central Valley water bill — his greatest administrative accomplishment — in late 1933. It brought him and his most implacable opponent, Senator John Inman, second from left standing, into a temporary alliance against the state's utility companies (courtesy of the California History Room, California State Library, Sacramento, California).

the people who pay him."[8] Many of the plan's supporters feared that opponents would seize on Rolph's comments to prove that the support of civil servants was being improperly coerced.

Inman, Rolph and others were unable to convince many people in southern California, or in the San Francisco area, that the water plan was in their interest, but skeptics did not come to the polls in sufficient numbers to defeat it. The referendum took place six days before Christmas, and only 34 percent of eligible voters cast ballots. To the amazement of its supporters, the project was approved by 20,000 votes. The *Union* called it "one of the greatest victories the people of this state have ever attained" — one gained over "almost invulnerable opposition."[9] The narrowness of the victory margin meant that the joint efforts of Rolph and Inman had been crucial to success. Even at this point, the final success of the Central Valley Project was not assured, and many years were still to elapse before it became a reality, but Rolph's efforts meant that it was safely on its way.

In the fight for the Central Valley Project, Rolph looked, sounded, and acted like a leader and a visionary. He applied steady pressure over a long period of time, he found common cause with political enemies, he lobbied successfully for federal aid, and he saw years before most of his contemporaries that the need for water would become critical to the state's future development. Why was he able to attain this singular success when so many of his other efforts resulted in failure? The best explanation is that he strongly believed in — and had considerable experience with — large public projects. The financial crisis may have overwhelmed him, as it did many other politicians of the era. But his San Francisco days had taught him how to build.

30

1934 — Recovery and Ruin

Though the water plan's success had given Rolph some positive publicity as the year came to an end, his advisors worried greatly about the public's continuing belief that the governor was somehow responsible for the sales tax. Two of their primary goals were to stop "a penny for Jimmy" from becoming a deadly campaign slogan for some opponent and to convince voters that the Depression — not Rolph's extravagance — had wrecked the state's finances. To their horror, the popular *Saturday Evening Post* carried an article about "Jimmy and his pennies" in September.

Still, Rolph and his advisors continued to work behind the scenes on a campaign strategy. The governor planned to increase his travel schedule — to accept all invitations that promised a good crowd. He would hammer home the message that he had tried to balance the budget but the legislature would not let him. He would point out that he had provided unemployment relief, overseen the passage of the Central Valley Water Plan, saved state employees from a salary cut at the hands of the legislature, and put a heart into government. And he would, of course, rely on the personal charm that had gotten him where he was — appealing to people who "can't understand deficits but enjoy a good handshake with the governor."[1]

Rolph could also depend on the smoothly running political machine that had served him so well in previous contests. He had made a point, at some risk to his credibility, of rewarding loyalists with important jobs. Now he would call in his chits. About this, he had no hesitancy. One Robert W. Kenny, whom Rolph appointed to a municipal court judge vacancy in 1931, found that his responsibilities included assisting in the governor's campaign. A letter to Kenny from a Rolph assistant in early 1934 expressed appreciation for "all the fine effort you are putting forth in support of his candidacy for reelection this year" and asking Kenny to drop a line to the campaign's San Francisco office describing "conditions ... in and around L.A."[2]

Rolph uses a boot jack. Attired in custom-made leather boots — he was said to own over 40 pairs — and with a fresh flower in his lapel, the governor hit the road in February 1934 to talk things over with the people (courtesy of the California History Room, California State Library, Sacramento, California).

The wild card was Rolph's health. He did not seem to be recovering quickly from his recent illness, and people suspected that he was still a sick man. Publicly, he said: "There's nothing the matter with my health that would prevent me from running,"[3] and as Thanksgiving 1933 came and went, he had every intention of doing so. On December 30, he narrowly escaped serious injury when his car skidded and crashed on the ferry landing in San Francisco. Though he had bruises on his chest and legs, he was eating a hearty meal an hour later. The incident seemed to highlight his resilience rather than his vulnerability.

On January 5, Rolph told the media that he would travel during the spring to talk things over with the people.[4] Though he had not yet decided to commit himself to the race, the announcement reflected a new sense of optimism among the governor and his aides that an economic upturn would make 1934 a good year in which to run. The state finance department reported that revenues from the hated sales tax were surpassing earlier expectations and might swallow the deficit all by themselves. Publicly, Rolph said: "We have had trying times—at last daylight is breaking through."[5]

Rolph continued to link himself in every way possible with the national administration's economic program, predicting that 1934 would be "the year in which recovery and Roosevelt will be written in synonymous terms."[6] In mid–January, as the president's birthday approached, he helped to organize a local celebration that he hoped would be "the greatest event in the history of Sacramento." Pointing to Roosevelt's battle with infantile paralysis, Rolph asserted that "his recovery ... is responsible in no small part for our recovery."[7]

Identifying with Roosevelt showed how skillfully Rolph sized up the state's political landscape. In the current national emergency, Americans were rallying behind the president's attempts to fashion effective recovery measures; critical reaction to his experimental and scattershot approach had not yet set in. Though no prominent Democrat had yet declared for governor in 1934, Rolph sought to prevent any eventual rival from portraying him as out of tune with Washington.

In fact, Roosevelt's disregard of the growing federal budget deficit enabled Rolph to argue that he, too, had rightly put jobs and recovery ahead of financial discipline. His use of the 1931 state surplus for public works— for which he was still being criticized—could be justified retroactively as beating the federal government to the punch. The *Sacramento Union* recognized the Rolph strategy but considered it flawed: "What did we get for all the money spent?" it asked.[8]

In early February, Lieutenant Governor Merriam and left-leaning attorney Sheridan Downey officially declared their candidacies for governor. Asked by the press what he thought of Merriam's announcement, Rolph replied: "Just say the governor smiled."⁹ A few days later, former governor C.C. Young likewise entered the race, but he was not given much of a chance. As the *Union* pointed out, Young had "lost many a vote by failing to smile at the right moment."¹⁰ The leaders of both major parties conceded that Rolph's well-oiled campaign machinery gave him the early lead and that, if he won the primary, only a reasonably popular Democrat—nowhere on the horizon—could beat him in the general election.¹¹

A day or two after Merriam and Downey entered the race, Rolph called in one of his aides at midnight and said: "I've decided to go. Tell everybody to get ready."¹² He designated February 9 as the beginning of a six-week tour of the state, accompanied by several leading officials of his administration. "This won't be a political trip," he said publicly. Its purpose would be to "make an accounting to my fellow Californians of what I've done as governor." In once again visiting every county, he intended to use planes, trains, automobiles, "and roller skates if necessary."¹³

The long schedule of towns to be visited sounded to the *Union* like a "train caller's endurance contest." Many reporters worried that the governor was taking a big risk with his health by making such ambitious plans. Behind the scenes, Matt Sullivan and Theodore Roche were said to oppose the trip. But Rolph hit the road again, covering 300 miles and making 10 speeches on the first day alone.

During the first couple of weeks, he showed the indomitable energy that was his trademark.¹⁴ He began the trip in the Central Valley town of Fresno and was given a friendly reception in gratitude for his strong support of the state water plan. After a swing through southern California, he stopped in San Luis Obispo, where he made an evening address. He showed some signs of weariness when it was over and had to be helped to his room, but he was the first one to rise in the morning and rousted everyone else out of bed. Continuing north to King City, he visited the high school, but finding that the students were in an assembly, he wrote on the blackboard: "I came to visit you but you weren't here. Please give my love to your mamas and your papas and your teacher."¹⁵

By this time, Rolph was approaching the limits of his endurance. In Santa Cruz, his daughter Annette expressed concern about his "manifest fatigue" and urged him to rest, but he said no.¹⁶ The next day, he collapsed, but after a short nap in the car, he was ready to go again. On February 24, as the governor stopped briefly in San Francisco (on what turned out to be his last public appearance there), reporters, who were oblivious to his worsening condition, exclaimed that he had worn out the corps of officials accompanying him. The next day, Rolph departed from his schedule and rose three hours earlier than planned so he could visit a condemned prisoner at San Quentin.

Rolph was buoyed by the warmth of the crowds in Napa and Sonoma on the 27th. He moved on toward Marysville that day, making 16 stops and as many addresses. He took a detour during the afternoon to call on his 90-year-old aunt and caught a chill standing in the rain without his hat. He spoke at Marysville that night and attended an American Legion dance, but he had no lunch or dinner, and it was midnight before he sat down to a meal of mushrooms and minced chicken. The next morning, while packing his suitcase, he collapsed again.[17]

Rolph was driven immediately to San Francisco. There, on March 1, doctors announced that he had been confined indefinitely to St. Francis hospital, suffering from mild congestion of the lungs and a marked gastrointestinal disturbance.[18] Over the next several days, however, Rolph seemed to improve and grow restless, at one point asking nurses for his pants and some oysters. But his doctor signaled that this was no temporary indisposition, warning that the governor needed many more weeks of complete rest.

When Rolph was finally released on April 1, he did not return to Sacramento but instead went to stay at the ranch of a close friend, Walter Linforth, near Santa Clara, where he remained in seclusion. After a time, against his doctors' orders, he arose from his bed, drove to his suite of offices in San Francisco, signed papers, and made upbeat remarks. But rumors began to circulate that he had suffered a stroke. On May 2, as he was signing college diplomas, he suffered yet another relapse and was returned to the hospital.

Rolph held a final press conference in May. It was clear to the newsmen covering the event that the governor had in fact had a stroke. His hand hung limp and swollen at his side, his speech was slightly slurred, and he tried to conceal a partially paralyzed left leg by dragging it into place. Despite his obvious distress, he was courteous and cheerful — a performance one reporter described as "darn plucky." The press corps got together afterward and agreed not to make his condition public.

A few days after the press conference, Rolph issued a statement saying he would not seek reelection. "Twenty-three years of public service ... have left me broken in both health and fortune. The loss of fortune has not troubled me greatly or held me back. But without sound health, I could not undertake the strenuous activities of a campaign or four more years of the intense labors and anxieties of the governorship."[19] A day after making the announcement, he was back at his desk in the San Francisco Civic Center, but this burst of energy was only temporary.

30. 1934—Recovery and Ruin

Rolph spent his final days at the Linforth ranch. His family made him as comfortable as possible. One day, Annie, son Jimmy, and Tim Reardon drove him to his own ranch and showed him the home they had prepared for his retirement. A few days after that happy trip, he fell into a coma, but he revived on May 31 and asked an aide to find out the expiration date of a reprieve he had given a convicted murderer. On June 2, he died. Fittingly, he was taken to San Francisco, where he lay in state under the rotunda of the civic center he had built over 20 years before.

Reports differed on the exact cause of his death. The *Chronicle* wrote that, according to his doctors, the governor had died of progressive cardiovascular disease with a terminal pneumonia.[20] The *Union*, by contrast, gave the official version — heart attack and lung congestion complicated by kidney trouble, high blood pressure, gastrointestinal disturbances, and complete physical exhaustion.[21] These were serious and probably insurmountable medical problems, but Rolph had complicated the task of his own recovery by steadfastly refusing to get the rest his doctors said he needed.

31

A Final Accounting

At the outset, we observed that historians have judged Rolph a misfit and an anachronism, a man whose time had passed, a man without the brains or the courage to make hard choices. Lieutenant Governor Merriam, in his eulogy, found a nicer way to say much the same thing—Rolph "represented the old school—not the hustle-bustle citizen of today but the old native citizen of romance and filled with love for his fellow men."[1]

All these characterizations contain elements of truth. Every politician whose worldview was formed during the less complicated and more prosperous 1910s and 1920s was out of his time in the 1930s. Rolph was one of the many leaders of the era who could not see or adapt to the fundamental changes taking place. President Roosevelt was helped to understand the new economic environment by a brain trust of brilliant thinkers. By contrast, Rolph drew upon friends who were as intellectually limited as he was. At great cost, he clung instead to his view of the politician as cheerleader and symbol. When it came to political campaigns, however, he was surprisingly modern. He embraced the revolutions in communications and transportation and was quick to see their potential in courting votes.

It is true that the governor did not have a wide-ranging intellect. In fact, his appeal to the public was partly based on the perception that he was an ordinary man placed in extraordinary circumstances. But neither was he deficient in brain power, despite his limited education. His success in business and politics required an ability to strategize and to outmaneuver his rivals. Many of his speeches were models of precision and perceptiveness, if not eloquence. He certainly relied more on his gut than his brain, but that was a reflection of his values and personality rather than an inability to think things through.

Rolph showed throughout his life in business and politics that he had courage. As a shipping executive, he accepted the need to take great financial risks in order to make substantial profits. As mayor and governor, he went his own way on many issues—for example, the San Francisco municipal railway and the Central Valley water project — at the cost of alienating powerful people. He was not afraid to publicly confront prominent state senators who were opposed to his programs. His aides remarked upon his physical courage, which he demonstrated by flying without hesitation in all kinds of weather.

But his courage had limits. He had an acute sense of realism and well-honed political survival skills, which caused him to stop short of offending a few powerful people who could help him stay in office. He compromised on many issues rather than make enemies of men like William Randolph Hearst and Herbert Fleishhacker.

A better explanation for Rolph's lack of political effectiveness is that he simply did not take hold as governor. He lacked the will to do what had to be done. Rather than seeking ideas from the many policy experts in Sacramento, it was easier to fall back on familiar sources of advice. Rather than trying to understand the details of tax policy or reapportionment, it was easier to hit the road and seek the human connections that made his life worth living. His disengagement may have reflected some lack of confidence. Perhaps he felt at a disadvantage in a strange and unfamiliar policy arena, or was intimidated by legislators and bureaucrats who had been working on state issues for many years.

Things might have been different if Rolph had taken office with a set of detailed policy goals. But he had never been a student of state government and had no clear idea what he wanted to do. He was left with a program based primarily on instinct and limited experience. First and foremost, he would put a human face on state government. Second, he would support the kind of large-scale public projects with which he had become identified as mayor. And third, he would follow through on his one firm campaign pledge — to spend down some of the budget surplus to stimulate the economy. But these limited objectives did not constitute an agenda.

The failure to take hold was tellingly illustrated in an anecdote passed down by one Louis Heilbron, who had represented the state government in discussions in Washington about possible relief measures. Heilbron found himself attending a conference in Rolph's office in 1933 that included state officials, cabinet officers and community leaders. While the discussion was going on, Rolph "called most of his friends from San Francisco to ask them what he should do with respect to these monies [relief funds] which he anticipated coming in from the Federal Government." Two conversations were going on in the room, he continued — one by Rolph over the phone and one by the others in the room "to determine what was actually to be achieved."

Attempting to draw Rolph back into the general discussion, his personal attorney said: "Now, Governor, would you just pay attention for a few moments" and motioned for Heilbron to explain federal relief requirements to him. Later, the conversation turned to the question of who might head a new relief agency. As soon as a consensus emerged, Rolph said: "Well, if that's the best man, I'll call him," and he immediately did so.[2]

Though unwarranted conclusions should not be drawn from such fragmentary evidence, the story appears to show a governor who was easily handled and who brought little of his own thinking into policy debates. We see him relying on old cronies for advice, even as he sits in a room containing the real experts on the subject at hand. And we hear in the words of his attorney a slightly impatient and patronizing tone, which suggests that, even three years into his term, Rolph still needed basic tutorials in order to understand and act upon the issues facing him. On the other hand, this glimpse shows that Rolph welcomed, and even encouraged, the expression of many points of view. Many public officials are headstrong and ignore good advice. Rolph was humble enough to realize that he did not have all the answers.

And he was confident enough of his executive skills to be able to chair large meetings and handle the inevitable dissent. For example, Rolph once invited a large, disparate group of people to a potentially rancorous meeting on the Central Valley water project. When one attendee said he had a minority view, Rolph said: "Oh, you come right up to the platform, we shall be glad to hear you; get up and tell us what you think." The speaker came away impressed with this demonstration of inclusiveness, calling Rolph a very fine person and one who understood public relations better than any previous governor.[3]

Rolph's lack of engagement with the issues and with people who could help him raises the question of how badly he wanted to be governor in the first place. He made the decision to run in 1929, when his personal finances were at a low ebb. He was not only broke, but deeply in debt. His options seemed limited. The prospect of a sixth term as mayor did not fill him with enthusiasm. He could return to the business world, but that course carried considerable risk. He had just turned 60. In October the stock market had collapsed. Leaving public service would mean starting from scratch during an economic downturn at an advanced age.

Becoming governor may have seemed the best way to continue the kind of life he enjoyed, to fulfill his obligations to his family, and to make contacts that could be financially useful to him in retirement. Rolph's decision to seek reelection in 1934 following a term of nearly constant disappointments may have been determined by the same grim realities—a need for a high income and a lack of attractive alternatives.

Though absence of political will was key, other problems contributed to Rolph's lack of success. He brought a limited mayoral perspective to the vastly different task of running California. Unlike San Francisco, which was concrete and palpable, California was an abstraction — "not an opening, parade or dedication, but a map on the wall, a series of densely worded bills piled high each morning."[4] Rolph was good at handling issues that had a human dimension, but he had little appetite for policy nuances. When asked to compare his current job with his previous one, he sighed and said that being mayor was "like being the head of a great family where you get to know everyone."[5] He could not get to know every Californian, though he certainly tried.

Some of Rolph's missteps were due to his inability to transfer his highly personal governing style to Sacramento. He had always preferred to work through a small circle of intimates — loyal men in whom he had complete trust. When he moved to the capital in January 1931 he left behind the staff that had served him so well and on whom he had come to depend. Most of these people decided to stay in San Francisco, where salaries were higher and they could be near friends and family. Others, like Theodore Roche and Ed Rainey, did take posts in the capital, but Rolph chose to appoint them to full-time administrative jobs with high salaries rather than keep them in the executive mansion as staff advisors.

Early in his tenure, Rolph was surrounded by strangers or holdovers from the Young administration. According to his private secretary, the governor at first did not even know how to use the phone. In this unfamiliar environment, with new and untested assistants, he tried to handle too many petty details himself. His staff often failed him. For example, he could have been spared embarrassment in the Ebright affair (see page 107) if he had not been misinformed about when Ebright's term ended. This kind of error would not have happened, said Rolph's personal secretary, David Taylor, if the vigilant and politically wise Rainey had been on the job.[6]

Rolph also lacked a good press secretary — someone who would protect him from the media, as had been done in San Francisco, and would see that positive articles came out to balance the negative ones. The result was an abundance of stories that focused on nonsubstantive matters, such as his love of ceremony and his practice of sending whiskey to condemned prisoners. The six-day holiday episode in 1931 (see pages 117–118) seemed the best example of a botched press operation, in which his half-serious musings were translated by staff into a policy pronouncement.

Being weak on policy details and having few fixed goals for his governorship, he also needed people who were skilled in translating his general ideas and beliefs into specific, achievable legislation that would make sense to sympathetic lawmakers. But he did not believe he could trust the people in Sacramento who knew policy. So he spent his weekends in San Francisco conferring with members of his kitchen cabinet and other old friends, who may have known less about state issues than he did. And he appointed loyalists, rather than experts, to high state offices.

Rolph came to the governorship at a time when the importance of a career civil service, untainted by political considerations, was becoming recognized. Though as mayor he had paid lip service to the concept, he was never able to let go of the idea that everyone who worked for the state owed personal allegiance to the man at the top. A certain amount of spoils to loyalists was tolerated during normal times, but as a merit-based bureaucracy promised a more efficient and professional state government, the governor was increasingly seen by other political players as working against the public good. He made his attitude crystal clear when he said: "If there isn't a Rolph man qualified for the job, then I'm in favor of abolishing the job."[7]

Rolph's disastrous relations with the state legislature clearly undermined his chances for success. Greater assertiveness might have earned him more respect. "When the iron hand is needed," wrote one journalist about the governor, "the velvet glove will not do."[8] But Rolph used neither the iron hand nor the velvet glove. Instead, he fired broadsides at the lawmakers that accomplished little beyond stirring up more enmity. It irritated him that they had the temerity to criticize him and the independence to get away with it. In a fit of pique, he once said: "I have no use for the Senate."

This legislature and this governor, in any event, were like oil and water. The culture of Sacramento was dignified, substantive, and formal, and it valued process as well as outcome. Rolph was unorthodox. He made up the rules as he went along. He once paid an unscheduled and highly irregular visit to the Assembly gallery, mingling with the tourists and other observers of the legislative process. Arising from his seat, he astonished the speaker by announcing that he had a special guest with him. He then introduced banker Herbert Fleishhacker, who was incongruously attired in a dinner jacket.[9] Rolph's spontaneity was well intentioned, but the lawmakers found the appearance of the governor and his major financier awkward and undignified.

To many of the legislators, Rolph was simply not a serious person. Somehow he had managed to beat C.C. Young, a very serious person, a student of state government, a man who played by the rules and knew how the system worked. Now Rolph and his San Francisco mafia were in charge. If he were to have any chance of gaining a measure of acceptance, he would have to earn their respect. But the members of the legislature may have seemed to the new governor like so many stuffed shirts. He had teased Senator Inman once by suggesting that he should get away and have a few laughs. By and large, these were not men he would enjoy hunting with or meeting after work for a drink. Of course, his open hostility was a tactical error. Warring with the lawmakers, said state Senator Arthur Breed, "is not a smart thing to do. Get along with them whether you like them or not."[10]

It is ironic that one of the most energetic men ever to hold the governorship should have spent so little time on the traditional duties of the office. His vacations and tours of the state were not scheduled around state business but the other way around; in fact, they often seemed a convenient pretext for escaping the capital when the pressure mounted. His propensity to appoint commissions to study problems while he pursued inconsequential tasks reinforced the impression that he was a figurehead leader. It also encouraged legislators and others to go around the governor when they wanted to get something done — as during the search for a revenue plan in 1933.

For a man who valued tolerance and harmony, Rolph must have found Sacramento appallingly contentious. Pressures built on every side — from office seekers, from labor unions, from the rich and powerful whose help he needed if he wanted to be reelected, from the fractious legislature, from the heads of his own departments, from the utility companies. Sometimes he resisted those pressures and did what he thought was right, but other times political expediency took over and he played to public opinion. Still other situations required the critical and prompt can't-please-'em-all decisions Rolph hated to make.[11]

Rolph's problems in Sacramento could have easily been predicted after a close reading of his personality and record as mayor. Well before he became governor, he was being criticized for reigning without governing. His habit of delegating substantive work to associates and commissions so that he could devote his time to his representational tasks made it unlikely that he would be an activist, policy-minded governor. A man who would rather shed a cheerful light than slay dragons would not thrive in an environment laced with hostility and naked ambition.

Even his fabled compassion was a potential handicap. As early as the 1906 earthquake, Rolph's colleagues in the Mission Relief Association were noticing that his concern for the suffering of individual San Franciscans interfered with his focus on the task at hand. He wanted to rush out and personally console each victim rather than tend to business in his office. Twenty-five years later, Rolph was still choosing to help the person in front of him rather than the hundreds of thousands who waited for him to act.

Two other troubling traits, in evidence many years before he became governor, were his restlessness and his addiction to crowds. The physical need to be in motion and to release his enormous energy made him a poor fit for the sedentary duties of a mayor or governor. His constant appearances before the public displayed his human qualities—his love of people and craving for human contact—but at times seemed compulsive and counterproductive. It was said of Roosevelt that he had a first-class temperament. The same cannot be said of Rolph.

And yet after three years of difficulties, mistakes and setbacks, Rolph had a fighting chance for reelection in 1934. His ability to escape the weight of his poor choices speaks volumes about what American voters look for—and often fail to find—in their candidates for elective office. His charm, high spirits, and simple humanity were not only endearing and attractive, but often were all that mattered to the public. He inspired sympathy when he admitted: "I may make mistakes, but I am trying to do the best I can." It was easy to root for him and to be forgiving when he failed.

His personal style spoke to people on an emotional level. Of the thousands of Californians who showed up for his hundreds of public appearances, the vast majority had never seen a governor face to face. His arrival in their hometowns must have been a special moment. He showed by his actions that he cared about people like them. Perhaps they had read something critical about him, but now he had come all the way to their town, at considerable expense, to share his optimism about the future and to listen to their concerns. Governors had never done that before, and it was bound to make a lasting impression.

When asked what they liked about their governor, a surprising number of people expressed pride that Rolph was so well known around the country. Perhaps it was the state's enduring love of celebrity and admiration for colorful personalities that enhanced his appeal. Like a Hollywood star, Rolph photographed well and had a flair for showmanship, in sharp contrast to the wooden and aloof chief executives of past years.

For Rolph, the true measure of government's effectiveness was the quality of the daily interaction between citizen and elected official. His heavy emphasis on constituent relations meant that even when he was in his office working, he may not have been attending to state business. By April, he was receiving 300 pieces of mail a day, and his staff was under instructions to acknowledge each one. The governor himself was said to devote an hour or two a day to letter writing.[12]

Rolph knew that the affection of the citizens of California counted more than the esteem of legislators or bureaucrats. Most people who followed the news in 1933 and 1934 were tuned into the national drama of Roosevelt's first term rather than the seemingly inconsequential maneuverings of Sacramento politicians. The electorate was changing rapidly as immigrants flocked to the state, which meant that mistakes made two years ago, or even two months ago, were less likely to be remembered when it came time to cast a ballot. The most significant reality that Rolph had somehow to overcome was that governors, like presidents, tend to be well thought of during periods of prosperity and unjustly blamed for hard times.

He also tried to take advantage of those unexpected but critical developments that thrust a chief executive temporarily into the spotlight, forcing him to act and be judged as a leader. Three high-profile issues helped to shape reaction to Jim Rolph and his gubernatorial tenure—the Tom Mooney case, the San Jose kidnapping, and the passage of the unpopular sales tax. All received considerable media attention over an extended period of time.

As we have seen, Rolph's stands on the first two issues resonated positively with the state's sober and conservative middle class, which was frightened of radicalism and horrified about the kidnapping of children as a means of extorting money from frantic parents. His instincts were correct about the impact of the sales tax as well, but he could neither use his veto without seeming irresponsible nor escape his share of the blame for the tax, though he certainly tried.

Without public opinion polls, it is difficult to judge whether Rolph's popularity held up throughout his term or ebbed as criticism of his actions grew. But it seems probable that the people were of two minds about their governor—continuing to view him with affection even as their concerns about his policies mounted. Californians sensed a reservoir of good intentions[13] behind his occasional naïveté and consequently excused his frequent lapses. At the same time, they suspected that the very qualities they admired—for example, his unbounded optimism—were clouding his judgment. Relying on random anecdotal evidence, he would say reassuringly: "You can see a better feeling coming along." His belief in his own words lessened his sense of urgency about the worsening unemployment problem.

Of course, the Depression continued long after Rolph's death. Not until the U.S. entry into World War II seven years later did the country's economy—brought to life by the mighty engine of defense spending—truly begin to recover. Briefly, in 1934, things appeared to brighten somewhat, providing a window of opportunity that might have brought victory to a healthy Rolph in the November election. Instead it brought victory to Frank Merriam, who overcame his lack of charisma to prove that the season of Republican supremacy in California had not yet passed. He bested the noted novelist and socialist Upton Sinclair in a bitter campaign that fall.

Though every year in that tragic decade was dismal, the Rolph years were the most dispiriting. The state's downhill slide began in 1931, and in 1933 the nadir was reached. It was Rolph's exquisite bad luck to have been governor at exactly the wrong time. Like Hoover, he took office to widespread acclaim and public expectation that his personal attributes would match up well with his new responsibilities. But, like the president, he was engulfed by the economic emergency. As the fortunes of both men tumbled, their assets were noticed less than their liabilities.

The uncertainty in Sacramento about how to combat the Depression mirrored the uncertainty in Washington among Hoover and his lieutenants. Like Hoover, Rolph believed that relief was appropriately the job of local government, and, besides, it was easy to grasp at straws and believe that the problem would resolve itself when prosperity returned. Once Roosevelt took office in March 1933, the explosion of governmental creativity that he unleashed made all state governments look slow and cautious. To Rolph's credit, he recognized Roosevelt's genius, and in fact tried to hitch his wagon to the Roosevelt star. His strongly felt identification with ordinary people — as seen in his love of campaigning, his delight in dressing like a workingman, his sympathy for men in prison, his pride in carrying a union card — showed that he might have been more comfortable as a Democrat.

In its obituary of Rolph, the *Sacramento Union*, for all its criticism of the governor over the previous four years, saw him headed toward reelection if he had remained healthy. Now that he was gone, the *Union* predicted, Californians would begin to appreciate the man more. He had gained in popularity in the last several months, and he died without realizing that the crowd had come back to him. His administration was everything but a failure, the paper concluded. He advertised the state far and wide, and he brought many improvements. True, he did not keep people employed, but then what state had? Against economic forces beyond his control, "he tried as hard and did as much for the people as any executive in his position could possibly have done."[14]

In a time when people had little to laugh about, Rolph made them feel better about their plight. Said one historian: "The buoyancy of his disposition and his unorthodox mannerisms seemed to cast a pleasant spell on many."[15] In a tribute to his former boss, longtime crony Ed Rainey recalled that President Wilson had lamented: "I wish the people loved me." Rolph, said Rainey, knew that love.[16] We are left to wonder whether love alone might have been enough to bring him a second term.

A large part of Rolph's appeal was that he had overcome a serious personal setback — the devastation of his finances — without succumbing to bitterness. As John McNab remembered, when Rolph's business career lay in ruins, "he did not quail. With his dreams shattered and his security swept into the flood, he lifted his head with a smile and carried on."[17] Californians may have been attracted to him in part because of his optimism and charisma, but they also knew that the true measure of a man's character is how he reacts to adversity.

Until Rolph's media campaign of 1930, the voters did not have enough information to decide whether they liked a candidate or not. Rolph was the first politician to sell his personality, rather than his resume, to the public. Today, likeability is the subtext whenever Americans step into the voting booth. People still hunger for the qualities that made Rolph so appealing. And politicians have heard the message — that being perceived as ordinary, as "just folks," brings greater electoral success than being seen as a member of the elite.

In the end, the Jim Rolph story is an American tragedy. He never thought of himself as a politician, though he became one of the best politicians of his era. He ran for mayor in order to bring people together and to assist in the development and expansion of the city he loved, but he came to love being mayor more than the job itself. When his fortune collapsed, he rededicated himself to public service but without knowing what he wanted to accomplish beyond winning the next election. His governorship, instead of being the culmination of a wildly successful career, exposed his flaws and came close to crushing his spirit.

It is accurate to say, as many historians have, that the Rolph administration failed to show political leadership and imagination in dealing with the Depression. But it is less clear how much the welfare of ordinary people could have been improved even by a creative and vigorous governor. Under the adverse conditions Rolph faced, failure was hardly a disgrace.

Besides, he would have argued, and most Californians would have agreed, that he succeeded on his own terms. As fortunes and livelihoods disappeared in a crisis that cast doubt on the success of the entire national experiment in democracy and capitalism, one man brought a message of hope, cheer, and reassurance to every corner of the state. Who can doubt that a moment of exposure to Sunny Jim's ebullient personality made facing the next day easier?

Chapter Notes

Preface

1. Will Irwin, quoted in T.H. Watkins and R.R. Olmsted, *Mirror of the Dream: An Illustrated History of San Francisco* (San Francisco: Scrimshaw Press, 1976), p. 151.
2. *The Memoirs of Ray Lyman Wilbur*, Stanford University, 1960, p. 395.
3. Cited in Merritt S. Barnes, "James Rolph, Jr.: Master of the Political Winds," *The American West* 15, no. 6 (November-December 1978): 13.
4. Paul Smith, quoted in Kevin Starr, *Endangered Dreams: The Great Depression in California* (New York, Oxford University Press, 1996), p. 149.
5. Duncan Aikman, "California's Sun God," *The Nation*, January 14, 1931, p. 35.
6. Barnes, "Master of the Political Winds," p. 8.
7. Berkeley, 1936.
8. Jerry Flamm, *Hometown San Francisco: Sunny Jim, Phat Willie, and Dave* (San Francisco: Scottwall, 1994).
9. "California During the Early 1930s: The Administration of James Rolph, Jr., 1931–1934," *Southern California Quarterly* 63, no. 3 (1981), pp. 262–282.

Introduction

1. *San Francisco Chronicle*, June 4, 1934.
2. *San Francisco Chronicle*, June 8, 1934.
3. *Sacramento Union*, June 3, 1934.
4. *San Francisco Chronicle*, June 3, 1934.
5. Quoted in John B. McGloin, *San Francisco: The Story of a City* (San Francisco: Presidio Press, 1978), p. 301.
6. Harry Farrell, *Swift Justice: Murder and Vengeance in a California Town* (New York: St. Martin's Press, 1992), p. 17.
7. Flamm, *Hometown San Francisco*, p. 3.
8. Watkins and Olmsted, *Mirror of the Dream*, p. 213.
9. Sally Stanford, *The Lady of the House* (New York: Putnam, 1966), p. 76.
10. Harry Carr, "California's Whoopee Governor," *Los Angeles Times Sunday Magazine*, March 22, 1933, p. 4.
11. Herbert L. Phillips, *Big Wayward Girl: An Informal Political History of California* (Garden City, NY: Doubleday, 1968), p. 59.
12. David Wooster Taylor, *The Life of James Rolph, Jr.* (San Francisco: Committee for Publication of the Life of James Rolph, Jr., 1934), p. 83.
13. Flamm, *Hometown San Francisco*, p. 2.
14. Tom Bellew, "James Rolph, Jr.," *San Francisco Chronicle*, June 26, 1934.
15. Flamm, *Hometown San Francisco*, p. 2.
16. Elenore Meherin, "Life of Jim Rolph," San Francisco *Call-Bulletin*, January 16, 1931.
17. Theodore Bonnet, *San Francisco Chronicle*, June 3, 1934.
18. Moses Rischin, "Sunny Jim Rolph: The First 'Mayor of All the People,'" *California Historical Society Quarterly*, Summer 1974, p. 165.
19. Tom Bellew, *San Francisco Chronicle*, June 20, 1934.
20. Carr, "California's Whoopee Governor," p. 4.
21. Sidney H. Kessler, "Mayor Jimmy Rolph: An Institution," *Sunset*, June 1928, p. 54.
22. Rischin, "Sunny Jim Rolph," p. 170.
23. Earl Behrens in the *San Francisco Chronicle*, June 3, 1934.
24. Flamm, *Hometown San Francisco*, p. 53.
25. Bonnet, *San Francisco Chronicle*, June 3, 1934.
26. Aikman, "California's Sun God," p. 35.
27. It now stands in the foyer of the home of Rolph's granddaughter, Nancy Rolph Welch, in Emerald Hills, California.
28. Barnes, "Master of the Political Winds," p. 8.
29. Herman G. Goldbeck, *The Political*

Career of James Rolph, Jr.: A Preliminary Study, master's thesis, University of California at Berkeley, 1936, p. 160.
30. Barnes, "Master of the Political Winds," p. 9.
31. Carol Hicke, *The 1911 Campaign of James Rolph, Jr., Mayor of All the People*, Master's thesis, San Francisco State University, June 1978, p. 25.
32. Meherin, San Francisco *Call Bulletin*, January 6, 1931.
33. Henry Miles Muheim, "My Life with the Lone Eagle," *American Heritage* 48 (May-June 1997), p. 84.
34. Rischin, "Sunny Jim Rolph," p. 170.
35. Hicke, p. 26. On rare occasions, his assiduous courtship of the entire electorate led to mistakes. One evening, crisscrossing the city to attend a series of meetings had left him near exhaustion when he arrived at his final appearance shortly after midnight. Addressing a neighborhood improvement club, he began: "Revered clergy and brother masons." Staffers whispered urgently in his ear, but he just kept right on talking as though nothing was amiss. (Earl "Squire" Behrens, *Inside California: A Reporter's Journal*, edited by William R. Gruer, unpublished manuscript, California Historical Society, San Francisco, p. 23.)

Chapter 1

1. Meherin, San Francisco *Call Bulletin*, December 24, 1930.
2. Meherin, San Francisco *Call Bulletin*, December 26, 1930.
3. Meherin, San Francisco *Call Bulletin*, December 20, 1930.
4. Taylor, *The Life of James Rolph, Jr.*, p. 33.
5. Details from Taylor, pp. 34–35.
6. Bellew, *San Francisco Chronicle*, June 6, 1934.
7. *Ibid*.
8. Rischin, "Mayor of All the People," p. 169.
9. Meherin, San Francisco *Call-Bulletin*, December 29, 1930.

Chapter 2

1. B.E. Lloyd, quoted in Watkins and Olmsted, *Mirror of the Dream*, p. 170.
2. Robert Glass Cleland, *California in Our Time (1900–1940)* (New York: Knopf, 1947), p. 11.
3. Bellew, *San Francisco Chronicle*, June 6, 1934.
4. Cleland, *California in Our Time*, p. 119.
5. Kessler, "Mayor Jimmy Rolph: An Institution," p. 18.
6. Meherin, San Francisco *Call-Bulletin*, December 31, 1930.
7. Meherin, San Francisco *Call-Bulletin*, January 2, 1931.
8. *Ibid*.
9. Robert Edward Lee Knight, *Industrial Relations in the San Francisco Bay Area, 1900–1918*, Berkeley, University of California Press, 1960, p. 89.
10. Meherin, San Francisco *Call-Bulletin*, January 7, 1930.
11. *San Francisco Call*, June 9–10, 1909; Bellew, *San Francisco Chronicle*, June 9, 1934. Rolph's partner, George Hind, was also opposed to his running for mayor because, Hind said, the firm needed him.
12. Meherin, January 5, 1930.
13. *San Francisco Chronicle*, October 23, 1909.
14. Hicke, *The 1911 Campaign of James Rolph, Jr.*, p. 16.
15. Cleland, *California in Our Time*, p. 12.
16. Meherin, San Francisco *Call-Bulletin*, January 6, 1930.
17. *Ibid*.
18. Hicke, *The 1911 Campaign of James Rolph, Jr.*, pp. 21, 25.
19. Hicke, p. 26.
20. Hicke, p. 78.
21. Meherin, San Francisco *Call-Bulletin*, January 6, 1930.
22. Goldbeck, *The Political Career of James Rolph, Jr.*, p. 12.
23. Meherin, San Francisco *Call-Bulletin*, January 7, 1930.
24. *San Francisco Examiner*, September 22, 1911.
25. According to one interpretation, labor was foolish to back Rolph. The candidate promoted an unrealistic vision of harmony between capital and labor, thus making workers forget that they had economic interests apart from those of their employers. "By embracing [Rolph], labor blurred the political lines and diluted the program that made it an alternative force to be reckoned with." Mary Ann Mason, "Neither Friends Nor Foes: Organized Labor and the California Progressives," in William Deverell and Tom Sitton, eds., *California Progressivism Revisited* (Berkeley, University of California Press, 1994), p. 59.

Chapter 3

1. Phillips, *Big Wayward Girl*, p. 62.
2. William M. Hines, "Our American Mayors: James Rolph, Jr., of San Francisco," *National Municipal Review* 18 (March 1929): p. 164.
3. Quoted in Mansel G. Blackford, *The Lost Dream: Businessmen and City Planning on the Pacific Coast, 1890–1920* (Columbus: Ohio State University Press, 1993), p. 59.
4. Segal, "James Rolph, Jr., and the Early Days of the San Francisco Railway," p. 16.

5. *Ibid.*
6. William Issel and Robert W. Cherny, *San Francisco, 1965–1932: Politics, Power and Urban Development* (Berkeley: University of California Press), 1986, p. 166.
7. Sister Clementia Marie Fisher, *James Rolph, Jr., 1869–1934: An Estimate of His Influence on San Francisco's History*, master's thesis, University of San Francisco, June 1965, p. 89.
8. Roger W. Lotchin, "John Francis Neylan: San Francisco Irish Progressive," in *The San Francisco Irish: 1850–1976*, James P. Walsh, ed., unpublished manuscript, Bancroft Library, Berkeley, California, 1978, p. 4.
9. Bellew, *San Francisco Chronicle*, June 16, 1934.
10. Hopkins, "The Man Who Keeps Mooney in Jail," p. 346.
11. Florence Holub in *The Noe Valley Voice*, April 1998.
12. Herbert Asbury, *The Barbary Coast: An Informal History of the San Francisco Underworld* (Garden City, NY: Garden City Publishing, 1933), p. 299.
13. *Ibid.*, p. 258
14. Gray Brechin, "Sailing to Byzantium: The Architecture of the Pan Pacific International Exposition," *California History*, Summer 1983, p. 117.
15. Paul C. Edwards, "The Rise and Decline of Jim Rolph," *San Francisco News*, August 9, 1933.
16. Bellew, *San Francisco Chronicle*, June 18, 1934.
17. *San Francisco Chronicle*, April 10, 1915.
18. Meherin, December 17, 1930.
19. Goldbeck, *The Political Career of James Rolph, Jr.*, p. 46.
20. Meherin, January 14, 1931.
21. Meherin, San Francisco *Call-Bulletin*, January 14, 1931.

Chapter 4

1. Quoted in McGloin, *San Francisco: The Story of a City*, p. 299.
2. See Curt Gentry, *Frame-up: The Incredible Case of Tom Mooney and Warren Billings* (New York: Norton, 1967), p. 361.
3. Flamm, *Hometown San Francisco*, p. 9.
4. Lotchin, "John Francis Neylan," p. 5.
5. Flamm, *Hometown San Francisco*, p. 38.
6. Contained in the James Rolph, Jr., papers, California Historical Society, San Francisco, note dated September 11, 1914.
7. Taylor, *The Life of James Rolph, Jr.*, p. 28.
8. Nancy Rolph Welch, the governor's granddaughter, disagrees with this assessment. She remembers being told by family members that he was "always around."

Chapter 5

1. Roger W. Lotchin, "The Darwinian City: The Politics of Urbanization Between the World Wars," *Pacific Historical Review* 48 (August 1979): 357–365.
2. Starr, *Endangered Dreams*, p. 288.
3. Knight, *Industrial Relations in the San Francisco Bay Area*, p. 321.
4. Barnes, "Master of the Political Winds," p. 9.
5. San Francisco *Labor Clarion*, November 23, 1917.
6. Tom Bellew, *San Francisco Chronicle*, June 23, 1934.
7. Meherin, San Francisco *Call-Bulletin*, January 16, 1931.
8. Bellew, *San Francisco Chronicle*, June 26, 1934.

Chapter 6

1. Unlabeled newspaper article in the Nancy Rolph Welch collection.
2. Details from Nancy Lund in the *Almanac*, February 11, 1998.
3. *San Francisco Examiner*, June 3, 1934.
4. Bellew, *San Francisco Chronicle*, June 17, 1934.
5. Rolph was unusual among shipowners in allowing his captains to take their wives on sea voyages. (Bellew, *San Francisco Chronicle*, June 23, 1934.)
6. Bellew, *San Francisco Chronicle*, June 22, 1934.
7. Cited in Flamm, *Hometown San Francisco*, p. 19.
8. Bellew, *San Francisco Chronicle*, June 22, 1934.
9. Flamm, *Hometown San Francisco*, p. 22.

Chapter 7

1. See H. Brett Melendy, "California's Cross-filing Nightmare: The 1918 Gubernatorial Election," *Pacific Historical Review* 33, 1964.
2. "Official log" of the Rolph 1918 campaign for governor, July 15-August 31, 1918, Rolph family files.
3. Bellew, *San Francisco Chronicle*, June 25, 1934.

Chapter 8

1. Meherin, San Francisco *Call-Bulletin*, January 18, 1931.
2. Fisher, *James Rolph, Jr., 1869–1934*, p. 129. Also, Meherin, January 18, 1931.

Chapter 9

1. Goldbeck, *The Political Career of James Rolph, Jr.*, p. 69.
2. All quotes from Barnes, "Master of the Political Winds," pp. 10–11.
3. Carol Hicke, *The 1911 Campaign of James Rolph, Jr.*, p. 49.
4. Francis A. Groff, "The Exposition Mayor," *Sunset Magazine* 28 (January 1912): 68.
5. Aikman, "California's Sun God," p. 36.
6. *Ibid*.
7. Rischin, "Sunny Jim Rolph," p. 172.
8. Hopkins, "The Man Who Keeps Mooney in Jail," p. 346.
9. Issel and Cherny, *Politics, Power and Urban Development*, p. 197.
10. Hopkins, "The Man Who Keeps Mooney in Jail," p. 345.
11. Hicke, *The 1911 Campaign of James Rolph, Jr.*, p. 25.
12. Rischin, "Sunny Jim Rolph," p.172.
13. Kessler, "Mayor Jimmy Rolph," p. 54.
14. Taylor, *The Life of James Rolph, Jr.*, p. 90.
15. Richard H. Frost, *The Mooney Case* (Stanford: Stanford University Press, 1968), p. 403. See also Merritt S. Barnes, "James Rolph, Jr.: Master of the Political Winds," *The American West* 15, no. 6 (November-December 1978): 10.
16. Goldbeck, *The Political Career of James Rolph, Jr.*, p. 123.
17. Edwards, "The Rise and Decline of Jim Rolph," August 10, 1933.
18. Hopkins, "The Man Who Keeps Mooney in Jail," p. 346.

Chapter 10

1. Edwards, *San Francisco News*, August 10, 1933.
2. Starr, *Endangered Dreams*, p. 287.
3. Quoted in Goldbeck, *The Political Career of James Rolph, Jr.*, p. 98.
4. Lotchin, "John Francis Neylan," p. 18.
5. *San Francisco Call and Post*, October 19, 1923.
6. Lotchin, "John Francis Neylan," p. 18.
7. M.M. O'Shaughnessy, *Hetch Hetchy: Its Origin and History* (San Francisco: Recorder, 1934), p. 110.
8. Fisher, *James Rolph, Jr., 1869–1934*, 95–96.
9. Quoted in Goldbeck, *The Political Career of James Rolph, Jr.*, p. 110.

Chapter 11

1. Speech by Matt Sullivan, James Rolph Papers, California Historical Society, San Francisco, 1927.
2. Issel and Cherny, *Politics, Power and Urban Development*, p. 180.
3. *San Francisco Chronicle*, June 3, 1934.
4. Flamm, *Hometown San Francisco*, p. 56.
5. Flamm, *Hometown San Francisco*, p. 29–30.
6. Upton Sinclair, *I, Candidate for Governor, and How I Got Licked* (New York: Farrar and Rinehart, 1935), p. 4.
7. Flamm, *Hometown San Francisco*, p. 50.
8. Barnes, "Master of the Political Winds," p. 12.
9. See, for example, Barnes, p. 12; and Watkins and Olmstead, *Mirror of the Dream*, p. 225.
10. Barnes, p. 12.
11. Flamm, *Hometown San Francisco*, p. 53.
12. Stanford, *The Lady of the House*, p. 78.
13. See Gerald Adams, *San Francisco Examiner*, July 29, 1983; and Flamm, p. 52.
14. Flamm, p. 53.
15. The San Francisco *Evening Post*, "after the 1911 election."
16. Flamm, *Hometown San Francisco*, p. 15–16.
17. Stanford, *The Lady of the House*, p. 79.

Chapter 12

1. Flamm, *Hometown San Francisco*, p. 46.
2. Flamm, p. 1.
3. According to Flamm, Reardon's handpicked candidate for sheriff tried to drop out of the race, believing he had no chance, but Reardon said: "If you do, you won't have a job here." (Flamm, *Hometown San Francisco*, p. 47.)
4. *San Francisco Chronicle*, October 24, 1927.
5. *Ibid.*, October 31, 1927.
6. Cited in Goldbeck, *The Political Career of James Rolph, Jr.*, p. 122, 124.
7. *Ibid.*, p. 116.
8. *San Francisco Chronicle*, November 7, 1927.
9. San Francisco *Call and Bulletin*, October 27, 1927.
10. *San Francisco Chronicle*, November 7, 1927.
11. *Ibid.*, October 24 and November 7, 1927.
12. San Francisco *Call and Bulletin*, October 24, 1927.
13. Cited in Flamm, *Hometown San Francisco*, p. 47.
14. Cited in Goldbeck, *The Political Career of James Rolph, Jr.*, p. 117.
15. *San Francisco Chronicle*, October 31, 1927.
16. Flamm, *Hometown San Francisco*, p. 38.
17. Letter from Irvin Keeler to the Rolph Campaign, September 17, 1927, Rolph papers, California Historical Society, San Francisco.

18. Behrens, *Inside California*, p. 25.
19. Cited in Flamm, *Hometown San Francisco*, p. 47.
20. *San Francisco Chronicle*, October 28, 1927.
21. *Ibid.*
22. *San Francisco Examiner*, November 4, 1927.
23. Lotchin, "John Francis Neylan," p. 24.
24. *San Francisco Examiner*, November 3, 1927.
25. Goldbeck, *The Political Career of James Rolph, Jr.*, p. 122.
26. Hines, "Our American Mayors," p. 166.
27. *San Francisco Chronicle*, November 3, 1927.
28. *Ibid.*, November 7, 1927.
29. *Ibid.*, November 8, 1927.
30. *San Francisco Examiner*, November 10, 1928.
31. James Rolph Papers, 1927 File, California Historical Society, San Francisco.
32. Fisher, *James Rolph, Jr., 1869–1934*, p. 101.
33. A picture taken by Tim Reardon shows a Sunday picnic at the Rolph ranch attended by dozens of public works employees, who were apparently trading their labor for food (Flamm, *Hometown San Francisco*).
34. Account in Flamm, p. 21.

Chapter 13

1. Bellew, *San Francisco Chronicle*, June 28, 1934, p. 11.
2. H. Brett Melendy and Benjamin F. Gilbert, *The Governors of California: Peter H. Burnett to Edmund G. Brown* (Georgetown, CA: Talisman Press, 1965), p. 351.
3. Cited in *ibid.*, p. 351.
4. Phillips, *Big Wayward Girl*, p. 57.
5. *Los Angeles Times*, August 13, 1930.
6. Cited in Goldbeck, *The Political Career of James Rolph, Jr.*, pp. 140–41.
7. Sinclair, *I, Candidate for Governor*, p. 15.
8. *San Francisco Examiner*, July 17, 1930.
9. Goldbeck, *The Political Career of James Rolph, Jr.*, p. 137.
10. *Los Angeles Times*, August 21, 1930.
11. Cited in *ibid.*, August 13, 1930.
12. Goldbeck, *The Political Career of James Rolph, Jr.*, p. 138.
13. Rolph's limousine carried a vase filled with flowers to supply his daily fresh boutonniere. (Flamm, *Hometown San Francisco*, p. 58.)
14. Aikman, "California's Sun God," p. 35.
15. *San Francisco Chronicle*, June 3, 1934.
16. *Ibid.*, August 13, 1930.
17. Flamm, *Hometown San Francisco*, p. 58.
18. Taylor, *Life of James Rolph, Jr.*, p. 100.
19. Flamm, p. 3.
20. *San Francisco Examiner*, August 5, 1930.
21. Letter to Ray Taylor, Rolph Papers, California Historical Society, San Francisco, May 1922.
22. *Beverly Hills Citizen*, June 12, 1930.
23. *San Francisco Examiner*, August 23, 1930.
24. *San Francisco Chronicle*, August 9, 1930.
25. *San Diego Union*, August 28, 1930.
26. Gladwin Hill, *Dancing Bear: An Inside Look at California Politics* (Cleveland: World, 1968), p. 74.
27. *Los Angeles Times*, August 24, 1930.
28. *San Francisco Examiner*, August 12, 1930.
29. *San Francisco Chronicle*, July 29, 1930.
30. *Ibid.*, August 14, 1930.
31. *Ibid.*, September 21, 1930.
32. *San Diego Union*, August 28, 1930.

Chapter 14

1. David M. Kennedy, *Freedom from Fear: The American People in Depression and War* (New York: Oxford University Press, 1999), pp. 56–57.
2. David Nasaw, *The Chief: The Life of William Randolph Hearst* (Boston: Houghton Mifflin, 2000), p. 437.
3. Consistent with his tendency to believe anecdotal evidence from friends rather than reports and statistics, he told the Rotary Club on January 16 that some of his colleagues in the shipping business had noticed an increase in shipping volume of late, which suggested to him that the downturn was coming to an end.
4. Carey McWilliams, *Factories in the Field: The Story of Migratory Farm Labor in California* (Boston: Little, Brown, 1939).
5. Aikman, "California's Sun God," pp. 35, 37.
6. Hearst telegram to Neylan, August 30, 1931.
7. Tom Bellew, *San Francisco Chronicle*, June 28, 1934.
8. *Sacramento Union*, January 8, 1931.
9. Franklin Hichborn, *California Politics, 1891–1939* (Santa Clara, CA: J.R. Haynes Foundation, 1950), p. 2603.
10. Details from Ruth A. Ross and Barbara S. Stone, *California's Political Process* (New York: Random House, 1973), pp. 81–117.
11. *Sacramento Union*, January 7, 1931.
12. *Ibid.*
13. Budget Message to the Assembly, January 12, 1931, *Assembly Journal*, p. 297.
14. *Sacramento Union*, January 7, 1931.
15. *Ibid.*, January 5, 1931.
16. Rolph's meeting with the jobless army, on a cold, windy day, fizzled when only a few workers got in to hear the governor and they did not seem much interested in his remarks (*Sacramento Union*, January 8, 1931).

17. *San Francisco News*, January 27, 1931.
18. *Sacramento Union*, January 13, 1931.

Chapter 15

1. Merrell Farnham Small, "The Office of the Governor Under Earl Warren," Regional Oral History Office, University of California, Berkeley, California, p. 185.
2. *San Francisco News*, February 18, 1931.
3. *Sacramento Union*, February 18, 1931.
4. *Ibid.*, July 17, 1931.
5. *Ibid.*, July 18, 1931.
6. *Ibid.*, October 11, 1931.
7. Helen Valeska Bary, "Labor Administration and Social Security: A Woman's Life," Regional Oral History Office, University of California, Berkeley, California, 1972, pp. 165–66.
8. *Sacramento Union*, February 3, 1931.

Chapter 16

1. *Assembly Journal*, January 23, 1931.
2. Rolph address to Senate, *Senate Journal*, January 23, 1931.
3. *Sacramento Union*, January 6, 1931.
4. Thomas S. Barclay, "Reapportionment in California," *Pacific Historical Review*, June 1936, p. 110.
5. *Ibid.*, p. 104.
6. *Ibid.*, p. 111.
7. *Ibid.*, p. 106.
8. *Sacramento Union*, May 16, 1931.
9. *Ibid.*, May 18, 1931.
10. *Ibid.*, May 20, 1931.
11. Leland Cutler, *America Is Good to a Country Boy* (Stanford, CA: Stanford University Press, 1954), pp. 135–136.
12. *Sacramento Union*, June 20, 1931.

Chapter 17

1. *Sacramento Union*, October 27, 1931.
2. *Ibid.*, March 6, 1931.
3. *Ibid.*, July 12, 1931.
4. *Ibid.*, April 29, 1932.
5. *Ibid.*, August 7, 1931.
6. *Ibid.*, August 9, 1931.
7. State employees, however, were more enthusiastic.
8. *Sacramento Union*, August 10, 1931.
9. *Ibid.*, August 14, 1931.
10. Quoted in *ibid.*, June 21, 1931.

Chapter 18

1. Kennedy, *Freedom from Fear*, p. 85.
2. Loren B. Chan, "California During the Early 1930s: The Administration of James Rolph, Jr., 1931–34," *Southern California Quarterly* 63, no. 3 (1981): 268.
3. *Sacramento Union*, October 2, 1931.
4. *Ibid.*, September 29, 1931.
5. Taylor, *Life of James Rolph, Jr.*, p. 108.
6. Details from S. Rexford Black, *Report on the California State Labor Camps*, California State Unemployment Commission, July 1932, pp. 9–10.
7. See, for example, *Sacramento Union*, February 8, 1932.

Chapter 19

1. *Sacramento Union*, June 14, 1931.
2. Phillips, *Big Wayward Girl*, p. 60.
3. *Sacramento Union*, June 15, 1931.
4. Quoted in Gentry, *Frame-Up*, p. 337–338.
5. Richard H. Frost, *The Mooney Case* (Stanford, CA: Stanford University Press, 1968), p. 404.
6. According to Frost, it was this attorney—the idealistic and influential Aaron Sapiro—who spearheaded the effort to get Rolph to pardon Mooney, and he recruited the reluctant Walker for this task.
7. *New York Times*, November 19, 1931.
8. *San Francisco Chronicle*, November 19, 1931.
9. *In the Matter of the Application Made on Behalf of Thomas J. Mooney for a Pardon*, Sacramento, California, April 21, 1932, p. 91.
10. *New York Times*, December 2, 1931.
11. *Sacramento Union*, December 2, 1931.
12. *Ibid.*, December 6, 1931.
13. Starr, *Endangered Dreams* p. 217.
14. Taylor, *The Life of James Rolph, Jr.*, p. 51.
15. Frost, *The Mooney Case*, p. 403.
16. Quoted in Hopkins, "The Man Who Keeps Mooney in Jail," p. 346.
17. See Frost, *The Mooney Case*, p. 409.
18. According to Gentry, when Rolph referred the case to Sullivan, Mooney knew it was over (Gentry, p. 361).
19. Frost, *The Mooney Case*, p. 404.
20. Gentry, *Frame-Up*, p. 361.
21. Starr, *Endangered Dreams*, p. 217.
22. *Sacramento Union*, April 22, 1932.
23. *Ibid.*, April 23, 1932.
24. *Los Angeles Times*, April 22, 1932.
25. *San Francisco Chronicle*, April 22, 1932.
26. Quoted in the *Sacramento Union*, May 1, 1932.
27. *Ibid.*

Chapter 20

1. Marquis James and Bessie Rowland James, *Biography of a Bank—The Story of the*

Bank of America (New York: Harper, 1954), p. 356. According to the authors, Bank of America president A.P. Giannini contributed $200,000 to the campaign during a time when he was watching every penny (p. 356).
  2. *Sacramento Union*, May 8, 1932.
  3. *Stockton Record*, May 4, 1932.
  4. Quoted in the *Sacramento Union*, May 27, 1932.
  5. *Ibid.*, May 8, 1932.
  6. A hint that Rolph risked not being taken seriously was a *Sacramento Union* headline on May 29: "Governor Faces Heavy Picnic Schedule."
  7. *Ibid.*, September 2, 1932.
  8. *Ibid.*, May 8, 1932.
  9. *Ibid.*, May 24, 1932.
  10. *Ibid.*, June 21, 1932.
  11. *Ibid.*, June 22, 1932.
  12. *Ibid.*, July 13, 1932.
  13. *Ibid.*, July 26, 1932.
  14. *Ibid.*, January 15, 1932.
  15. *Ibid.*, February 11, 1932.
  16. *Ibid.*, March 24, 1932.
  17. *Ibid.*, June 30, 1932.
  18. *Ibid.*, July 1, 1932.
  19. *Ibid.*, June 11, 1932.

Chapter 21

  1. *Sacramento Union*, October 18, 1932.
  2. *Ibid.*, August 10, 1932.
  3. *Ibid.*, September 4, 1932.
  4. *Ibid.*, September 9, 1932.
  5. *Ibid.*, September 12, 1932.
  6. Rolph's biographer and personal secretary, David Wooster Taylor, believed that Rolph should have had more, rather than fewer, San Francisco loyalists around him as protection from a press corps that was biased against him.
  7. *Sacramento Union*, September 12, 1932.
  8. *Ibid.*, October 8, 1932.
  9. *Ibid.*, October 7, 1932.
  10. The *Sacramento Union* ran a contest in October 1932 that captured the public reaction to the high-level discord. Readers were asked to supply a final line to this limerick:
  Jimmy Rolph up and shouted, "You're fired!"
  Turned round and yelled out, "You are hired."
  That started a fight.
  Is Rolph wrong or right?
  The winning entry was:
  It depends—are you fired, or hired?
  11. *Ibid.*, October 16, 1932.
  12. *Ibid.*, October 18, 1932.
  13. *Ibid.*
  14. *Ibid.*, October 15, 1932.
  15. *Ibid.*, October 26, 1932.
  16. Quoted in *ibid.*, January 19, 1933. Though Rolph was battered for the low quality of his appointments, Earl Lee Kelly, the new head of public works, was a talented administrator and politician. Over time, serving both Rolph and his successor, Frank Merriam, he acquired considerable influence over personnel selections. He had a strong character and a creative streak. Later, he did well as a vice president of the Bank of America and even considered running for governor in 1946.
  17. *New York Times*, October 23, 1932.

Chapter 22

  1. *Sacramento Union*, July 5, 1932.
  2. James E. Hartley, Steven M. Sheffrin, and J. David Vasche, "Reform During Crisis: The Transformation of California's Fiscal System During the Great Depression," *Journal of Economic History* 56, no. 3, p. 666.
  3. Marvel M. Stockwell, *Studies in California State Taxation* (Berkeley: University of California Press, 1939), p. 169.
  4. *Sacramento Union*, November 26, 1932.
  5. Understanding the budget was becoming so difficult that, during the next administration, the legislature would create a committee to provide objective advice to its members on budgetary matters, and Vandegrift would become its first chairman.
  6. Flamm, *Hometown San Francisco*, p. 60.
  7. *Sacramento Union*, August 19, 1932.
  8. Hichborn, *California Politics, 1891–1939*, p. 2615.
  9. James and James, *Biography of a Bank*, p. 356.
  10. *Sacramento Union*, January 1, 1933.

Chapter 23

  1. Quoted in Kennedy, *Freedom from Fear*, p. 111.
  2. Richard Lowitt, *The New Deal and the West* (Bloomington: Indiana University Press, 1984), p. 175.
  3. *Sacramento Union*, January 4, 1933.
  4. *Ibid.*
  5. *Sacramento Bee*, January 4, 1933.
  6. *Sacramento Union*, January 4, 1933.
  7. *Los Angeles Times*, January 5, 1933.
  8. *Sacramento Union*, January 7, 1933.
  9. *Ibid.*, January 6, 1933.
  10. *Los Angeles Times*, January 6, 1933.
  11. *San Francisco Examiner*, January 5, 1933. According to the *Sacramento Union*'s John Lee, several Rolph supporters in the Senate went to the governor and asked: "Shall we kill [the investigation]?" Rolph is alleged to have told them that he never ran from a fight (*Sacramento Union*, January 1, 1934).

12. *San Francisco Chronicle*, January 11, 1933.
13. *Ibid.*
14. *Sacramento Union*, January 15, 1933.
15. *Ibid.*, July 18, 1931.
16. *Ibid.*, February 5, 1933.
17. *Ibid.*, February 24, 1933.
18. *Ibid.*, February 23, 1933.
19. *Ibid.*, February 1, 1933.
20. *Ibid.*, February 27, 1933.
21. *Ibid.*, May 12, 1933.
22. Governor's Message to the Senate, *Senate Journal*, May 11, 1933, p. 2783.
23. *Ibid.*, pp. 2773, 2776–2777, 2782.
24. *Ibid.*, p. 2781.
25. *Sacramento Union*, April 29, 1933.
26. *Ibid.*, May 13, 1933.
27. *Ibid.*, February 23, 1933.
28. *Ibid.*, February 24, 1933.
29. Taylor, *The Political Career of James Rolph, Jr.*, p. 123.

Chapter 24

1. Albert A. Romasco, *The Poverty of Abundance: Hoover, the Nation, and the Depression* (New York: Oxford University Press, 1965), pp. 224–225.
2. *Sacramento Union*, June 4, 1933.
3. Hartley, "Reform During Crisis," p. 673.
4. *Sacramento Union*, January 4, 1933.
5. *Ibid.*, March 12, 1933.
6. *Ibid.*, April 25, 1933.
7. *Ibid.*
8. *Los Angeles Examiner*, April 29, 1933. Longtime advisor Eustace Cullinan drafted the veto message. As a joke, Cullinan threw in this "line of hokum": "All the world is aware that I love horses, but I am at a point where I must make my choice between the home and the stable, and in that situation, I take my stand firmly on the side of the home and so veto the bill." Rolph used the line, showing that pressure had not dulled his sense of humor—or perhaps it captured his sentiments exactly (Eustace Cullinan remembers the "early days" in *The Recorder*, undated but after Rolph's death, from the Nancy Rolph Welch collection).
9. More evidence of Rolph's successful cultivation of Hearst (or vice versa) was the governor's attendance at the wedding of the publisher's son, George, at San Simeon in June. (*Sacramento Union*, June 27, 1933.)
10. *Ibid.*, May 8, 1933.
11. Some historians assert that Rolph was in favor of Proposition One. (See, for example, Stockwell, *Studies in California State Taxation*, p. 168.) If he was, he was careful not to say so publicly, allowing him to claim later that he had opposed any tax increases.
12. *Sacramento Union*, June 7, 1933.
13. *Ibid.*, June 22, 1933.
14. *Ibid.*, June 29, 1933.
15. *Ibid.*, July 7, 1933.
16. *Ibid.*, July 4, 1933.
17. *Ibid.*, July 6, 1933.
18. *Ibid.*, June 18, 1933.
19. *Ibid.*
20. *Ibid.*, May 24, 1933.
21. *Ibid.*, July 18, 1933.
22. *Ibid.*, July 23, 1933.
23. *Ibid.*, July 26, 1933.
24. He once said, according to Phillips (*Big Wayward Girl*): "I wish I could have been governor in Governor Young's years. I'd have shown them how to entertain!"
25. *Sacramento Union*, July 9, 1933.
26. *Ibid.*, July 29, 1933.
27. *Ibid.*, August 11, 1933.
28. *Ibid.*, August 12, 1933.
29. *Ibid.*, August 19, 1933.
30. *Ibid.*, August 12, 1933.
31. *Ibid.*
32. Chan, "California During the Early 1930s," p. 279.
33. Stockwell, *Studies in California State Taxation*, p. 111.
34. See Hartley, "Reform During Crisis," p. 666.

Chapter 25

1. Taylor, *The Life of James Rolph, Jr.*, p. 22.
2. *Ibid.*, p. 11.
3. *San Francisco Chronicle*, June 3, 1934.
4. Taylor, *The Life of James Rolph, Jr.*, pp. 12–13.
5. Rolph's former chauffeur, Charlie Bovey, who is now 104, reports that he drove the governor into the mountains for some recreation at about this time, but that he almost immediately had to bring him back to Sacramento because of extreme altitude sickness. This may have been one more manifestation of his worsening condition.
6. *Sacramento Union*, August 31, 1933.
7. *Ibid.*, September 25, 1933.
8. "I took care of it for two years," the friend told journalist Jerry Flamm. "It was fortunate that I did. When he died, his wife had the money from the insurance policies." (Flamm, *Hometown San Francisco*, p. 59.)
9. Taylor, *The Life of James Rolph, Jr.*, p. 81.

Chapter 26

1. Lowitt, *The New Deal and the West*, p. 178.
2. *Sacramento Union*, January 4, 1933.
3. Cletus E. Daniel, *Bitter Harvest: A History*

of California Farmworkers, 1870–1941 (Ithaca, NY: Cornell University Press, 1981), p. 158.
4. *Ibid.*, p. 164.
5. According to Daniel, commodity prices in 1933 had spiked upward, allowing any willing cotton grower to offer a higher wage to the pickers (*ibid.*, p. 179).
6. *Ibid.*, p. 165.
7. Starr, *Endangered Dreams*, pp. 76–77.
8. *Ibid.*, p. 77.
9. *Sacramento Union*, October 11, 1933.
10. Daniel, *Bitter Harvest*, p. 202.
11. *Sacramento Union*, October 13, 1933.
12. See Daniel, *Bitter Harvest*, pp. 204–217, for an account of Creel's bold efforts to dictate a solution to both sides.

Chapter 27

1. *Alameda Times-Star*, May 12, 1933.
2. *Sacramento Union*, July 10, 1933.
3. *Ibid.*, August 19, 1933.
4. *Ibid.*, July 26, 1933.
5. *Ibid.*, July 7, 1933.
6. *Ibid.*, August 7, 1933.
7. *Ibid.*, August 19, 1933. Of course, this judgment turned out to be premature.
8. *Ibid.*, June 15, 1933.
9. *Ibid.*, August 31, 1933.
10. *Ibid.*, October 3, 1933.
11. *Ibid.*, November 19, 1933.

Chapter 28

1. *Sacramento Union*, October 16, 1933.
2. The governor's granddaughter remembers growing up with bars on her windows because fears of kidnapping were so strong.
3. Farrell, *Swift Justice*, pp. 69, 113–114.
4. *Sacramento Union*, November 27, 1933.
5. *New York Times*, November 28, 1933.
6. Cited in Farrell, *Swift Justice*, p. 139.
7. Cited in *ibid.*, p. 146.
8. Quoted in James J. Rawls and Walton Bean, *California: An Interpretive History* (Boston: McGraw-Hill, 1998), p. 319.
9. Quoted in Brian McGinty, "Shadows in St. James Park," *California History* 57, Winter 1978–79, p. 301.
10. Cited in Farrell, *Swift Justice*, p. 241.
11. Rolph's remarks were reported with only slight variations in most of the country's major newspapers, but the governor's secretary, James Wooster Taylor, claimed that Rolph had used the following qualifying phrase: "While the law should have been permitted to take its course...."
12. Quoted in Farrell, *Swift Justice*, p. 267.
13. *Sacramento Union*, November 28, 1933.
14. *Ibid.*, November 29, 1933.

15. *Ibid.*, December 3, 1933, Rolph's secretary and biographer, David Wooster Taylor, believed that the governor's comments stopped kidnapping in California for several months. (Taylor, *The Life of James Rolph, Jr.*, p. 112.)
16. Rolph later claimed that letters to him were 10–1 in favor of his stand throughout the aftermath of the event. (See Tom Bellew, "Story of Rolph," *San Francisco Chronicle*, June 29, 1934.) Sister Clementia Marie Fisher has written that Rolph received 267 supportive letters and 57 critical ones. (Fisher, *James Rolph, Jr.*, p. 126.
17. Quoted in the *Sacramento Union*, November 28, 1933.
18. Cited in Farrell, *Swift Justice*, p. 273.
19. Quoted *ibid.*, p. 271.
20. Quoted in Frost, *The Mooney Case*, p. 469.
21. All quotes from the *Sacramento Union*, November 29, 1933.
22. Quoted in McGinty, "Shadows in St. James Park," p. 302.
23. *Sacramento Union*, November 30, 1933.
24. *Ibid.*, December 7, 1933.
25. Quoted in Bellew, "Story of Rolph," *San Francisco Chronicle*, June 29, 1934.
26. Cited in Farrell, *Swift Justice*, p. 274.
27. *Ibid.*
28. *Sacramento Union*, December 8, 1933.
29. *Ibid.*, December 1, 1933.
30. *Ibid.*, December 2, 1933.

Chapter 29

1. *Sacramento Union*, July 13, 1932.
2. Quoted in Lawrence B. Lee, "California Water Politics: Genesis of the Central Valley Project, 1933–44," *Journal of the West* 24, October 1985, p. 66.
3. *Sacramento Union*, October 5, 1933.
4. *Ibid.*, October 6, 1933.
5. *Ibid.*, November 3, 1933.
6. *Ibid.*, December 16, 1933.
7. *Ibid.*, December 17, 1933.
8. *Ibid.*, October 14, 1933.
9. *Ibid.*, December 21, 1933.

Chapter 30

1. *Sacramento Union*, August 25, 1933.
2. Robert W. Kenny Correspondence and Papers, Bancroft Library, Berkeley, California.
3. *Sacramento Union*, September 28, 1933.
4. *Ibid.*, January 6, 1934.
5. *Ibid.*, January 1, 1934.
6. *Ibid.*
7. *Ibid.*, January 25, 1934.
8. *Ibid.*, January 28, 1934.
9. *Ibid.*, February 4, 1934.

10. *Ibid.*, February 16, 1934.
11. *Ibid.*, February 5, 1934.
12. David Wooster Taylor, *Los Angeles Examiner*, June 17, 1934.
13. *Ibid.*
14. He had not only regained his energy but also his sense of humor and his keen political instincts. Responding to an invitation to judge a baby contest in late January, he wrote: "No baby contests for me ... I was the judge of a baby contest once in San Francisco and I vowed I would never again judge a baby show. I value the good will of all mothers too much to judge their babies. Good luck to you. Hope you will be able to live it down after the show is over. I will pray for you." (*San Francisco Chronicle*, January 26, 1934.)
15. Bellew, *San Francisco Chronicle*, June 30, 1934.
16. *Ibid.*
17. *Ibid.*
18. *Sacramento Union*, March 2, 1934.
19. Bellew, *San Francisco Chronicle*, June 30, 1934.
20. *San Francisco Chronicle*, June 3, 1934.
21. *Sacramento Union*, June 3, 1934.

Chapter 31

1. *San Jose Mercury-Herald*, June 4, 1934.
2. Interview with Louis Heilbron, State Government Oral History Program, 1991–1992.
3. Louis Bartlett, "Louis Bartlett Memoirs," unpublished typescript, Regional Cultural History Project, University of California, Berkeley, 1957, pp. 177–185.
4. Kevin Starr, *San Francisco Examiner*, November 14, 1977.
5. *Sacramento Union*, January 16, 1932.
6. *Los Angeles Examiner*, June 15, 1934.
7. Barnes, "Master of the Political Winds," p. 13.
8. Paul Edwards, *San Francisco News*, August 12, 1933.
9. Behrens, *Inside California*, p. 28.
10. Arthur H. Breed, Jr., "Alameda County and the California Legislature," Regional Oral History Office, Berkeley, California, p. 35.
11. Flamm, p. 60.
12. *Sacramento Union*, April 22, 1931.
13. Phillips, *Big Wayward Girl*, p. 63.
14. *Sacramento Union*, June 3, 1934.
15. Phillips, *Big Wayward Girl*, p. 59.
16. *San Francisco Chronicle*, April 1, 1937.
17. *Ibid.*, April 2, 1937.

Bibliography

Unpublished Sources

Dissertations and Theses

Fisher, Sister Clementia Marie. *James Rolph, Jr., 1869–1934: An Estimate of His Influence on San Francisco's History*, master's thesis, University of San Francisco, 1965.

Goldbeck, Herman G. *The Political Career of James Rolph, Jr.: A Preliminary Study*, master's thesis, University of California, Berkeley, 1936.

Hicke, Carole E. *The 1911 Campaign of James Rolph, Jr., Mayor of All the People*, master's thesis, San Francisco State University, 1978.

Oral History Transcripts

Bary, Helen Valeska. "Labor Administration and Social Security: A Woman's Life." Regional Oral History Office, University of California, Berkeley, 1972.

Breed, Arthur H., Jr. "Alameda County and the California Legislature." Regional Oral History Office, University of California, Berkeley.

Dyer, Noel John. *Lawyer for the Defense*. Oral history transcript, University of California, Berkeley, 1988.

Heilbron, Louis. State Government Oral History Program, 1991–92.

Small, Merrell Farnham. "The Office of the Governor Under Earl Warren." Regional Oral History Office, University of California, Berkeley.

Archival Papers

Bartlett, Louis. *Louis Bartlett Memoirs*. Unpublished typescript, Regional Cultural History Project, University of California, Berkeley, 1957.

Behrens, Earl "Squire." *Inside California: A Reporter's Journal*. Unpublished manuscript, California Historical Society, San Francisco.

James Rolph Papers, California Historical Society, San Francisco.

Jesse Brown Cook Scrapbooks Documenting San Francisco History and Law Enforcement, ca. 1895–1936, Bancroft Library, Berkeley.

Lotchin, Roger W. "John Francis Neylan: San Francisco Irish Progressive," *The San Francisco Irish, 1850–1976*. Unpublished manuscript, Bancroft Library, Berkeley, 1978.

The Memoirs of Ray Lyman Wilbur, Stanford University, 1960.

Papers of John Francis Neylan, Bancroft Library, Berkeley.
Robert W. Kenny Correspondence and Papers, Bancroft Library, Berkeley.

Family Documents

Official Log of the Rolph 1918 Campaign for Governor, July 15-August 31, 1918, Rolph family files.

Published Sources

Books

Asbury, Herbert. *The Barbary Coast: An Informal History of the San Francisco Underworld*. Garden City, NY: Garden City Publishing Co., 1933.

Blackford, Mansel G. *The Lost Dream: Businessmen and City Planning on the Pacific Coast, 1890–1920*. Columbus: Ohio State University Press, 1993.

Byington, Lewis Francis. *The History of San Francisco, Vol. 1*. Chicago: S.J. Clarke, 1931.

Cleland, Robert Glass. *California in Our Time*. New York: A.A. Knopf, 1947.

Cutler, Leland W. *America Is Good to a Country Boy*. Stanford, CA: Stanford University Press, 1954.

Delmatier, Royce D., Clarence F. McIntosh, and Earl G. Waters, eds. *The Rumble of California Politics, 1848–1970*. New York: Wiley, 1970.

Deverell, William, and Tom Sitton, eds. *California Progressivism Revisited*. Berkeley: University of California Press, 1994.

Doerr, David R. *California's Tax Machine: A History of Taxing and Spending in the Golden State*. Sacramento: California Taxpayers' Association, 2000.

Farrell, Harry. *Swift Justice: Murder and Vengeance in a California Town*. New York: St. Martin's Press, 1992.

Flamm, Jerry. *Hometown San Francisco: Sunny Jim, Phat Willie, and Dave*. San Francisco: Scottwall, 1994.

Frost, Richard H. *The Mooney Case*. Stanford, CA: Stanford University Press, 1968.

Gentry, Curt. *Frame-up: The Incredible Case of Tom Mooney and Warren Billings*. New York: Norton, 1967.

Hichborn, Franklin. *California Politics, 1891–1939*. Santa Clara, CA: J.R. Haynes Foundation, 1950.

Issel, William, and Robert W. Cherny. *San Francisco, 1865–1932: Politics, Power and Urban Development*. Berkeley: University of California Press, 1986.

James, Marquis, and Bessie Rowland James. *Biography of a Bank: The Story of the Bank of America*. New York: Harper, 1954.

Kazin, Michael. *Barons of Labor: The San Francisco Building Trades and Union Power in the Progressive Era*. Urbana: University of Illinois Press, 1987.

Kennedy, David M. *Freedom From Fear: The American People in Depression and War, 1929–1945*. New York: Oxford University Press, 1999.

Knight, Robert Edward Lee. *Industrial Relations in the San Francisco Bay Area, 1900–1918*. Berkeley: University of California Press, 1960.

McGloin, John B. *San Francisco: The Story of a City*. San Francisco: Presidio Press, 1978.

Melendy, H. Brett, and Benjamin F. Gilbert. *The Governors of California: Peter H. Burnett to Edmund G. Brown*. Georgetown, CA: Talisman Press, 1965.

Nasaw, David. *The Chief: The Life of William Randolph Hearst*. Boston: Houghton Mifflin, 2000.
O'Shaughnessy, M.M. *Hetch Hetchy: Its Origin and History*. San Francisco: Recorder, 1934.
Perles, Anthony. *The People's Railway: The History of the Municipal Railway of San Francisco*. Glendale, CA: Interurban Press, 1981.
Phillips, Herbert L. *Big Wayward Girl: An Informal Political History of California*. Garden City, NY: Doubleday, 1968.
Putnam, Jackson. *Modern California Politics*. San Francisco: Boyd and Fraser, 1980.
Rawls, James J. and Walton Bean, *California: An Interpretive History*. Boston: McGraw-Hill, 1998.
Rogin, Michael Paul, and John L. Shover. *Political Change in California: Critical Elections and Social Movements, 1890–1966*. Westport, CT: Greenwood, 1970.
Romasco, Albert A. *The Poverty of Abundance: Hoover, the Nation, and the Depression*. New York: Oxford University Press, 1965.
Roos, Robert de. *The Thirsty Land: The Story of the Central Valley Project*. Stanford, CA: Stanford University Press, 1948.
Sinclair, Upton. *I, Candidate for Governor: And How I Got Licked*. New York: Farrar and Rinehart, 1934.
Stanford, Sally. *The Lady of the House*. New York: Putnam, 1966.
Starr, Kevin. *Endangered Dreams: The Great Depression in California*. New York: Oxford University Press, 1996.
Stockwell, Marvel M. *Studies in California State Taxation*. Berkeley: University of California Press, 1939.
Taylor, David Wooster. *The Life of James Rolph, Jr*. San Francisco: Committee for Publication of the Life of James Rolph, Jr., 1934.
Watkins, T.H., and R.R. Olmsted. *Mirror of the Dream: An Illustrated History of San Francisco*. San Francisco: Scrimshaw Press, 1976.
Whiteman, Luther, and Samuel L. Lewis. *Glory Roads: The Psychological State of California*. New York: Crowell, 1936.

Articles

Aikman, Duncan. "California's Sun God." *The Nation*, January 14, 1931.
Barclay, Thomas S. "Reapportionment in California." *Pacific Historical Review* 5 (June 1936).
Barnes, Merritt S. "James Rolph, Jr.: Master of the Political Winds." *The American West*, 15, no. 6 (November-December 1978).
Bellew, Tom. "The Life of James Rolph, Jr." *San Francisco Chronicle*, June 4–30, 1934.
Brechin, Gary. "Sailing to Byzantium: The Architecture of the Panama Pacific International Exposition." *California History* 62, no. 2 (Summer 1983).
Carr, Harry. "California's Whoopee Governor." *Los Angeles Times Sunday Magazine*, March 22, 1933.
Chan, Loren B. "California During the Early 1930s: The Administration of James Rolph, Jr., 1931–1934." *Southern California Quarterly* 63, no. 3 (1981).
Edwards, Paul C. "The Rise and Decline of Jim Rolph." *San Francisco News*, August 7–12, 1933.
"Governor Lynch and His Mob." *The Nation*, December 13, 1933.
Groff, Francis A. "The Exposition Mayor." *Sunset* 28 (January 1912).
Hartley, James E., Steven M. Sheffrin, and J. David Vasche. "Reform During Crisis:

The Transformation of California's Fiscal System During the Great Depression," *Journal of Economic History* 56, no. 3 (September 1996).
Hines, William M. "Our American Mayors: James Rolph, Jr., of San Francisco." *National Municipal Review* 18 (March 1929).
Hopkins, Ernest Jerome. "The Man Who Keeps Mooney in Jail." *The New Republic,* May 11, 1932.
Kessler, Sidney H. "Mayor Jimmy Rolph: An Institution." *Sunset,* June 1928.
Lee, Lawrence B. "California Water Politics: Depression Genesis of the California Water Project, 1933–1944." *Journal of the West* 24, no. 4 (October 1985).
Lotchin, Roger W. "The Darwinian City: The Politics of Urbanization Between the World Wars." *Pacific Historical Review* 48 (August 1979).
Lowitt, Richard. "The Great Depression and the West — Introduction." *Journal of the West* 24, no. 4 (October 1985).
McGinty, Brian. "Shadows in St. James Park." *California History* 57, no. 4 (Winter 1978–79).
Meherin, Elenore. "Life of Jim Rolph." *San Francisco Call-Bulletin,* December 17, 1930–January 20, 1931.
Melendy, H. Brett. "California's Cross-filing Nightmare: The 1918 Gubernatorial Election," *Pacific Historical Review,* Vol. 33, 1964.
Muheim, Henry Miles. "My Life with the Lone Eagle." *American Heritage* 48 (May-June 1997).
Rischin, Moses. "Sunny Jim Rolph: The First 'Mayor of All the People.'" *California Historical Society Quarterly* 53, no. 2 (Summer 1974).
Segal, Morley. "James Rolph, Jr., and the Early Days of the San Francisco Railway." *California Historical Society Quarterly* 43, no. 1 (March 1964).
Tygiel, Jules. "Where Unionism Holds Undisputed Sway: A Reappraisal of San Francisco's Union Labor Party." *California History* 62, no. 3 (Fall 1983).

Official and Semi-Official Publications

Assembly Journal, 49th and 50th Sessions, 1931–1933.
Black, S. Rexford. "Report on the California State Labor Camps." California State Unemployment Commission, July 1932.
Final Report of the Investigating Committee to the Senate of the State of California, Senate Journal, May 2, 1933.
In the Matter of the Application Made on Behalf of Thomas J. Mooney for a Pardon, Sacramento, California State Printing Office, April 21, 1932.
Governor's Message to the Senate, *Senate Journal,* May 11, 1933. Report and Recommendations of the California State Unemployment Commission, State of California, November 1932.
Rolph, James, Jr. "Governor Calls Water Victory the Greatest Event Since Gold Rush," *California Highways and Public Works,* January 1934.
Rolph, James, Jr. "Message of the Governor Concerning Pardons, Commutations and Reprieves Granted by Governor James Rolph, Jr., for Period 1931–33." Sacramento, California State Printing Office, 1933.

Reference Sources

Barclay, Thomas M. "James Rolph, 1869–1934." *Dictionary of American Biography,* Supplements 1–2, American Council of Learned Societies, 1944–58.

Magazines and Journals

Almanac
American Heritage
The American West
California Highways and Public Works
California Historical Society Quarterly
California History
Journal of Economic History

Journal of the West
The Nation
National Municipal Review
The New Republic
Pacific Historical Review
Southern California Quarterly
Sunset

Newspapers

Los Angeles Examiner
Los Angeles Times
New York Times
Sacramento Bee
Sacramento Union
San Diego Union
San Francisco Bulletin
San Francisco Call

San Francisco Call-Bulletin
San Francisco Call and Post
San Francisco Chronicle
San Francisco Daily News
San Francisco Evening Post
San Francisco Examiner
San Jose Mercury Herald
Stockton Record

Index

Agriculture Department (California) 107
Anti-Saloon League 94

Balzar, Frederick 137
Bank of America 149
Bank of California 20
Barbary Coast 22, 34–35, 39
Barnes, Merritt S. 2
Beery, Wallace 171
Behrens, Earl 11, 55, 73, 79, 148
Bovey, Charlie 216
Breed, Arthur 149, 156, 203
Brown, Edmund G. 4
Budget (California state) 2, 4, 93–95, 102–104, 111–112, 113–114, 140, 146–153, 160–161

California Historical Society 6
Cannery and Agricultural Workers Industrial Union 99, 174–177
Carrillo, Leo 184
Central Valley Water Plan 3, 103, 137–140, 151, 163, 179, 187–191, 199
Chan, Loren B. 6, 168
Chandler, Harry 162
Civil Service 136–137, 144–145, 189, 202
Civilian Conservation Corps 124
Creel, George 176–177
Cross-filing 56
Cullinan, Eustace 39–41, 67, 71, 153, 216
Cutler, Leland 112

Depression 1–2, 98–99, 121, 135, 140, 146, 152, 159–160, 174, 205–206
DeWitt, Kittle & Co. 19
Downey, Sheridan 194
Dreiser, Theodore 131

Earthquake of 1906 1, 5, 23–24, 26
Ebright, George 107, 201
Edwards, Paul C. 66
Eliot, Charles 49

Employees Association (California) State 140
Employers Association (San Francisco) 22

Farm Labor 99, 133, 174–178
Farrell, Harry 183, 185
Finn, Tom 78, 80, 83–84
Fitts, Buron 90–92, 94–96, 110, 181
Flamm, Jerry 6, 11, 42, 55, 74–75, 78–79, 92
Fleishhacker, Herbert 65–66, 68, 71, 131, 199, 202
Furuseth, Andrew 28

Garrison, Walter 144, 149, 154
Giannini, A. P. 214–215
Goldbeck, Herman G. 6
Golden Gate Bridge 86
Government (California state) 101, 118, 134, 143
Governor's Council 104–105, 117
Grange Recall 9, 155–156
Green, Jack 181

Hanna, Edward 121–122, 177
Harding, Warren 63
Hart, Brooke 182
Hearst, George 216
Hearst, William Randolph 35, 68–69, 82–84, 98, 100, 108, 162–163, 167, 199
Heilbron, Louis 199–200
Heney, Francis J. 26, 39, 57–58
Hetch Hetchy Water Project 25, 48–50, 64, 67–72, 79, 82–83, 86, 91, 187
Hichborn, Franklin 149
Hicke, Carol 28
Hind, George 20, 84, 210
Hind-Rolph Shipping Company 20, 54, 60
Hoover, Herbert 2, 85, 89, 97, 141, 148, 152, 168, 185, 187, 206
Hopkins, Ernest Jerome 33, 64

Industrial Relations Department (California) 108

Index

Inman, John 121–122, 124, 138–140, 142–144, 151, 153–157, 163, 188–190, 202–203

Johnson, Charles 106, 111–113, 144, 156, 180
Johnson, Hiram 4, 30, 32, 38, 39, 78, 90, 101, 104, 180

Kelly, Earl Lee 144, 215
Kennedy, David M. 98
Kenny, Robert W. 192

Labor unionism and strikes 18, 22, 50–51, 63, 152, 175–177, 210
Lavender, Rosie 9
Law and Order Committee 51
Legislature (California state) 1, 4, 5, 6, 98, 100–102, 109–113, 118, 121–122, 138–140, 153, 160–161, 164, 202
Levey, Edgar C. 110
Lewis, Sinclair 131
Lindbergh, Charles 13, 135, 183–184
Linforth, Walter 196–197
Little, Walter 110
Lotchin, Roger 47

Mayer, Louis B. 162
McCarthy, P.H. 26, 28–29
McFadden, Jimmy 75
McLeran, Ralph 71
McNab, Gavin 27, 40, 67, 75–76, 79, 128
McNab, John 40, 82, 140, 206–207
McSheehy, L. B. 69
McWilliams, Carey 99
Meherin, Elenore 6, 11
Melendy, H. Brett 90
Mencken, H. L. 74
Merchant's Exchange 21, 23, 25–26
Merriam, Frank 4, 97, 101, 121–122, 124, 142, 153–154, 157–158, 166, 180, 194–195, 198, 205, 215
Mission District 20, 25, 27–28, 53
Mission Promotion Association 21
Mission Relief Association 23–24, 38–40, 203
Mooney, Tom 6, 51, 125–133, 135, 138, 162, 181, 184, 205, 214
Motor Vehicle Department (California state) 108
Moulton, Dudley 155–156
Muir, John 49
Municipal Conference 27
Municipal Railway 31–32, 82, 91, 187, 199

National Governors Conference 137, 165–167, 183
National Recovery Administration 176–177, 180
New Deal 2
Neylan, John Francis 68–69, 71, 82–84, 98, 108

Oakland Bay Bridge 82, 84
O'Brien, Daniel 182
Older, Fremont 26, 130–131
Oneal, Louis 186
O'Shaughnessy, Michael 49, 67, 71, 83

Pacific Gas and Electric Co. 39, 40, 67–72, 79, 149, 153, 160
Page, Anita 76
Pan-Pacific International Exposition 26–27, 31, 35, 76
Phelan, James 22, 48–49, 59, 82
Portola Festival 26
Power, James 78–81, 83–84
Preparedness Day Parade 51, 126–127
Progressivism 2, 27, 30, 56, 62, 65, 67, 71, 83–84, 100
Prohibition 3, 30, 48, 57, 91, 94, 100, 163–164
Public Works Department (California state) 108

Racetrack Gambling Bill 162–164, 179
Rainey, Ed 40–41, 61, 74, 201, 206
Raker Act 50
Reagan, Ronald 4
Reapportionment 3, 109–111
Reardon, Tim 41–42, 61, 79, 103, 108, 145, 175, 197, 212, 213
Reichert, Irving 176
Republican County Committee 25, 79
Republican National Convention 141
Richardson, Friend 133
Riley, Ray 149, 151, 161, 168
Riley-Stewart Plan 161–164, 167, 169
Roche, Theodore 39, 58, 108, 128, 195, 201
Rogers, Will 1, 97, 167, 180, 184
Rolph, Annette 34, 41, 66, 76, 195
Rolph, Annie Reid 19, 28, 34, 41–43, 53, 76, 96, 101, 123, 172, 197
Rolph, Georgina 41
Rolph, James, Jr.: appearance 10–11, 27–28, 73; assessment 2, 4, 10, 64–65, 99, 179, 198–207; business career and finances 5, 11, 20–21, 53–55, 59–60, 65–66, 84–85, 172–173, 198, 200, 206–207; campaigns, general 12–13, 81, 92–93; and capital punishment 125–126; childhood 17–20; death 9, 10, 197, 201; health 1, 5–6, 73–75, 84, 122, 155–156, 170–172, 177–178, 181–182, 194; inaugural address 102–104, 109, 111; and 1906 earthquake 23–25; and 1911 campaign 12–13, 27–29; and 1915 campaign 35–37, 48; and 1918 campaign 56–58; and 1919 campaign 61; and 1923 campaign 69; and 1927 campaign 78–84; and 1930 campaign 5, 89–97; and organized labor 23, 25, 28, 81, 94, 103–104, 133; personality and style 10–12, 17, 19, 25–28, 32–33, 54, 57, 63, 92–93, 170; policies as mayor 25, 64–65, 86; political beliefs 2, 30, 72, 104; travel 3,

115–117, 122, 151, 195–196, 203; and World War I 50–52
Rolph, James, Sr. 17, 20, 34
Rolph, James, III 34, 41, 43, 69, 155, 197
Rolph, Mary 20
Rolph, William 43
Rolph, Landis and Ellis 105
Rolph Mail and Steamship Co. 60
Rolph Navigation and Coal Co. 53–54
Roosevelt, Franklin D. 2, 3, 12, 124, 147, 152, 160–161, 165, 176, 180, 185, 187, 188, 194, 198, 204, 206
Ruef, Abraham 23, 26, 39

Sailors' Union of the Pacific 25, 28
San Francisco, general 17–18, 22, 34, 80
San Jose kidnapping 6, 9, 182–186, 189, 205
Sapiro, Aaron 214
Schmitz, Eugene 23, 26, 37, 61
Senate Investigation of Rolph Administration 153–158, 161, 163
Shipowners Association of San Francisco 20, 25
Shipping Board, United States 55, 59
Sierra Club 49
Sinclair, Upton 74, 91, 131, 205
Social Welfare Department (California state) 108
Southern California Quarterly 6
Splivalo, Rheba Crawford 108
Spring Valley Water Company 86
Stanford, Sally 41, 75–76
Starr, Kevin 130
State Labor Camp Committee 122, 124
Stevens, William D. 57–58, 78, 89
Stewart, Fred 161
Sullivan, Matt 10, 18, 23–24, 27, 38–39, 58, 59, 73, 103, 128–134, 138, 140, 188–189, 195, 214

Supreme Court of California 58, 127
Symes, John 66, 155

Taft, William 76
Tammany Hall 79
Tax Research Bureau, California 147, 149, 151
Taxes, California State 147, 152, 159–169; income 147, 159, 165–169; property 147, 159, 161, 165–166, 169; sales 9, 121, 147, 159–160, 162, 165–169, 192, 194, 205
Taxpayers' Association, California 147
Taylor, David Wooster 43, 59, 74–75, 92–93, 122, 130, 170–171, 201, 215, 217
Trinity Academy 19
Turner, Roscoe 137

Unemployment 2, 121–122, 151, 192
Union Labor Party 23, 26–27, 79
United Railway Company 31, 67

Vandegrift, Rolland 112–113, 122, 140, 144, 147, 149, 151, 154–156, 161, 163–164, 167–168, 215

Walker, Jimmy 128–130, 132, 214
Warren, Earl 4, 106
Welch, Nancy Rolph 6, 123, 129, 132, 137, 141, 171, 182, 209, 211, 217
Wilson, Woodrow 50, 51, 58–59, 206
Women's Christian Temperance Union 94, 181

Young, C. C. 79, 84–85, 90–96, 101, 102, 104, 106–107, 124, 127, 131, 135, 140, 142, 147, 195, 202
Young, Milton K. 97

www.ingramcontent.com/pod-product-compliance
Lightning Source LLC
Chambersburg PA
CBHW032050300426
44116CB00007B/676